© 1985, 1991, 1999 by Winifred Aldrich

Blackwell Science Ltd, a Blackwell Publishing Company
Editorial Offices:
Osney Mead, Oxford OX2 0EL, UK
 Tel: +44 (0)1865 206206
Blackwell Science, Inc., 350 Main Street,
Malden, MA 02148-5018, USA
 Tel: +1 781 388 8250
Iowa State Press, a Blackwell Publishing Company, 2121 State
Avenue, Ames, Iowa
50014-8300, USA
 Tel: +1 515 292 0140
Blackwell Publishing Asia Pty Ltd, 550 Swanston Street,
Carlton South, Melbourne, Victoria 3053, Australia
 Tel: +61 (0)3 9347 0300
Blackwell Wissenschafts Verlag,
Kurfürstendamm 57, 10707 Berlin, Germany
 Tel: +49 (0)30 32 79 060

First published in Great Britain by
 Collins Professional and Technical Books 1985
Reprinted 1986, 1987
Reprinted by BSP Professional Books 1987, 1989
Second edition 1991
Reprinted 1992
Reprinted by Blackwell Science Ltd 1993, 1994, 1996, 1997
Third edition 1999
Reprinted 2003

Library of Congress
Cataloging-in-Publication Data
Aldrich, Winifred.
 Metric pattern cutting for children's wear and babywear:
from birth to 14 years/Winifred Aldrich. – 3rd ed.
  p. cm.
 Includes bibliographical references (p.).
 ISBN 0–632–05265–1 (hardcover)
 1. Children's clothing–Pattern design. 2. Infants' clothing
– Pattern design. 3. Garment cutting. I. Title.
 TT640.A43 1999
 646.4'072–dc21   99-19986
                                                       CIP

ISBN 0-632-05265-1

A catalogue record for this title is available from
the British Library

Set in 9/10pt Times
by DP Photosetting, Aylesbury, Bucks
Printed and bound in India by
Thomson Press (I) Ltd.

For further information on
Blackwell Publishing, visit our website:
www.blackwellpublishing.com

METRIC
PATTERN CUTTING
FOR CHILDREN'S WEAR
AND BABYWEAR

From birth to 14 years

Third Edition

WINIFRED ALDRICH

Blackwell
Science

CONTENTS

Acknowledgements

I would like to thank:

Alec Aldrich for his assistance with the technical drawings;

Ann Rodgers for her constructive analysis of the book and her experimental work with the blocks with the students at Loughborough College of Art and Design;

Howard Long for his work on the computer which was required to analyse the statistical data;

Richard Miles the Publisher for his professional advice and his production of this book;

the National Children's Wear Association of Great Britain and Northern Ireland for their interest and advice;

the British Standards Institution for their information on size designation of children's wear. Material based on BS 3728: 1982 and BS 7231: Part 1 and Part 2; 1990 is reproduced by permission of the British Standards Institution. Complete copies of the documents can be obtained by post from BSI Sales, 389 Chiswick High Road, London W4 4AL;

other members of the sizing committee for their permission to reproduce the size charts:
Dr. A. Ward, Loughborough University of Technology;

Mr. B.H. Moore, British Home Stores;
Mr. J. Dolman, National Children's Wear Association;
Mr. W.G. Gibson, Manchester Polytechnic.

I would also like to thank the staff of the play groups and schools listed below and the parents for consenting to the measurement of their children. Without their interest and co-operation I could not have written this book.

Quorn Nursery Group;
Dearnley Play Group;
Smithy Bridge Play Group;
Shelthorpe Play Group;
Woodhouse Eaves Baptist Play Group;
Loughborough Baptist Play Group;
St Paul's C. of E. School, Woodhouse Eaves;
New Parks House Primary School, Leicester;
New Parks House Junior School, Leicester;
Glenfield Hall County Junior and Infant School;
Hathern C. of E. Primary School;
Danemill County Primary School, Enderby;
New Parks Senior School, Leicester;
The Martin High School, Anstey;
Stonehill High School and Community College, Birstall;
The Bosworth College, Desford.

INTRODUCTION

There have been major changes in the design of children's clothes since the first edition of this book. The principal ones have been fashion influences and the development of new fabrics. Whilst a strong element of 'body related' *classic 'form' pattern cutting* remains, the popularity of easy-fitting styles and knitted fabrics has meant that *simple 'flat' pattern cutting* is used to construct a large proportion of garments. Therefore, the book is organised into two parts which demonstrate the different types of cutting. This is explained in Design and Pattern Cutting for Children's Wear, page 6.

Fashion and social influences have affected size groupings in the sale of clothes and in the development of garment ranges. The size groupings have been changed from the previous edition to reflect this. Although it is now necessary to organise the grading and pattern construction with reference to the garment ranges, it must be realised that this does not reflect the natural growth spurts and body changes that take place (ref. pages 7–8). The new size charts still reflect this in their size groupings.

Although there has been a strong movement towards separating boys' wear and girls' wear, some manufacturers in leisure and jersey wear are still producing unisex clothes. Therefore, the Unisex Size Chart with the reduced size range has been retained. If a reduced size chart specifically for boys or girls is required, measurements from alternative sizes in the main size charts can be used. Height intervals in the Unisex Chart provide a guide for the size labelling.

In 1982 when I began to plan this book, no recognised size chart was available on which one could base a system of pattern cutting for children's wear. The size chart offered by the British Standards Institution (BSI) had been withdrawn because it was considered to be out of date and they did not expect to be able to offer a new one for at least two years. It was apparent that a book on pattern cutting for children's wear was required by schools and colleges; therefore, I decided to begin a research project to measure children between two years and fourteen years.

A field study was undertaken; the measurements collected provided the necessary data required to produce size charts and to construct blocks. A total of 1,783 boys and girls were measured; account was taken of any differences which could have affected the study, for example, geographical areas, social class and ethnic grouping. The study was constructed to ensure that the children measured reflected the spread of children in the general population.

The results of the study were analysed and size charts were prepared based on the centilong system; the blocks constructed from the charts will fit a large proportion of children in each height interval.

Important Note on the British Standards Institution Size Charts BS 7231 Part 1 and Part 2
A major survey of children's measurements by the University of Loughborough for the British Standards Institution survey has now been completed. The raw data collected by the University is published in Part 1 of the Standard and a range of size charts constructed from this raw data are offered in Part 2.

The author has found the raw data in Part 1 to be particularly useful in the correlation of many of the findings in her own survey. However, she disagrees strongly with the way Part 2 has interpreted the raw data and the way the size charts have been constructed (see section 5). The measurements in Part 2 are calculated as crude increments and there are contradictions between the measurements of the different age groups. Therefore, the author has decided to continue to retain her own size charts, which were derived from her personal survey, and has used some supplementary measurements calculated from the raw data from Part. 1.

One may question why these BSI Part 2 size charts are included in the Appendix of this book. The British Standards Institution is an influential body and students entering industry will encounter these charts. It is essential that the students examine and discuss the positive and negative aspects of these charts during their college studies. It is therefore thought necessary that this book, written for clothing students, should offer them the opportunity to examine and discuss some of the problems raised by this major survey.

It is hoped that the book will be useful to students who wish to specialise in the manufacture of children's wear and that it will encourage more students to become interested in this field of design. There is an increasing demand for original designs which recognise the practical demands of a child's lifestyle. Many mothers now wish to design and make clothes for their children and these garments can be original yet inexpensive. The blocks can be used to draft designs for individual children; this is particularly useful when making patterns for children who are not standard size.

Many schools are encouraging their students to design their own patterns and a section on the developing figure has been included to assist teachers in senior schools in providing the correct blocks for the teenage figure.

I hope that this book will contribute to the increasing interest in children's wear design.

Winifred Aldrich

Design and Pattern Cutting for Children's Wear

Design

Since this book was first published, an enormous difference has taken place in attitudes to the design of children's clothes. Although French and Italian design, renowned for its use of high quality fabrics and decoration, remains at the top end of the market, children's wear is no longer a neglected area of design in Britain. The increasing quality of mass production garments from the Far East and developing countries has allowed designers to offer complex detailing and cut on low-cost garments. The use of new technological communications has reduced response times and increased the practicality of manufacturing off-shore.

The designer must understand the requirements and the lifestyle of babies and children at different ages. Changes in the social culture have generated the growth of children's departments directed by fashion. They mirror adult store lay-outs with co-ordinated ranges and frequent fashion style changes. Sportswear has been the most important influence on children's design; it has directed many new fabric developments, and changed methods of cut and manufacture.

The most difficult market is the sub-teen group. Boys' attitudes are fairly rigid, responding to peer pressure and group demands. Particular labels become important, the fashions often starting at street level. Girls in this age group are very fashion conscious, yet their figures may not have developed sufficiently to wear adult clothes. However, there comes a point when the sub-teen or early teenager does not want to be seen in a children's shop. Large or wealthy stores set up sections aimed directly at this group; the garments on offer can include ranges from the top designers. Other fashion retail outlets, which originally aimed at a 'teen–twenty' market have extended their size ranges downwards to fit smaller figures. This is possible because many of their garments are 'flat cut' in jersey fabric and with little body shaping.

Children's wear offers special opportunities to designers to experiment with colour, decoration and design detail. Fabric producers are targeting children's wear with special weaves and finishes, such as soft denim or felted fabrics. Garment designers work with fabric designers to produce new exciting prints.

The designer is responsible for providing information to those responsible for sourcing materials and manufacturing garments. The British Standard BS 7907: 1997, *The design and manufacture of children's clothing to promote mechanical safety* lays down precisely the areas for which the designer is responsible. This covers the materials of the garments and all the trimmings, fastenings and other components. It also states the ages below which certain components cannot be used. Wear and fit trials undertaken by manufacturers and retailers usually also include risk assessment. A child's every-day garment has to be made up in a fabric that will stand up to punishing wear and repeated launderings.

Any student wishing to design clothes for children must be aware of the changing shape of the child as it grows and the different proportions of different parts of the body. The proportions and lengths of children's garments are crucial. Students should experiment with shapes that are innovative yet practical, and they should also allow for the child's growth.

Pattern cutting

In earlier editions of this book, the size charts were constructed and divided in accordance with the way a child's body generally develops. Today, as was explained in the Introduction, clothes are designed and sold as ranges for particular target groups dictated by the large retailers. This has affected the groupings for pattern cutting. The revised size charts in the new edition are a response to the needs of pattern cutters.

SIMPLE 'FLAT' PATTERN CUTTING
(PART ONE)
The number of garments cut from simple 'flat' blocks has increased for three main reasons: the popularity of easy-fitting styles and sportswear, the increase in the use of knitted fabrics and the use of manufacturing methods that keep price levels low. Methods of computer grading encourage the re-application of existing grades, and this is easier when applying them to simple styles. The insertion of sleeve heads is faster when machined on 'the flat' with little ease in the sleeve head. Most garments constructed by simple flat cutting and manufacture lay flat when completed and therefore are easier to store, transport and package.

The attraction of these garments depends heavily on fabric design, simple but innovative shapes and decorative features. The flat blocks can be used for a wide range of garments, i.e. simple dresses, shirts, blouses, leisurewear, weatherwear, knitwear and nightwear. 'Flat' pattern cutting methods for these garments are demonstrated in Chapters 4–8. Some basic pattern cutting methods are applicable to both 'flat' pattern cutting and to classic 'form' cutting. These basic methods are located in Part Two, Chapters 10, 11 and 13.

CLASSIC 'FORM' PATTERN CUTTING
(PART TWO)
There remains a demand for school uniforms and also a small but steady demand for traditional tailored clothes and for well-cut high quality garments that refer directly to a child's shape. Classic 'form' pattern cutting is used for garments which have a close relationship with the body shape and which is achieved by pattern cutting. This is required mainly when working with fabrics without stretch characteristics or for cutting garments for traditional masculine and feminine shapes.

The Growth of Children and Adolescents

Designers of children's clothes should be aware of the way that a child's body shape changes as it grows and they should also be able to recognise the shape of a child at a particular stage. Well-designed children's clothes take account of the child's continually changing shape.

It is important to note that in previous editions of this book the size charts were constructed and divided in accordance with the way a child's body generally develops. Today, as explained in the Introduction, clothes are designed and sold as ranges for particular target groups dictated by the large retailers. This has affected the groupings for pattern cutting. The revised size charts in the new edition are a response to the needs of pattern cutters. However, by creating sub-divisions, they still reflect the uneven body shape changes that occur during children's growth.

The rapid growth and changing shape of the child from birth to age one means that close increments in sizing have to be made; this is done usually in three-month intervals. It is at this stage that weight and the age of the child are the predominant descriptions for garment selection, whereas height becomes the critical sizing division once a child begins to walk.

GENERAL FEATURES
The speed at which a child grows decreases steadily from birth onwards until puberty when the rate of growth accelerates (this acceleration is known as the 'adolescent spurt' or 'growth spurt'). Until the growth spurt occurs there appears to be little difference between boys and girls in the speed at which they grow.

The decrease in the rate of growth varies from approximately 8cm per year at three years to 5cm per year at ten years. Manufacturers have decided to accept a 6cm height interval as a base for a coding scheme, as this approximates to the average growth per year over this period. However, it must be noted that the range of heights in children in any particular age group is larger than the amount of growth that occurs in any one year, therefore a child's age is only a very crude guide or 'designation' of his/her expected stature. It is better to link other body measurements to height rather than age, and one must recognise that age on clothing labels is only a secondary description. During puberty, age ceases to have even a descriptive value as variations in height linked to heredity are further distorted by the variability of the onset of puberty and the growth spurt.

In early childhood there is little difference between the sexes. Significant differences begin to appear at about seven which means that by this age it is necessary to offer a size chart for each sex. Puberty brings dramatic differences between boys and girls, the onset of puberty occurring eighteen months to two years earlier in the girl.

Children of the same height can have variable arm and leg measurements and these differences become more apparent as the limb length increases.

Children in the North of England, Scotland and Northern Ireland have been found to be slightly smaller than average. This may be due in part to the greater numbers of working-class children in these areas. Significant differences can be found between children of classes 1 and 2 (managerial and professional occupations) and classes 4 and 5 (semi-skilled and unskilled occupations). Children from classes 1 and 2 appear to be taller (2–5cm) but not heavier than classes 4 and 5.

CHILDREN FROM BIRTH TO AGE SEVEN
The most apparent characteristic of a small child's shape is the size of its head: by the age of three the child's head has almost completed its growth. A small child has a head one fifth of its height while the adult's head is only one eighth. The head size of a child must be taken into account when designing openings on the bodice for the head to pass through.

From the age of two, the average child loses fat until about the age of eight. This 'slimming down' process is very apparent and it is generally spoken of in terms of the child 'losing his baby fat'.

Boys are often a little thinner than girls at this stage, but as the differences in measurements are small, a common size chart can be used. The most significant difference occurs on the hip/seat measurement and some manufacturers of boys' wear take account of this.

Toddlers have very little waist shaping and their stance gives them a hollow back and protruding stomach. These features decrease as the child grows and loses fat.

CHILDREN FROM AGE SEVEN TO PUBERTY

By the age of seven the posture of the child has straightened. From seven years to puberty the average child has a greater relative increase in body girth to height. Despite this increase, a girl's waist develops more shape. At this period the legs of children of both sexes grow faster than the trunk.

Although the speed at which a boy and a girl grows is similar until puberty, the average girl is slightly shorter than the average boy and slightly heavier. During this period, figure differences become more apparent, the most significant being the wider shoulders of the boy and the smaller waist and larger hips of the girl (the latter features are increasingly apparent as the girl enter puberty earlier than the boy).

BOYS AND PUBERTY

The average boy starts his growth spurt at about the age of thirteen and grows rapidly until the age of fifteen, then more slowly until he is seventeen, but as the timing of the spurt varies, height and age have little correlation at this time. Age, therefore, has little relevance on size charts at this stage. Boys often become thinner during this growth spurt but they begin to gain muscle.

Before puberty, leg length grows faster than trunk length, but during the period of peak growth the trunk grows faster than the limbs, the rate of growth of the shoulders is at a maximum and the rate of growth of the head accelerates slightly. Boys have two more years of growth than girls and therefore attain a greater final height.

GIRLS AND PUBERTY

Girls begin to grow quickly at about the age of eleven or twelve; however their growth spurt is shorter in duration than that of boys and proceeds at a slower rate. Because girls enter puberty earlier, a proportion of eleven to thirteen-year-old girls are taller than boys of the same age. Girls continue to get fatter during their growth spurt, but this is in the trunk rather than the limbs and a girl's hip size shows a particular increase.

The bust development of a girl is the most dramatic change in her shape. The early stages of development result in little bust prominence and it is only when the bust begins to develop a structural shape that a girl will require to have blocks which have bust darts. The age at which these different development stages of maturity are reached can differ widely, which means that children between ten and fourteen of similar height and weight can have very different bust measurements. Girls who have developing figures require a specific size chart and block construction as children's blocks are inadequate and women's blocks are too mature.

At this stage in a girl's development the relationship between height and age is now too variable to be recorded as yearly increments.

Tools and Equipment for Making Patterns

A student should aim to acquire a good set of equipment. However, some items are very expensive. The items marked with an asterisk denote those that are not essential immediately.

Working surface   A flat working surface is required. However, a tracing wheel will mark any polished or laminated top, therefore some protection must be given to his type of surface.

Paper   Strong brown paper or white pattern paper is used for patterns. Parchment or thin card should be used for blocks that are used frequently.

Pencils   Use hard pencils for drafting patterns (2H). Coloured pencils are useful for outlining complicated areas.

Fibre pens   These are required for writing clear instructions on patterns.

Rubber

Metric ruler and metre stick

Curved rules   These are used for drawing long curves.

Metric tape measure

Set square   A large set square with a 45° angle is very useful; metric grading squares can be obtained.

Compass   The compass is used for constructing patterns which are based on a circle.

Tracing wheel

Shears   Use separate shears for cutting cloth and paper as cutting paper will blunt the blades.

Sellotape

Pins

One-quarter and one-fifth scale squares   These are essential for students to record pattern blocks and adaptations in their notebooks.

Stanley knife

Tailor's chalk   This is used for marking out the final pattern onto the cloth and for marking alterations on the garment when it is being fitted.

Toile fabrics   Calico is used for making toiles for designs in woven fabrics. Make sure the weight of the calico is as close to the weight of the cloth as possible. Knitted fabric must be used for making toiles for designs in jersey fabrics; the toile fabric should have the same stretch quality.

Calculator   The calculator is now a common tool in all areas of skill as it eliminates the hard work of calculating proportions and it is accurate. If a calculator is not available use the table of aliquot parts on page 22.

French curves   Plastic shapes and curves are available in a range of sizes and they are useful for drawing good curves. A flexicurve which allows a shape to be manipulated is also available.

Pattern notcher   This is a tool which marks balance points by snipping out a section of pattern paper.

Pattern punch

Pattern hooks

Pattern weights   These keep pieces of pattern in position on the paper or cloth.

Model stands   Although not essential for a beginner, they are invaluable to the serious student for developing designs.

Computer equipment   Computer systems for cutting and grading patterns.

The equipment can be obtained at:
R.D. Franks Ltd, Kent House, Market Place, London W1
Eastman Machine Co. Ltd, Druro House, Station Estate, Eastwood Close, London E18 1BI
Morplan, 56 Great Tichfield Street, London W1P 8DX
Staples Group, Lockwood Road, Huddersfield HD1 3QW

Glossary

Definitions of terms used when drafting patterns.

BACK PITCH/FRONT PITCH   Point on body sections of the garment which match balance points on the sleeve, to ensure that the sleeve hangs correctly.

BALANCE MARKS   Marks or notches that denote positions where seams are joined together.

BLOCK   See page 20.

BUTTONSTAND   The distance between the button line and the front edge of the garment.

CIRCUMFERENCE   See 'constructing a circle' below.

CROTCH LINE   The seam line that joins the legs of trousers, passing between the legs.

DIMENSION   A measurement; in clothing terms it is the measurement of a specific place on the body generally understood by most people, e.g. waist, hip.

EASE   Extra allowance added to body measurements during block construction to allow for body movement and comfort.

ENCLOSED SEAMS   Seams which have seam allowances hidden from view, e.g. inside a collar, facing or cuff.

FITTING LINES   The lines along which a garment must be seamed when it is assembled.

FLY   A flap to conceal buttons. Is also the term for the front fastening on men's trousers.

GIRTH   A measurement around the body.

GRAIN LINE   A line marked on a pattern. The pattern is placed on the fabric with the line parallel to the selvedge.

NETT   A term which means that there is no seam allowance included in the pattern.

RADIUS   See 'constructing a circle' below.

SCYE   Armhole.

SEAT WEDGE   The wedge that is opened on the back crutch line of trousers to increase the seat angle.

SLEEVE HEAD   The section of the sleeve from scye depth line to top of sleeve.

The definitions for the following terms are given in the section on collars (page 122): STYLE LINE, ROLL LINE, STAND, FALL, BREAK POINT, BREAK LINE.

CONSTRUCTING A CIRCLE

Many patterns use circles as a base for their construction.

The circumference of a circle is the measurement around a circle.

The radius is a line from the centre of the circle to the outer edge.

To construct a circle the radius must be known. The circle can then be drawn with a compass or more primitively with a pencil and ruler.

In pattern cutting the waist or wrist measurement is known and one may be required to construct a circle whose circumference is exactly that measurement. The following calculation can be made to obtain the radius required to construct a circle.

Radius = circumference divided by 6.28

Working example   Waistline measurement is 55cm. Construction of a circle is required whose circumference is 55cm.

Radius = 55 ÷ 6.28 = 8.76

Construct a circle as a diagram with a radius of 8.76cm; its circumference will be 55cm.

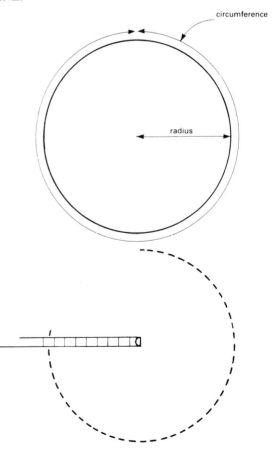

1   THE BASIC PRINCIPLES, SIZING AND SIZE CHARTS

Methods of Measuring Body Dimensions

Body measurements are taken over light underclothes with the child barefoot. The natural waistline should be identified with a piece of tape or elastic.

A: Height   The child's height and other vertical measurements are taken with the child standing erect with the feet together. The height measurement is taken from the head crown to the soles of the feet.

B: Chest/bust   The maximum girth measurement under the armpits with the tape passing over the shoulder blades and across the chest or bust.

C: Waist   The measurement of the natural waist girth measurement with the child's abdomen relaxed.

D: Hip/seat   The horizontal measurement taken round the fullest part of the seat.

E: Across back   The measurement taken across the back from armscye to armscye mid-way between the cervical and the base of the armscye.

F: Neck size   The girth measured around the base of the neck touching the cervical and the top of the front collar bone.

G–H: Shoulder   The measurement taken from the base of the side neck to the shoulder edge.

I: Upper arm   The girth measured around the upper arm mid-way between the shoulder and the elbow. The measurement is taken with the arm bent.

J: Wrist   The girth measured at the base of the arm over the wrist bone.

K–L: Scye depth   The measurement from the cervical to a line which touches the base of the armscye (armscye line).

K–M: Neck to waist   The measurement taken from the cervical to the waistline.

M–N: Waist to hip   The measurement taken from the waistline to the hip/seat line.

K–O: Cervical height   The measurement taken from the cervical to the soles of the feet.

M–P: Waist to knee   The measurement taken from the centre back waistline to the crease at the back of the knee.

Q–R: Body rise   The measurement is taken on a seated figure from the side waistline to the top of the stool. This measurement can also be calculated by measuring M–O (waist height) and subtracting S–O (inside leg) from M–O.

S–O: Inside leg   The measurement taken from the crotch to the soles of the feet.

H–T: Sleeve length   The measurement from the shoulder edge to the wrist bone.

U: Head circumference   The horizontal girth of the head.

V: Vertical trunk   The measurement taken from the centre of one shoulder, down the back, under the crotch returning over the abdomen and chest to the original shoulder position.

W: The girth measured at the base of the leg just above the ankle bone.

X–Y: The measurement of the foot from the heel to the top of the big toe.

EXTRA MEASUREMENTS (GARMENTS)
Extra measurements are standard measurements of specific parts of basic garments. They are offered as a guide to be used when drafting basic blocks. They are:

Cuff size, two-piece sleeve
Cuff size, shirts
Trouser bottom width
Jeans bottom width.

Drafting the Blocks for Individual Figures

The blocks can be drafted for individual figures by substituting the personal measurements of a figure for the standard ones shown in the standard size charts on pages 16–19 and 161. Successful blocks can only be drafted if the personal measurements are taken accurately in the correct position on the body. The description of the measurements listed above should be read carefully before measuring the figure.

All the body measurements listed should be taken except the scye depth and the waist to hip. These measurements are difficult to take accurately, therefore they should be taken from the standard size charts

(pages 16–19 and 161) using the child's height as a reference.

The dart size for blocks for girls with developing figures should be taken from the size chart on page 161 after reference to the notes on the development of the bust.

When the figure has been measured the individual measurements should be checked against a list of standard measurements for the height group of the child. If significant differences are apparent, the figure should be re-measured and checked to see if it is in fact wider or narrower than the average figure.

Body measurements

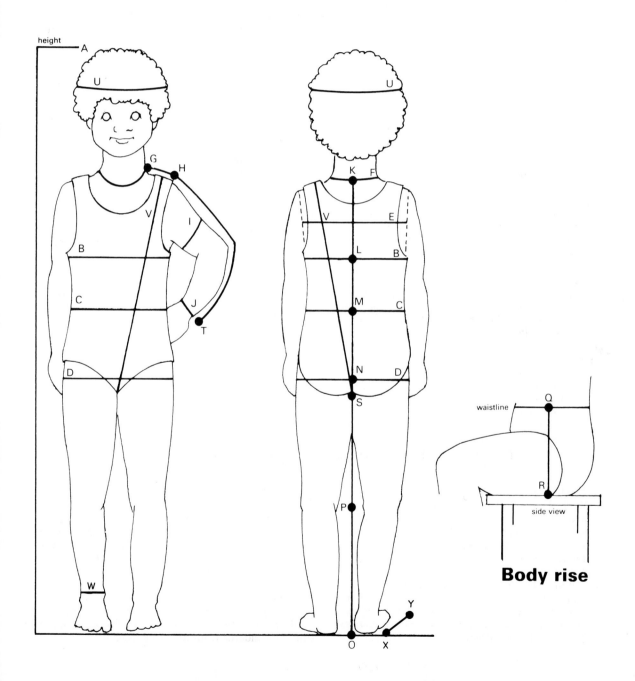

Body rise

Metric Sizing and Size Charts

The sizing of children's garments available in shops which are not a part of the multiple chain stores is somewhat chaotic. A move was made by the British Standards Institution in 1982 (BS 3728) to designate size by the height dimension and this is being accepted by an increasing number of small manufacturers. Some manufacturers are using this system for children up to the age of eleven but see it as less useful for older children where the correlations of girth and limb length to height become more variable. For this group they prefer to mark the garments with chest or bust, waist, hip and inside leg measurements.

SIZE DESIGNATION
In June 1990, the British Standards Institution published their specification for size designation for children's wear and recommendations of body dimensions for children (BS 7231).

The primary aim of these British Standards is the establishment of a size designation system which indicates the body size of the child or infant that a garment is intended to fit. Provided that the shape of the child or infant's body has been accurately determined, this system will facilitate the choice of garments that fit.

The size designation system is based on body and not garment dimensions. Choice of garment measurements is normally left to the designer and the manufacturer, who are concerned with style, cut and other fashion elements and must make allowance for garments normally worn beneath a specific garment.

CONTROL DIMENSIONS
Control dimensions are the dimensions of the body given on labels to enable consumers to buy clothes that fit.

The basic control measurement of all infants' and children's garments is height. The height interval used for labelling purposes should be 6cm based on a specified fixed point, e.g. 98cm, 104cm, 110cm.
Infants (boys and girls up to 104cm)   Height is the control dimension.
Girls (females who have not completed their growth)   For all forms of outerwear, height will always be given. Other control measurements will be given depending on the area of the body the garment will cover and the type of garment; these are bust, waist and hip. Foundation garments will include bust and underbust girth.
Boys (males who have not completed their growth)   For all forms of outerwear, height will always be given. Other control measurements given will be chest, waist and hips. Neck measurements will be given for uniform and formal shirts.

LABELLING
The size designation on a label should have the control dimensions in centimetres of the intended wearer of the garment.

Garment measurements are not included in the size designation, but where they are considered to be of value they can be added as additional information and indicated separately.
Additional information includes:
1. extra body measurements, e.g. inside leg lengths are usually included in trouser labels;
2. extra garment measurements;
3. the approximate age of the child that the garment will fit.
Where size designation is supplemented by additional information this information should be separated from the size designation as shown in the diagrams.

It is recognised that age alone is an unreliable guide to fit as children's stature in relation to age is very variable. However its retention in addition to height, indicating the average child, is supported by the National Children's Wear Association as they state that many garments are purchased without the child being present.

Examples of information on garment labels

Weight	8 kg
Approx. age	6 months

(a) Infant's dress

Height	128 cm
Chest girth	60 to 65
Approx. age	8 years

(b) Vest, jumper or jacket

Height	116 cm
Waist girth	50 to 55
Approx. age	6 years

(c) Skirt or shorts

The information offered in the section on Size Designation is published with the permission of the British Standards Institution (see page 4).

SIZE CHARTS – HISTORICAL BACKGROUND

In 1982, when this book was first written, it was realised that the British Standards Institution's survey, done by the University of Loughborough, was going to take some years. Because of the expected delay the author undertook a smaller scale survey (see the Introduction). The size charts offered in this book are based on this personal survey. The BSI survey was completed and published in 1990. It was published in two parts: Part 1 contains raw data from the Loughborough University survey shown in centile tables; Part 2 contains size charts commissioned by the technical committee.

Part 2 of the survey has been heavily criticised for the way it interpreted the raw data in Part 1 (see page 184) and the crude construction of the size charts which contain many anomalies, contradictions and some distorted measurements that are not suitable for cutting patterns. Therefore, the author decided to retain her own size charts in the main body of the book. She found that a great deal of the raw data collected in Part 1 of the Loughborough survey correlated closely with the data collected in her survey. She argues that the main size charts offered in the main section of the book, which were constructed from her survey, are valid and of a sounder construction than those offered in Part 2 of the BSI Standard.

The author's calculations from the raw data from Part 1 of the Loughborough survey have been used to provide the supplementary body measurements on page 186 and to extend the main measurement charts (page 16) for babies.

As stated in the introduction, students may encounter BSI size charts when they enter industry; they should be aware of the value of Part 1 and of ways of interpreting it. They should also be aware of the anomalies in Part 2; some BSI Part 2 size charts are included in the Appendix of this book. See page 184 for further discussion of the charts and the inclusion of some supplementary measurements from Part 1.

SIZE CHARTS – THE CENTILONG SYSTEM

The centilong system is an accepted European practice of designating different sizes by height intervals. This practice has been accepted by the ISO, BSI and most British manufacturers. The centilong system bases children's sizing intervals on height, the interval between the sizes being based on 6cm at specific points i.e. 98cm, 104cm, 110cm, which roughly correspond with age intervals. The fixed points are mid-way in a size range.

For example: the range for the 110cm size label will be from 107 to 112.9cm height. A child who is 108.5cm in height will be seen as a size 110cm.

The changing shape of the growing child, and the different figure changes of the sexes, means that the different size charts have to be offered for specific groups. The following size charts are offered in this book:

1. Size chart for boys and girls, 56–98cm height (approx. age birth–3 years); page 16.
2. Size charts for girls – undeveloped figures, 104–152cm height (approx. age 4–12 years); page 17.
3. Size chart for boys, 104–170cm height (approx. age 4–14 years); page 18.
4. Size chart for unisex sizes 80–164cm height (approx. age 1–14 years) in 'two size' groupings; page 19.
5. Size chart for girls – developing figures, 146–164cm height (approx. age 11–14 years); page 161.

RETAIL SIZE RANGES

Retail size range groupings vary. They vary between stores where the marketing team decide how the range will target its particular customer base. There can be variations within the same store where different product groups may offer overlapping size ranges. This can be very confusing, and particularly affects the transition from babywear to toddler's garments.

The division of the size ranges in this book reflects the *general trends* in clothing marketing in 1998, and each group can be extended into another range using the appropriate measurements. The book has been planned to be flexible but still offer accurate and well-fitting blocks appropriate to the product type. The grading decisions, complex or simplistic (dependent on range and style), proceed from a sound theoretical base. This book has also been planned to offer the means of constructing garments to individual measurements.

Important Notes

It is advisable that students should read the section on the growth of children and adolescents (page 7). This offers an explanation of the uneven growth and body shape changes that result in the different measurement increments between the sizes in the charts. Although the book has revised the size group divisions in the size charts, the work still proceeds from a sound theoretical base that relates to the growth of children.

Useful world-wide anthropometric data collected by the University of Nottingham for ergonomics can be obtained from the Consumer Safety Unit of the Department of Trade and Industry.

Standard Body Measurements   Birth–3 years

Boys and girls, 58–98cm height, approximate age birth–3 years

Important note The standard measurements in this block are taken from the 75th centile of sizing surveys. They have been calculated so that when they are used to construct the blocks, the blocks will fit approximately 75% of babies or children in the height interval. The measurements have been marginally adjusted for easy size labelling and to give sensible grading intervals. However, the balance over a range of size has been maintained.

		56	64	72	80	86	92	98
HEIGHT		56	64	72	80	86	92	98
APPROXIMATE WEIGHT (kg)		4–5	6–7	8	9–10	11–12	–	–
APPROXIMATE AGE		birth	3m	6m	12m	18m	2	3
B	CHEST	40	43	46	49	51	53	55
C	WAIST	38	41	44	47	49	51	53
D	HIP/SEAT	40	43	46	50	52	54	56
E	ACROSS BACK	16.8	18	19.2	20.4	21.2	22	22.8
F	NECK SIZE	22.5	23.5	24.5	25.5	26	26.5	27
G–H	SHOULDER	4.4	5	5.6	6.2	6.6	7	7.4
I	UPPER ARM	14.2	15.2	16.2	17.2	17.6	18	18.4
J	WRIST	9.6	10.4	11.2	12	12.3	12.6	12.9
K–L	SCYE DEPTH	9.6	10.2	10.8	11.4	12	12.6	13.2
K–M	BACK NECK–WAIST	17	18.2	19.4	20.6	21.8	23	24.2
M–N	WAIST–HIP	–	–	–	–	–	11.4	12
K–O	CERVICAL HEIGHT	–	–	–	–	–	75.5	80.8
M–P	WAIST–KNEE	–	–	–	–	–	32	34
Q–R	BODY RISE	11.4	12.4	13.4	14.4	15.4	16.4	17.4
S–O	INSIDE LEG	19	23	27	31	34.5	38	41.5
H–T	SLEEVE LENGTH	19.5	22	24.5	27	29.5	32	34.5
U	HEAD CIRCUMFERENCE	42.5	44.5	46.5	48.5	49.5	50.5	51.5
V	VERTICAL TRUNK	72	77	82	87	92	97	102
W	ANKLE GIRTH	11	12	13	14	14.5	15	15.5
X–Y	FOOT LENGTH	8.4	9.6	10.8	12	13	14	15
Measurements (garments)								
CUFF SIZE, TWO-PIECE SLEEVE		–	–	–	–	–	10	10.2
CUFF SIZE, SHIRTS		–	–	–	–	–	15	15.4
TROUSER BOTTOM WIDTH		–	–	–	–	–	15.5	16
JEANS BOTTOM WIDTH		–	–	–	–	–	13.5	14

Standard Body Measurements   Girls (undeveloped figures) 4–12 years

Important note The standard measurements in this block are taken from the 75th centile of sizing surveys. They have been calculated so that when they are used to construct the blocks, the blocks will fit approximately 75% of children in the height interval. The measurements have been marginally adjusted for easy size labelling and to give sensible grading intervals. However, the balance over a range of sizes has been maintained.

Girls, 104–152cm height, approximate age 4–12 years

		104	110	116	122	128	134	140	146	152
A	HEIGHT APPROXIMATE AGE	4	5	6	7	8	9	10	11	12
B	CHEST	57	59	61	63	66	69	72	75	78
C	WAIST	54	56	58	59	60	61	62	63	64
D	HIP/SEAT	59	62	65	68	71	74	77	80	83
E	ACROSS BACK	23.6	24.4	25.2	26	27.2	28.4	29.6	30.8	32
F	NECK SIZE	27.5	28	28.5	29	30	31	32	33	34
G–H	SHOULDER	7.8	8.2	8.6	9	9.5	10	10.5	11	11.5
I	UPPER ARM	18.8	19.2	19.6	20	20.8	21.6	22.4	23.2	24
J	WRIST	13.2	13.5	13.8	14.1	14.4	14.7	15	15.3	15.6
K–L	SCYE DEPTH	13.8	14.4	15	15.6	16.2	16.8	17.4	18	18.6
K–M	BACK NECK–WAIST	25.4	26.6	27.8	29	30.2	31.4	32.6	33.8	35
M–N	WAIST–HIP	12.6	13.2	13.8	14.4	15	15.6	16.2	16.8	17.4
K–O	CERVICAL HEIGHT	86.1	91.4	96.7	102	107.4	112.8	118.2	123.6	129
M–P	WAIST–KNEE	36	38	40	42	44	46	48	50	52
Q–R	BODY RISE	18.4	19.2	20	20.8	21.6	22.4	23.2	24	24.8
S–O	INSIDE LEG	45	48.5	52	55.5	59	62	65	68	71
H–T	SLEEVE LENGTH	37	39.5	42	44.5	47	49.5	52	54	56
U	HEAD CIRCUMFERENCE	52.5	52.9	53.3	53.7	54.1	54.5	54.9	55.3	55.7
W	ANKLE GIRTH	16	16.5	17	17.5	18	18.5	19	19.5	20

Extra measurements (garments)

	104	110	116	122	128	134	140	146	152
CUFF SIZE, TWO-PIECE SLEEVE	10.4	10.6	10.8	11	11.5	12	12.5	13	13.5
CUFF SIZE, SHIRTS	15.8	16.2	16.6	17	17.5	18	18.5	19	20
TROUSER BOTTOM WIDTH	16.5	17	17.5	18	18.5	19	19.5	20	20.5
JEANS BOTTOM WIDTH	14.5	15	15.5	16	16.5	17	17.5	18	18.5

Standard Body Measurements   Boys 4–14 years

Boys, 104–170cm height, approximate age 4-14 years

Important note The standard measurements in this block are taken from the 75th centile of sizing surveys. They have been calculated so that when they are used to construct the blocks, the blocks will fit approximately 75% of children in the height interval. The measurements have been marginally adjusted for easy size labelling and to give sensible grading intervals. However, the balance over a range of sizes has been maintained.

A	HEIGHT	104	110	116	122	128	134	140	146	152	158	164	170
	APPROXIMATE AGE	4	5	6	7	8	9	10	11	12	13	– – – –	– 14
B	CHEST	57	59	61	64	67	70	73	76	79	82	86	90
C	WAIST	54	56	58	60	62	64	66	68	70	72	74	76
D	HIP/SEAT	58	61	64	67	70	73	76	79	82	85	89	93
E	ACROSS BACK	24	24.8	25.6	26.8	28	29.2	30.4	31.6	32.8	34	35.6	37.2
F	NECK SIZE	27.5	28	28.5	29	30	31	32	33	34	35	36	37
G–H	SHOULDER	8	8.5	9	9.5	10	10.5	11	11.5	12	12.5	13.1	13.7
I	UPPER ARM	18.8	19.2	19.6	20	20.8	21.6	22.4	23.2	24	24.8	25.8	26.8
J	WRIST	13.4	13.6	13.8	14	14.4	14.8	15.2	15.6	16	16.4	16.8	17.2
K–L	SCYE DEPTH	13.8	14.4	15	15.6	16.4	17.2	18	18.8	19.6	20.4	21.4	22.4
K–M	BACK NECK–WAIST	25.8	27	28.2	29.4	30.8	32.2	33.6	35	36.4	37.8	39.4	41
M–N	WAIST–HIP	12.6	13.2	13.8	14.4	15	15.6	16.2	16.8	17.4	18	18.8	19.6
K–O	CERVICAL HEIGHT	86.1	91.4	96.7	102	107.4	112.8	118.2	123.6	129	134.4	139.8	145.2
Q–R	BODY RISE	18	18.8	19.6	20.4	21.2	22	22.8	23.6	24.4	25.2	26.2	27.2
S–O	INSIDE LEG	45	48.5	52	55.5	59	61	65	68	71	74	77	80
H–T	SLEEVE LENGTH	37	39.5	42	44.5	47	49.5	52	54.5	57	59	61	63
U	HEAD CIRCUM.	52.5	53	53.5	54	54.5	55	55.5	56	56.5	57	57.4	57.8
	Extra measurements (garments)												
	CUFF SIZE, TWO-PIECE SLEEVE	10.4	10.6	10.8	11	11.5	12	12.5	13	13.5	13.8	14	14.2
	CUFF SIZE, SHIRTS	15.8	16.2	16.6	17	17.5	18	18.5	19	20	20.5	21	21.5
	TROUSER BOTTOM WIDTH	16.5	17	17.5	18	18.5	19	19.5	20	20.5	21	21.5	22
	JEANS BOTTOM WIDTH	14.5	15	15.5	16	16.5	17	17.5	18	18.5	18.8	19	19.2

Standard Body Measurements   Unisex 1–14 years

Unisex 80–164cm height

The measurement chart has been constructed for companies who specialise in leisurewear or who wish to produce a reduced size range. The chart is unisex; note that the main differences between girls' and boys' figures are their waist and hip measurements; a compromise between their measurements is given in this chart.
All the measurements have been calculated so that when they are used to construct the blocks, the blocks will fit approximately 75% of children in the height interval.

A	HEIGHT	80	92	104	116	128	140	152	164
	APPROXIMATE AGE	–1	1–2	3–4	5–6	7–8	9–10	11–12	13–14
B	CHEST	49	53	57	61	67	73	79	85
C	WAIST	46	50	54	58	61	64	67	70
D	HIP/SEAT	50	55	60	65	72	78	84	90
E	ACROSS BACK	20.4	22	23.6	25.2	27.6	30	32.4	34.8
F	NECK SIZE	25.5	26.5	27.5	28.5	30	32	34	36
G–H	SHOULDER	6.4	7.2	8	8.8	9.8	10.8	11.8	12.8
I	UPPER ARM	17.2	18	18.8	19.6	21	22.4	23.8	25.2
J	WRIST	12.2	12.8	13.4	14	14.6	15.2	15.8	16.4
K–L	SCYE DEPTH	11.4	12.6	13.8	15	16.4	17.8	19.2	20.6
K–M	BACK NECK–WAIST	20.6	23	25.4	27.8	30.2	33	35.8	38.6
M–N	WAIST–HIP	10.2	11.4	12.6	13.8	15	16.5	18	19.5
K–O	CERVICAL HEIGHT	64.2	75	85.8	96.6	107.4	118.2	129	139.8
M–P	WAIST–KNEE	28	32	36	40	44	48	52	56
Q–R	BODY RISE	14.2	16	17.8	19.6	21.4	23.2	25	26.8
S–O	INSIDE LEG	31	38	45	52	58	64	70	76
H–T	SLEEVE LENGTH	27	32	37	42	47	51.5	56	60.5
U	HEAD CIRCUMFERENCE	48.5	50	51.5	53	54	55	56	57
W	ANKLE GIRTH	14	15	16	17	18	19	20	21

Extra measurements (garments)

		80	92	104	116	128	140	152	164
	CUFF SIZE, SHIRTS	15	15.4	15.8	16.2	17	18	19	21
	TROUSER BOTTOM WIDTH	15	15.5	16.5	17.5	18.5	19.5	20.5	21.5
	JEANS BOTTOM WIDTH	13	13.5	14.5	15.5	16.5	17.5	18.5	19

Using the Blocks

A block is a foundation pattern from which style adaptations are made. The blocks include the amount of basic ease required for the function of the garment block (e.g. a coat block has more ease than a dress block).

In the clothing industry, the blocks are constructed to standard (average measurements) such as those given in the size charts on the previous pages. Because the size range is wide (birth to 14 years), different blocks are used at different stages, particularly for classic clothes that require a closer and distinct body fit. A list of the blocks

is given below; note that size is designated by the height of the child.

Girls with developing figures require blocks that allow for the bust shape, hence blocks with a dart allowance should be used (pages 162–166).

A block can be drafted to fit an individual figure using personal measurements (page 12).

The blocks do not include any seam allowance. This must be added after the pattern is completed.

Types of Block

This edition of the book has been designed to demonstrate the two different types of cutting that are currently in operation in the garment industry. The division is possibly most evident in children's clothing, where a large proportion of garments are not tailored or shaped to fit the body (classic 'form' cutting). Instead, they are cut from 'flat' blocks to produce simple shapes and to allow the front body parts to be similar to the back parts.

This can be done when:
1. the garment style is cut wide and fits very easily around the figure;
2. the fabric to be used has stretch characteristics and will therefore fit easily around the body shape.
Many leisurewear manufacturers will cut only from flat blocks. They are useful in that they offer simpler grading and are more appropriate to the methods of manufacture.

Part One: The 'Flat' Blocks

Babywear (birth–2 yrs)
GIRLS AND BOYS 58–92cm height
1 **Jersey Body Blocks** (page 24)
2 **Woven Fabric Body Block** (page 24)
3 **Overgarment Block** (page 24)
4 **Kimono Block** (page 24)
5 **Trouser Blocks** (page 26)
6 **Sleepsuit Block** (page 28)

Girls and Boys (1–14 yrs)
GIRLS AND BOYS 80–164cm height
1 **Body block** (page 38)
2 **Shirt Block** (page 38)
3 **Overgarment Blocks** (page 40)
4 **Kimono Blocks** (pages 40–42)
5 **Tee Shirt and Knitwear Blocks** (page 44)
6 **Jeans Block** (page 46)
7 **Trouser Blocks** (page 48)
8 **Underwear Blocks** (page 50)

Part Two: The Classic Blocks: ('Form' Cutting)

Girls (1–12 yrs) Boys (1–14 yrs)
GIRLS AND BOYS 80–98cm height
GIRLS (UNDEVELOPED FIGURES) 104–152cm height
BOYS 104–170cm height
1 **Bodice Blocks** – infants and girls (page 88)
2 **Dress Blocks** – girls (page 90)
3 **Formal Coat Block** – infants and girls (page 92)
4 **Overgarment Block** – infants (page 92)
5 **Overgarment Blocks** – boys and girls (page 94)
6 **Blazer Block** – boys and girls (page 96)
7 **Shirt Blocks** – infants, girls and boys (page 102–105)
8 **Skirt Block** – girls (page 142)
9 **Trouser Blocks** – boys and girls (page 152)

Girls – Developing Figures (11–14 years)
GIRLS 146–164cm height
1 **Bodice Block** (page 162)
2 **Dress Block** (page 164)
3 **Overgarment Block** (page 166)
4 **Trouser Block** (page 168)
5 **Skirt Block** (page 170)

From Block to Finished Pattern

The block pattern ... is the basic pattern from which adaptations are made. The block chosen is traced or 'wheeled' on to pattern paper to produce a working pattern.

The working pattern ... is used for cutting and adapting to achieve the final shapes required for the final pattern. Complicated designs may require a number of working shapes to be cut before the final shape is achieved. At this stage it is necessary to have as much information as possible written on the pattern.

The final pattern ... is the pattern from which the garment will be cut. It must have all the information required to make up the garment written on the pattern. The final pattern has to be very accurate; all pattern pieces which have to be joined together should match exactly. If ease is included in a seam this should be marked by notches. The pattern should have smooth lines and curves. Curved rules and shapes are excellent aids in the making of 'professional' curves, particularly at the neck and armhole.

Adapting the Blocks – Basic Points

The blocks include the correct amount of ease that is required for the function of the block (e.g. a coat block has more ease than a dress block). Before commencing any adaptation the following points should be considered.

1. Choose the correct blocks; it is very important that the type of garment is related to the type of block. The classic blocks are useful for conventional formal types of garments that are directly related to the child's body shape. They are used if well-fitting one-piece or two-piece sleeves are required. For loose-fitting less formal garments use the easy-fitting 'flat' blocks.

2. Decide the length; lengthen or shorten the block.

3. Make any adjustments to armholes or necklines before proceeding with drafting style lines or collars.

If this procedure is followed the correct basic shape will be achieved. This means that any styling will have the correct proportions.

Seam Allowances

Patterns used in industry have seam allowances added. Designers often adapt patterns from blocks which include seam allowances. This is a difficult task for a beginner. Students will find that it is easier to work with nett patterns (those without seam allowances) especially during the development of complicated styles. The seam allowance can be added when the adaptation of the pattern is completed. The amount of seam allowance required in specific places is usually:

basic seams (e.g. side seams, style seams) 1.5cm.
enclosed seams (e.g. collars, facings, cuffs) 0.5cm.
hem depth depends on shape and finish 1–5cm.

special seams (e.g. welt seam) often require different widths of seam allowance on matching seam lines.

Fabrics which fray easily may require a wider seam allowance.

The width of the seam allowance must be marked on each piece of pattern by lines or notches.

Nett patterns are often produced for individual garments and the seam allowances are chalked directly on to the fabric lay. These garments are often cut with a standard 1.5cm seam allowance around enclosed seams as well as basic seams. The enclosed seams of individual garments can be trimmed during making-up.

Pattern Instructions

To enable the garment to be made up correctly the following instructions must be marked on the pattern.

1. The name of each piece.
2. Centre back and centre front.
3. The number of pieces to be cut.
4. Folds.
5. Balance marks ... these are used to ensure that pattern pieces are sewn together at the correct points.
6. Seam allowances ... these can be marked by lines round the pattern or notches at each end of the seam. If the pattern is nett (has no seam allowance) this must be marked on the pattern.

7. Construction lines ... these include darts, buttonholes, pocket placings, tucks, pleats, decorative stitch lines. Construction lines are marked directly on the pattern or indicated by punch holes.

8. Grain lines ... these indicate how the pattern must be positioned on the fabric. Mark the grain lines on the separate pattern pieces before the working pattern is cut into sections. Once it is in pieces it can be difficult to establish the correct grain, particularly if the pattern has been through a number of development stages.

Aliquot Parts

If a calculator is not available for working out fractional parts, the following table can be used.
Figures in columns marked with an asterisk are calculated to one decimal place.

NECK SIZE (cm)

	$*^1/_8$	$*^1/_5$
22.5	2.8	4.5
23	2.9	4.6
23.5	2.9	4.7
24	3	4.8
24.5	3.1	4.9
25	3.1	5
25.5	3.2	5.1
26	3.2	5.2
26.5	3.3	5.3
27	3.4	5.4
27.5	3.4	5.5
28	3.5	5.6
29	3.6	5.8
30	3.8	6
31	3.9	6.2
32	4	6.4
33	4.1	6.6
34	4.3	6.8
35	4.4	7
36	4.5	7.2
37	4.6	7.4

CHEST, WAIST AND HIP SEAT (cm)

	$*^1/_{16}$	$*^1/_{12}$	$*^1/_6$	$^1/_4$	$^1/_2$
38	2.4	3.2	6.3	9.5	19
39	2.4	3.3	6.5	9.75	19.5
40	2.5	3.3	6.5	10	20
41	2.6	3.4	6.8	10.25	20.5
42	2.6	3.5	7	10.5	21
43	2.7	3.6	7.2	10.75	21.5
44	2.75	3.7	7.3	11	22
45	2.8	3.8	7.5	11.25	22.5
46	2.9	3.8	7.6	11.5	23
47	2.9	3.9	7.8	11.75	23.5
48	3	4	8	12	24
49	3.1	4.1	8.2	12.25	24.5
50	3.1	4.2	8.3	12.5	25
51	3.2	4.3	8.5	12.75	25.5
52	3.3	4.3	8.7	13	26
53	3.3	4.4	8.8	13.25	26.5
54	3.4	4.5	9	13.5	27
55	3.4	4.6	9.2	13.75	27.5
56	3.5	4.7	9.3	14	28
57	3.6	4.8	9.5	14.25	28.5
58	3.6	4.8	9.7	14.5	29
59	3.7	4.9	9.8	14.75	29.5
60	3.8	5	10	15	30
61	3.8	5.1	10.2	15.25	30.5
62	3.9	5.2	10.3	15.5	31
63	3.9	5.3	10.5	15.75	31.5
64	4	5.3	10.7	16	32
65	4.1	5.4	10.8	16.25	32.5
66	4.1	5.5	11	16.5	33
67	4.2	5.6	11.2	16.75	33.5
68	4.3	5.7	11.3	17	34
69	4.3	5.8	11.5	17.25	34.5
70	4.4	5.8	11.7	17.5	35
71	4.4	5.9	11.8	17.75	35.5
72	4.5	6	12	18	36
73	4.6	6.1	12.2	18.25	36.5
74	4.6	6.2	12.3	18.5	37
75	4.7	6.3	12.5	18.75	37.5
76	4.8	6.3	12.7	19	38
77	4.8	6.4	12.8	19.25	38.5
78	4.9	6.5	13	19.5	39
79	4.9	6.6	13.2	19.75	39.5
80	5	6.7	13.3	20	40
81	5.1	6.8	13.5	20.25	40.5
82	5.1	6.8	13.7	20.5	41
83	5.2	6.9	13.8	20.75	41.5
84	5.3	7	14	21	42
85	5.3	7.1	14.2	21.25	42.5
86	5.4	7.2	14.3	21.5	43
87	5.4	7.3	14.5	21.75	43.5
88	5.5	7.3	14.7	22	44
89	5.6	7.4	14.8	22.25	44.5
90	5.6	7.5	15	22.5	45
91	5.7	7.6	15.2	22.75	45.5
92	5.8	7.7	15.3	23	46
93	5.8	7.8	15.5	23.25	46.5

Part One: Simple 'Flat' Pattern Cutting Babywear

2 SPECIFIC BABYWEAR BLOCKS

Approximate age: birth–2 years

SIZING

The blocks in this section are for specific garments for babies and toddlers. For example, very young babies need particular types of easy-fitting garments with wide openings and simple fastenings. Babies and toddlers who still wear nappies require trousers which are specially designed to accommodate them. However, many ranges designed for toddlers, such as dresses, shirts and tee shirts, are graded down into babywear sizing; this can be done by using the sizing on page 16.

NOTE

Some basic cutting methods are applicable to both 'flat' pattern cutting and to classic 'form' cutting; for example, some sleeve, collar and skirt adaptations. These basic methods are located in Part Two, Chapters 10, 11 and 13.

The 'Flat' Body Blocks For Babywear

For babies and toddlers sizes 56–92cm height

MEASUREMENTS REQUIRED TO DRAFT THE
BLOCKS
(e.g. 64cm height, approx. age 3 months)
Taken from the size chart on page 16 for standard
measurements (8cm and 6cm height intervals).

Chest	43cm
Across back	18cm
Neck size	23.5cm
Shoulder	5cm
Scye depth	10.2cm
Back neck to waist	18.2cm
Sleeve length	22cm
Wrist	10.4cm

Jersey Body Blocks

The main figures construct the basic jersey block, the
figures in brackets give an easier fitting shape.

Back and front sections
Square down and across from 0.
0 – 1 Back neck to waist; square across.
0 – 2 Finished length; square across.
0 – 3 Scye depth: plus 2cm (3cm); square across.
0 – 4 $^1/_2$ measurement 0–3; square across.
0 – 5 $^1/_4$ scye depth minus 1.75cm; square across.
0 – 6 $^1/_5$ neck size plus 0.2cm (0.7cm); square up.
6 – 7 1.5cm. Draw in the back neck curve.
3 – 8 $^1/_2$ across the back plus 2cm (3cm); square up to 9 and 10.
10–11 0.5cm; join 7–11.
3 –12 $^1/_4$ chest plus 3cm (5cm); square down to 13 and 14.

Draw in the armscye shape to touch points 11, 9, 12.
0 –15 $^1/_5$ neck size minus 1cm (0.5cm); draw in front neck.

Sleeve
Square down from 0.
0 – 1 $^1/_2$ measurement 0–3 on body block minus 1cm.
0 – 2 Sleeve length minus 3cm (4cm); square across.
0 – 3 The measurement of the armhole curve from 11–12.
2 – 4 $^1/_2$ wrist plus 2cm (3cm); join 3–4.
Divide 0–3 into seven sections; mark points 5, 6, 7, 8, 9, 10.
Draw in the sleeve head:
raise the curve at 6, 0.2cm;
raise the curve at 9, 1cm (1.5cm).

Woven Fabric Body Block

Use the instructions for the *basic jersey block* with the
following modifications.

Back section
3 – 8 $^1/_2$ across the back plus 1.5cm; square up to 9 and 10.

Front section
9 –16 0.5cm.
Draw a line 0.4cm below the line squared out from 5.
7 –17 The measurement 7–11; draw front shoulder line to touch the new line at point 17.
Draw in the front armscye shape as shown in diagram to touch points 17, 16, 12.

The 'Flat' Overgarment Block for Babywear

For babies and toddlers sizes 56–92cm height

Back and front sections
Square down and across from 0.
0 – 1 Back neck to waist; square down.
1 – 2 Extend to finished length.
0 – 3 $^1/_4$ chest: plus 6cm; square down to 4 and 5.
0 – 6 1.5cm.
0 – 7 Scye depth; plus 4cm; square out to 8.
0 – 9 $^1/_2$ measurement 6–7; square out.
0 –10 $^1/_4$ scye depth minus 2cm; square out.
0 –11 $^1/_5$ neck size plus 0.8cm; draw back neck curve.
7 –12 $^1/_2$ across back plus 3.5cm; square up to 13 and 14.
14–15 0.75cm; join 11–15.
Draw in the back armscye shape as shown in diagram to touch points 15, 13, 8.
0 –16 $^1/_5$ neck size plus 1cm; draw in front neck curve.

Sleeve
Square down from 0.
0 – 1 $^1/_2$ measurement 6–7 on body block minus 1cm; square across.
0 – 2 Sleeve length minus 3cm; square across.
0 – 3 The measurement of the armhole curve from 15–8.
2 – 4 $^2/_3$ measurement 1–3; join 3–4.
Divide 0–3 into six section; mark points 5, 6, 7, 8, 9.
Draw in the sleeve head:
hollow the curve 0.3cm at point 5;
raise the curve at 8 and 1cm.

KIMONO BLOCK ADAPTATION
Most babies' overgarments are constructed using the
kimono block adaptation (see the instructions on page 40).
Many jersey overjackets are constructed from the kimono
adaptation, using the easy-fitting jersey block as the base.

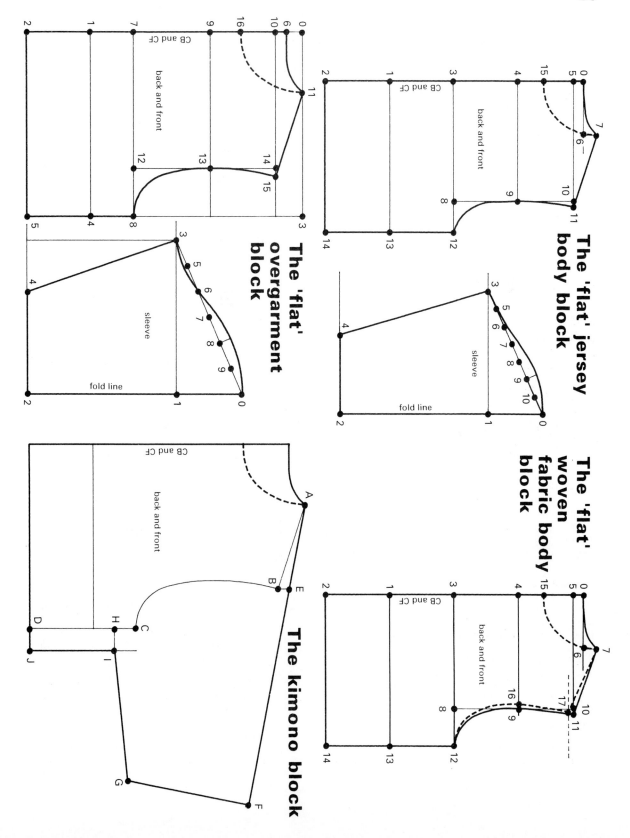

25

The 'flat' jersey body block

The 'flat' woven fabric body block

The 'flat' overgarment block

The kimono block

The 'Flat' Trouser Blocks

For babies and toddlers sizes 56–92cm height

MEASUREMENTS REQUIRED TO DRAFT THE BLOCKS
(e.g. 64cm height, approx. age 3 months)
Taken from the size chart on page 16 for standard measurements (8cm and 6cm height intervals).

Hip/seat	43
Body rise	12.4
Inside leg	23

Easy-fitting Two-piece Trouser Block

An easy-fitting trouser block shaped especially to accommodate nappies.

Front section
Square both ways from 0.
0 – 1 Body rise plus 4.5cm; square across.
1 – 2 Inside leg measurement minus 2cm; square across.
1 – 3 $1/2$ the measurement 1–2; square across.
1 – 4 $1/4$ hip/seat plus 5cm; square up to 5.
4 – 6 $1/3$ the measurement 4–5.
4 – 7 $1/4$ the measurement 1–4 minus 1cm.
Joint 5–6 and 6–7 with a curve to touch a point 1.75cm from 4.
4 – 8 $1/2$ measurement 1–4 minus 0.5cm; square down to 9 and 10.
10–11 $1/3$ measurement 1–4 plus 1cm.
Join 1–11 with a curve; mark point 12 on knee line. Straighten the line 4cm above point 11.
10–13 = 10–11.
9 –14 = 9–12. Join 7–14.
Draw front inside leg seam; curve the line inwards 0.25cm from 7–14; continue the curve to point 13. Straighten the line 4cm above point 13.

Back section
5 –15 2cm; square up 2cm to 16.
0 –17 1.5cm; join 16–17.
4 –18 $1/2$ the measurement 4–5.
7 –19 The measurement 4–7 minus 0.5cm.
19–20 0.5cm.
Join 16–18 and 18–20 with a curve to touch a point 2.75cm from 4.
1 –21 0.7cm
13–22 is $1/2$ the measurement 3–12.

Draw a curved side seam from 17 through point 21 and 22 to point 11. Straighten the line 4cm above point 11.
9–23 = 9–22. Join 20–23.
Draw back inside leg seam; curve the line inwards 0.4cm from 20–23; continue the curve to point 13. Straighten the line 4cm above point 13.

One-piece Trouser Block

The one-piece trouser block is a simple shape; it is used mainly for leggings and jersey trousers.
The main figures will give the leggings shape; the figures in the brackets give an easy-fitting shape.

Front section
Square down and across from 0.
0 – 1 Body rise plus 2cm (4.5cm); square across.
1 – 2 Inside leg measurement minus 2cm; square across.
1 – 3 $1/2$ the measurement 1–2; square across.
1 – 4 $1/4$ hip/seat measurement plus 1cm (5.5cm); square up to 5.
4 – 6 $1/3$ the measurement 4–5.
4 – 7 $1/4$ the measurement 1–4 minus 0.5cm.
Join 5–6 and 6–7 with a curve touching a point 1.75cm from 4.
2 – 8 $3/4$ measurement 1–4 plus 1cm; square up to 9.
9 –10 1cm (1.5cm); join 7–10.
Draw front inside leg seam; curve the line inwards 0.25cm from 7–10; continue the curve to point 8. Straighten the line 4cm above point 8.

Back section
5 –11 2cm; square up 2cm to 12. Join 12–0.
4 –13 $1/2$ the measurement 4–5.
7 –14 The measurement 4–7 minus 0.5cm (1cm).
14–15 0.5cm.
Join 12–13 and 13–15 with a curve touching a point 2.75cm (3cm) from 4.
10–16 1cm; 8–17 = 1.5cm. Join 15–16.
Draw back inside leg seam; curve the line inwards 0.4cm from 15–16; continue the curve to point 17. Straighten the line 4cm above point 17.

Creating a Front/back Trouser Pattern
Trace round back section (heavy line).
Trace round front section (dotted line).
Mirror the front and place the side seams together.

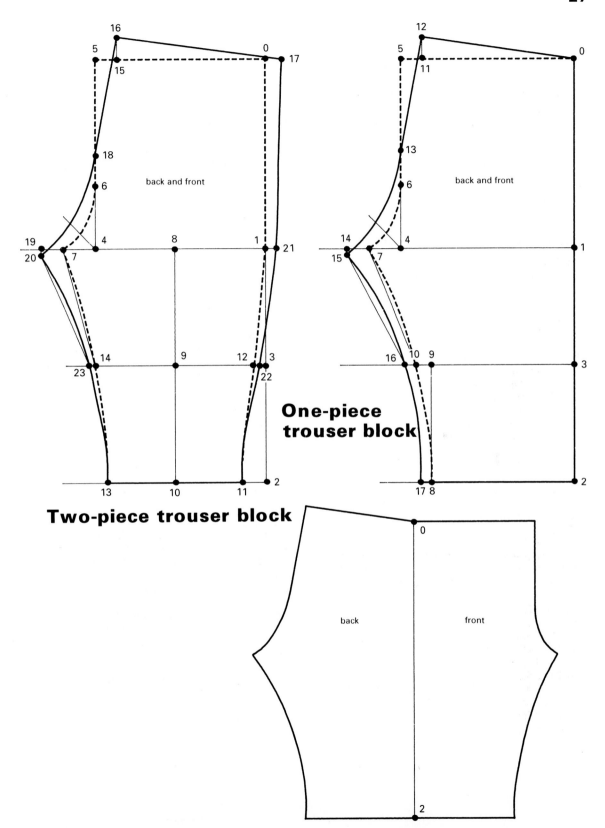

**One-piece
trouser block**

Two-piece trouser block

The One-piece Sleepsuit Block

For babies and toddlers sizes 56–92cm height

This block adaptation is based on the basic 'flat' jersey block. It is used for sleepsuits for very young babies. The adaptation can also be based on the easy-fitting jersey block to create a variety of one-piece designs for older babies and toddlers. See adaptations on page 32.

MEASUREMENTS REQUIRED TO DRAFT THE BLOCKS
(e.g. 64cm height, approx. age 3 months).
Taken from the size chart on page 16 for standard measurements (8cm and 6cm height intervals).

Hip/seat	43
Body rise	12.4
Inside leg	23
Foot length	9.6

Body sections

Trace off the body and sleeve sections of the basic 'flat' jersey body block (ref. page 24).
Mark points 1, 13, 15. Square down from 1 and 13.
1 –16 body rise plus 5cm; square across to 17.
16–18 inside leg meas. minus 3cm; square across to 19.
16–20 7cm; square across to 21.
12–22 $\frac{1}{2}$ measurement 12–13.
22–23 0.5cm.
17–24 $\frac{1}{2}$ measurement 13–17.
24–25 0.5cm.
19–26 $\frac{1}{6}$ meas. 18–19 minus 1cm; join 26–21.
Draw in curved side seam through points 12, 23, 25, 21.

Back section

18–27 $\frac{1}{6}$ meas. 18–19 plus 1cm; join 16–27.
Mark point 28 on the line from 20.
27–29 $\frac{1}{2}$ measurement 26–27; square down.
29–30 $\frac{1}{3}$ foot meas. plus 0.5cm. Draw back foot shape.

Front section

30–31 = 29–30. Draw front foot shape.
Add 1.5cm buttonstand from 15–16. Mark points 32, 33.
Join 33–27.

Foot piece

Trace off back and front foot; join along line 26–27.

Gusset

Square both ways from 0.
0 – 1 5cm.
Construct a line from 1 to touch the vertical line from 0.
1 – 2 measurement = 16–28 on body block.
Mirror the line to construct a diamond shaped gusset.

The sleepsuit usually has neck and cuff ribs, and is often constructed with ankle ribs instead of the foot section. The front and leg sections are open to approx. 4cm above point 27, faced with fine ribbing and fastened with popper studs.

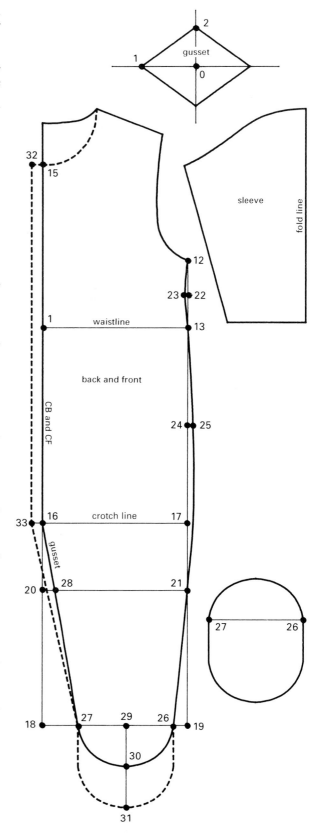

Part One: Simple 'Flat' Pattern Cutting Babywear

3 SPECIFIC BABYWEAR ADAPTATIONS

Approximate age: birth–2 years

NOTE

Many of the 'flat' pattern cutting methods for children's wear in Chapters 5–8 can also be used for babywear; for example dresses, pinafores, fleecy tops and anoraks. The adaptations in this chapter focus on the type of garments worn by very young babies, babies who are crawling, and toddlers who are still wearing nappies.

Some basic pattern cutting methods are applicable to both 'flat' pattern cutting and to classic 'form' cutting; for example some sleeve, collar and skirt adaptations. These basic methods are located in Part Two, Chapters 10, 11 and 13.

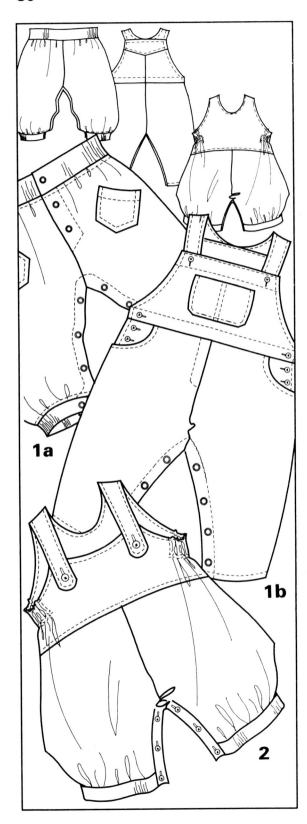

1a

1b

2

1 TROUSERS

Most trouser designs can be adapted for babywear using the babywear trouser block as a base. It is also important to open the inside leg seam to allow for nappy changing. The following examples show two adaptations: 1a (jersey fabric) and 1b (woven fabric – basic dungarees).

1a JERSEY TROUSERS

Front and back trousers   Shorten at hem by depth of cuff rib. Shorten at waist by depth of cuff rib.
Add centre front fly extension width = 3cm length = 8cm.
Draw in patch pocket.
Mark point A and B on the back inside leg seam; C and D on front inside leg seam.
Front rib facing   Construct a rectangle; length = meas. A–B; width = 2cm.
Mark stud positions.
Back rib facing   Construct a rectangle length = 2 × meas. C–D; width = 4cm. Mark stud positions.
Fly facing   Trace off fly facing.
Pockets   Trace off patch pocket; add 3cm extension to the top edge.

1b BASIC DUNGAREE TROUSERS

The basic adaptation for dungaree trousers is shown on page 76. These instructions can be used for babywear using the babywear trouser block for the trousers and the easy-fitting jersey body block for the bib. The leg opening allows for nappy changing.
Front and back trousers   Mark point A and B on the back inside leg seam; C and D on front inside leg seam.
Draw a facing line 3cm in from front inside leg seam.
Mark stud or buttonhole positions.
Front facing   Trace off facing.
Back facing strip   Construct a rectangle length = 2 × meas. A–B; width = 5cm. Mark stud or button positions.

2 TROUSERS – EXTRA FULLNESS

Trace off the one-piece flat trouser block and the easy-fitting jersey body block for the bib. Add 1–2cm to the side seam, 3cm to waistline. Mirror the front sections. Adjust the back and front waistline of the trousers at centre front and back to the same meas. as body block.
Front bib   Trace off front body block. Add 3cm to waistline. Draw in bib shape and strap. Mark buttonhole. Draw in facing line. Trace off front bib section.
Back bib   Trace off body block. Draw in bib shape. Place front strap to back strap; leave 1cm gap at shoulder. Draw facing line. Trace off back bib section with strap.
Back and front facings   Trace off facings.
Back and front trousers   Shorten trousers to length required. Add 1.5cm at both inside leg seams. Shorten by cuff rib depth.
Leg opening   Construct the appropriate leg opening shown above. This depends on the fabric used.

ONE-PIECE VERSION

Join bibs to full length trousers along the waistline. Draw in side seam with a curvy shape.

1 Trousers 1a

1 Trousers 1b

2 Trousers 2

One-piece version

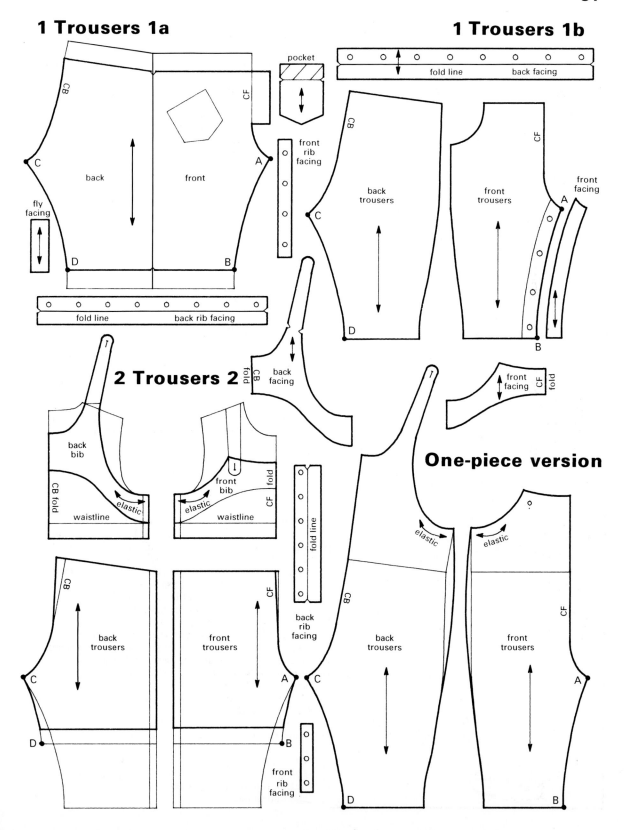

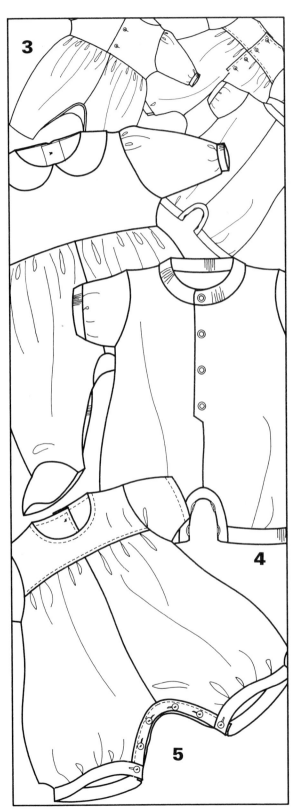

3   ROMPER 1 (JERSEY)

A placket fastening runs from 4cm above the hemline of each leg and around the top edge of the back gusset.

Body sections   Trace off the easy-fitting version of the sleepsuit block. Widen the hemline 0.25cm at each side. Draw in high waistline. Draw 2 vertical lines to hem. Mark points 28 and 16; mark point A 4cm above hemline. Trace off back; add buttonstand, mark buttonholes, add extended facing (ref 1b, page 120). Trace off front, mirror.

Collar   Construct two-piece flat collar (ref. 4 page 124).

Sleeve   Trace off sleeve. Shorten sleeve by ribbed cuff depth. Draw vertical line approx. 3cm from centre line. Cut up line; open approx. 3cm. Re-draw top curve.

Back and front trousers   Trace off trousers; cut up vertical lines and open approx. 3–4cm at waistline. Mirror front trousers. Mark B and C at hem. B–D and C–E = 1.5cm. Draw curve from D–E, raised 2cm.

Gusset   Construct sleepsuit gusset.

Placket   Construct a rectangle; length = 2 × meas. A–16; width = 4cm. Draw centre fold line; mark studs.

Foot piece   F–G = foot length plus 1.5cm. F–H = $\frac{1}{2}$ F–G minus 1cm. I–J = meas. of the curve D–E. J–K = E–C I–L = B–D. Draw curves from I–J and L–K.

Toe piece   Trace off toe piece from I–J.

4   ROMPER 2 (JERSEY)

Body sections   Trace off the easy-fitting version of the sleepsuit block. Shorten to length required. Mark points A at waist, B at crotch, C at hem. B–D = 3cm. B–E = $\frac{1}{2}$ A–B minus 1cm. D–F = 3cm. Join F–C. Re-draw side seam with a curvy line. Shorten leg length by cuff rib depth. Trace off back. Trace off front and mirror. Mark depth of front opening; add buttonstand, mark studs, add extended facing (ref. 1b, page 120).

Sleeve   Trace off sleeve. Shorten sleeve; then shorten again by ribbed cuff depth.

Gusset strip   Construct a rectangle; length = 2 × meas. C–F; width = 4cm. Draw centre fold line; mark studs.

5   ROMPER 3

Body sections   Trace off basic body block; mirror front. Draw in yoke lines. Trace off lower body sections; mark points A, B, C. A–D = A–B; square down. C–E = body rise plus 5cm. E–F = 3cm; square across to G. F–H = leg length required; square across to I. I–J = 1.5cm.

Back   G–K = $\frac{1}{2}$ meas. E–C. G–L = 3.5cm. Join K–L and L–J with curves. Mark back opening; add buttonstand, mark buttonholes, add extended facing (ref 1b, page 120).

Front   G–M = $\frac{1}{3}$ meas. E–C. G–N = 2.5cm. Join M–N and N–J with curves.

Front and back yokes   The yokes are double faced. Trace off front and back yoke; add buttonstand and buttonholes to back yoke section.

Gusset strip   Construct a rectangle; length = meas. L–J plus N–J; width = 4cm. Draw centre fold line; mark buttonholes.

Leg cuff   Construct rectangle; length = approx 20cm; width = 4cm. Draw centre fold line. Mark button position and buttonhole.

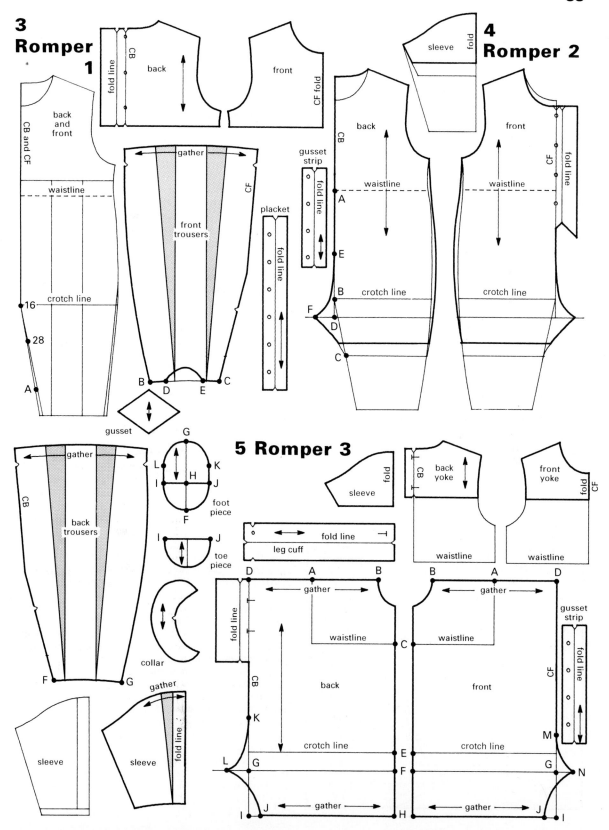

3 Romper 1

back and front
CB and CF
waistline
crotch line
16
28
A
back
CB
fold line
front
CF fold
gather
front trousers
CF
placket
fold line
gusset
gather
back trousers
CB
sleeve
gusset strip
fold line
A
E
B
F
D
C
crotch line
back
CB
waistline

4 Romper 2

front
CF
fold line
waistline
crotch line
sleeve
fold

G
L K
I H J
F
foot piece
I J
toe piece
collar
F G
sleeve
gather
sleeve
fold line

5 Romper 3

sleeve
fold
back yoke
CB
waistline
front yoke
CF
fold
waistline
leg cuff
fold line
D A B
gather
waistline
C
B A D
gather
waistline
gusset strip
CF
fold line
fold line
CB
back
front
K
crotch line
E
crotch line
M
L G
F
G N
I J
gather
H
gather
J I

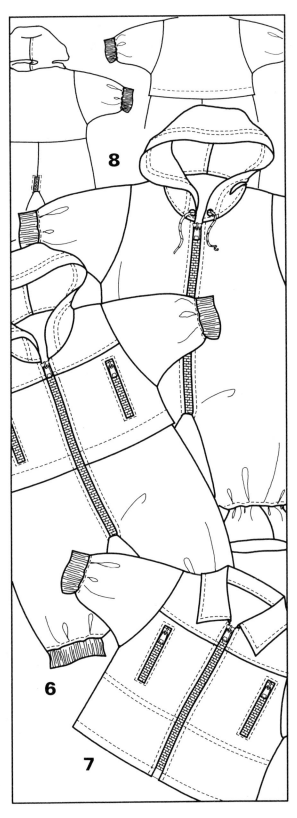

Many different kinds of easy-fitting snowsuit and jacket designs are constructed from the kimono block.
The snowsuits are shown with an attached hood. They also can be constructed with a convertible collar (ref. 2, page 122), but with a separate hood (ref 1, 2, page 128).

6 SNOWSUIT 1

Body sections Trace off the kimono block (adapted from the overgarment block).
Draw in armhole line. Mark A at shoulder, B at underarm. Draw in a 1cm dart. B–C = $\frac{1}{2}$ meas. A–B, B–D = $\frac{1}{2}$ B–C. B–E = B–D. Shorten sleeve by rib cuff depth.
Add 3cm below waistline; mark points F and G.
Mirror front block.
Lower neckline for attached hood 1 (ref. 1, page 128).
Draw in zip line; this is $\frac{1}{2}$ meas. of the zip from the centre front line. Mark points H and I.
Draw front yoke line, pocket position and pocket facing.
Trace off back and front sections; add 2cm below F–G and H–I to create tuck.
Mark tuck stitch line 2cm above F–G and H–I.
Front yoke Trace off front yoke.
Sleeve Trace off sleeve; cut up line D–E; open approx. 3cm. Re-draw top curve and underarm seam curve.
Front trousers Shorten trousers by ribbing depth.
Add 0.5cm at crotch point.
Draw in zip line down the full length of the crotch $-\frac{1}{2}$ meas. of the zip from the centre front line.
Mark point J at front waistline. J–K = H–I.
Add 0.5cm at inside leg hem, 1cm at outside leg hem.
Draw in new side seam and inside leg seam with curves.
Back trousers Shorten trousers by ribbing depth.
Add 1cm at crotch point. Add 1cm at centre back, mark point L. Draw new crotch line.
Extend front zip line to approx 6cm from crotch point.
Add 0.5cm at inside leg hem, 1cm at outside leg hem.
L–M = F–G. Draw in new side seam and inside leg seam.
Pockets Trace off the pocket bag and pocket facings.
Hood Construct hood 1 (ref. 1, page 128).

7 OVERJACKET

This illustration shows the top section of Snowsuit 1 lengthened to create an overjacket. It also has a convertible collar.

8 SNOWSUIT 2

This version has a one-piece front, but has a two-piece back to keep the extra 'seat rise' at the centre back. It also demonstrates the construction of attached 'snow shoes'.
Body sections Construct the back and front as above without the tuck and without the front yoke and pockets.
Join the front body section to the front trousers at H–I.
Foot piece 1 Construct rectangle; width approx. 4cm; length = foot length plus 3.5cm. Mark points A and B.
Draw a foot curve from A–B. Measure the length.
Mirror the foot shape along the line A–B.
Foot piece 2 C–D = meas. of the curve A–B,
C–E = 4.5cm; square out. C–F = $\frac{2}{3}$ meas. C–D; square up to G.
Join G–D with a curve.

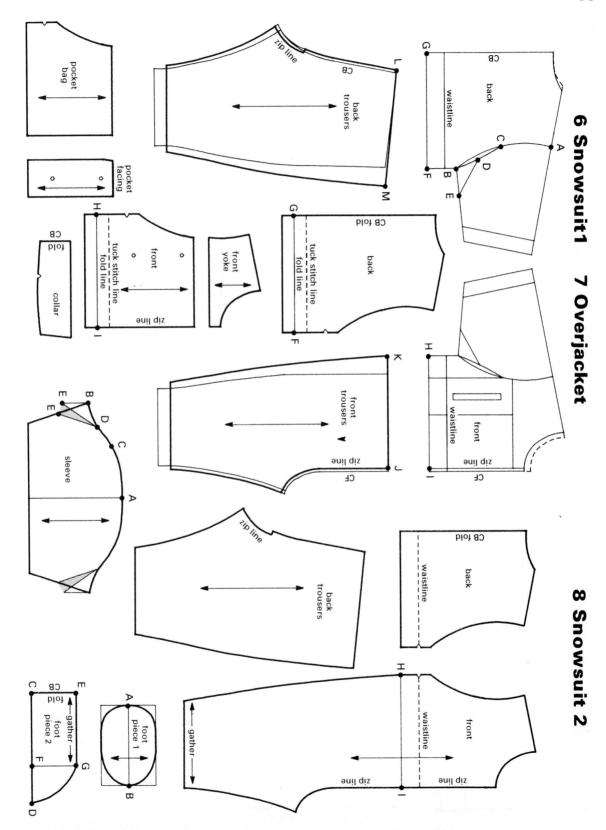

6 Snowsuit1   7 Overjacket

8 Snowsuit 2

pocket bag

pocket facing

collar

front yoke

front

back

zip line

back trousers

CB

waistline

back

CB

front trousers

CF

zip line

front

CF

zip line

waistline

sleeve

zip line

back trousers

back

CB fold

waistline

foot piece 2

fold CB

gather

foot piece 1

front

waistline

zip line

gather

tuck stitch line fold line

tuck stitch line fold line

CB fold

fold CB

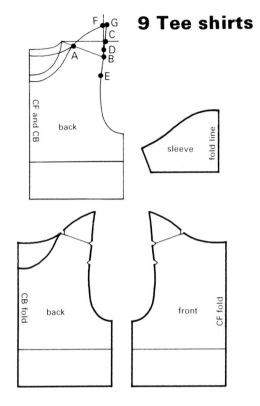

9 Tee shirts

10 Gathered knickers 1

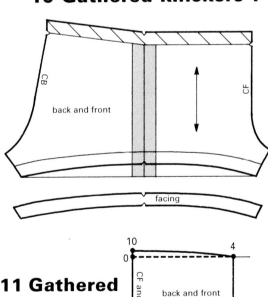

facing

11 Gathered knickers 2

9 TEE SHIRTS

Basic tee shirts and adaptations are drafted from the jersey blocks on page 24. Most tee shirts for babywear have neck fastenings so that they can be pulled easily over the baby's head. The wide-necked tee shirt with foldover flaps at the shoulder is a common neck adaptation.

Body sections   Trace off the jersey block required. Lower front and back neck approx. 1cm.
Widen the neck approx. 2cm. Draw new neck curves.
Mark point A at new neck point, B at shoulder point.
Square out from A; square out from B to point C.
D is $\frac{1}{2}$ the meas. B–C. Mark flap point E on the armhole (approx. 2.5cm from B). D–F = D–E. F–G = 0.5cm.
Draw in flap from A–G and B–G.
Trace back section. Trace and mirror front section.

10 GATHERED KNICKERS 1

Trace off the one-piece trouser block to length required.
Mirror front section.
Open the side seam by approx. 4cm; re-draw waistline.
Draw a curved hemline, raise 2cm at side seam.
Draw in facing. Trace off facing.
Add 2cm extension for elastication at waistline.

11 GATHERED KNICKERS 2

Square down and across from 0
0 – 1 body rise plus 6cm; square out.
1 – 2 $\frac{1}{3}$ measurement 0–1; square out.
1 – 3 3cm; square out.
0 – 4 $\frac{1}{4}$ hip measurement plus 6cm; square down to 5.
3 – 6 4cm; square up to 7.
7 – 8 0.5cm; 8–9 0.5cm. Join 5–9.
Draw back leg curve 6, 9, 5 raising it 1cm.
Draw front leg curve 6, 8, 5 raising it 2cm.
0 –10 1cm; draw in back waistline.
Trace back section. Trace and mirror front section; join along line 3–6.

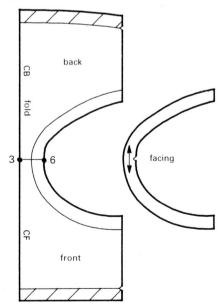

Part One: Simple 'Flat' Pattern Cutting Boys and Girls

4   THE 'FLAT' BLOCKS

Approximate age: 1–14 years

SIZING

Many of the blocks and adaptations are for basic garments aimed at children aged 1–14 years; however, some blocks, i.e. basic body blocks and jersey blocks, can be drafted or graded down for babies and toddlers. In this case, use the size chart on page 16.

The blocks are not constructed to fit closely to the body form and will be unisex if drafted from the Unisex Size Chart on page 19. If garments are to be constructed for a particular sex, then use the separate girls or boys size charts on page 17 and 18.

NOTE 1

Some basic pattern cutting methods are applicable to both 'flat' pattern cutting and to classic 'form' cutting; for example, some sleeve, collar and skirt adaptations. These basic methods are located in Part Two, Chapters 10, 11 and 13.

NOTE 2

Most adaptations in Chapters 5–8 suggest that the front block is mirrored before adaptation. This allows students to get a better understanding of the body shape. However, in industry the back and front of simple 'flat' garments frequently face the same way. This enables many of the size grades to be the same on the back and front sections and is particularly useful when computer grading.

The 'Flat' Body Block and Shirt Block

For boys and girls, sizes 80–164cm height
Useful blocks for easy-fitting flat shapes in simple dresses and blouses in woven and jersey fabrics

MEASUREMENTS REQUIRED TO DRAFT THE BLOCKS

(e.g. 104cm height, approx. age 3–4 years).
Taken from the Unisex size chart (12cm height intervals).
Refer to the size charts pages 16, 17 and 18 for standard measurements (6cm height intervals).
The main figures construct the basic body block. To construct the shirt block use the figures in brackets and the shirt sleeve instructions.

Chest	57cm
Across back	23.6cm
Neck size	27.5cm
Shoulder	8cm
Scye depth	13.8cm
Back neck to waist	25.4cm
Waist to hip	12.6cm
Sleeve length	37m
Wrist	13.4cm

Back and front sections

Square down and across from 0.

0 – 1 back neck to waist plus 1.25cm; square down.
1 – 2 waist to hip: square across.
0 – 3 $1/4$ chest:
  sizes 80–116cm height   plus 3cm (4.5cm)
      122–164cm height   plus 3.5cm (5.5cm);
  square down to 4 and 5.
0 – 6 1.25cm.
6 – 7 scye depth:
  sizes 80–116cm height   plus 1.5cm (2.5cm)
      122–164cm height   plus 2cm (3.5cm);
  square across to 8.
6 – 9 $1/2$ measurement 6–7; square out.
6 –10 $1/4$ scye depth minus 2cm; square out.
0 –11 $1/5$ neck size plus 0.3cm; draw back neck curve.
7 –12 $1/2$ across back:
  sizes 80–116cm height   plus 1.5cm (3cm)
      122–164cm height   plus 2cm (4cm);
  square up to 13 and 14.
14–15 sizes 80–116cm height   plus 1cm
      122–164cm height   plus 1.25 cm; join
  11–15.
Draw in back armscye shape to touch points 15, 13, 8.

Front section

0 –16 $1/5$ neck size; draw in the front neck curve.

13–17 sizes 80–116cm height   0.6cm
      122–164cm height   0.9cm
Draw a line below the line squared out from 10:
  sizes 80–116cm height   0.5cm
      122–164cm height   0.75cm;
11–18 The measurement 11–15; draw front shoulder line
  to touch the new line at point 18.
Draw in the front armscye shape as shown in diagram to touch points 18, 17, 8.
Note For a waisted garment, the front waistline can be lowered 1cm at point 1 on sizes up to 116cm height.

Sleeve – body block

Square down from 0

0 – 1 $1/2$ measurement 6–7 on body block plus 1cm; square across.
0 – 2 Sleeve length minus 1cm; square across.
0 – 3 The measurement of the armhole curve from 15–8.
2 – 4 $2/3$ measurement 1–3 plus 0.5cm; join 3–4.
Divide 0–3 into six sections; mark points 5, 6, 7, 8, 9.
Draw in the sleeve head:
hollow the curve 0.4cm at 5;
raise the curve at 8; sizes 80–116cm height   1.25cm
      122–164cm height   1.5cm.

Sleeve – shirt block

Square down from 0.

0 – 1 $1/3$ measurement 6–7 on body block; square across.
0 – 2 Sleeve length minus 3cm; square across.
0 – 3 The measurement of the armhole curve from 15–8.
2 – 4 $2/3$ measurement 1–3 minus 0.5cm; join 3–4.
Divide 0–3 into five section; mark points 5, 6, 7, 8.
Draw in the sleeve head:
hollow the curve 0.3cm at point 5;
raise the curve between 7 and 8;
  sizes 80–116cm height   1cm
      122–164cm height   1.25cm.

Note – Sleeve pitch points

Some sleeve adaptations require pitch points on the sleeve and body sections.
Mark point 6 on the sleeve as a pitch point with a notch.
Measure the distance 3–6.
Measure along the armhole of the body sections the same distance. Mark the pitch points with a notch.

The 'Flat' Sleeveless Body Block

Trace off the body block along the back armhole line.
Draw in front neckline.
Mark points, 5, 8, 13, 15 on the block.
8–A 1.25cm; square down to B.
A–C 1cm; square across for new scye depth line.

13–D 1.5cm.
15–E 1.75cm along the shoulder line.
Draw in new armhole curve to touch points E, D, C.

The 'flat' body and shirt block

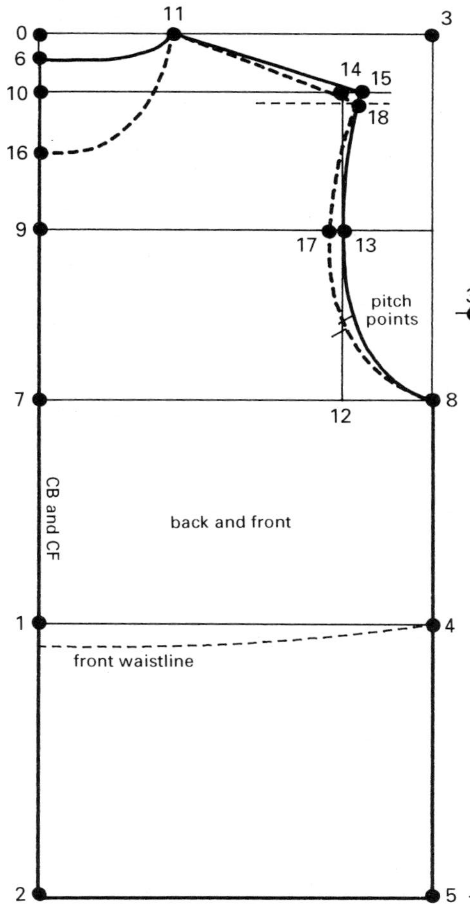

The body sleeve   The shirt sleeve

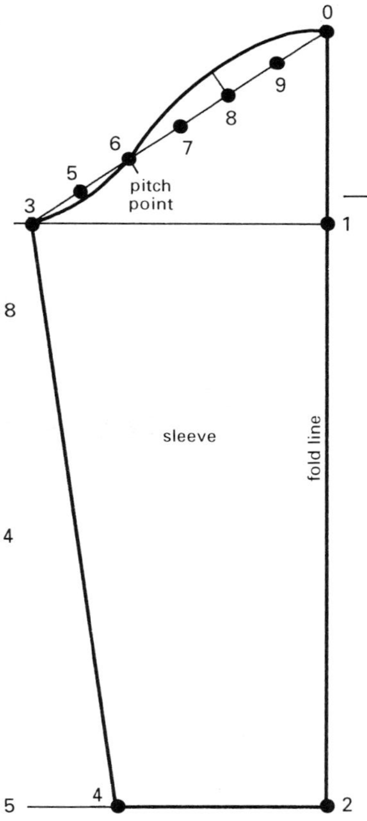

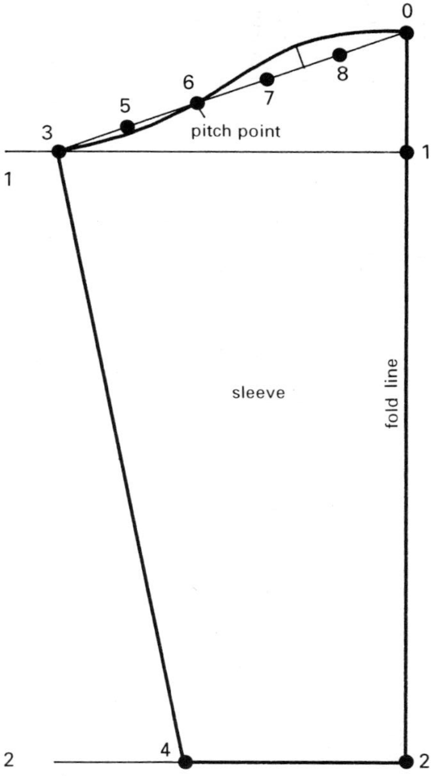

The 'flat' sleeveless body block

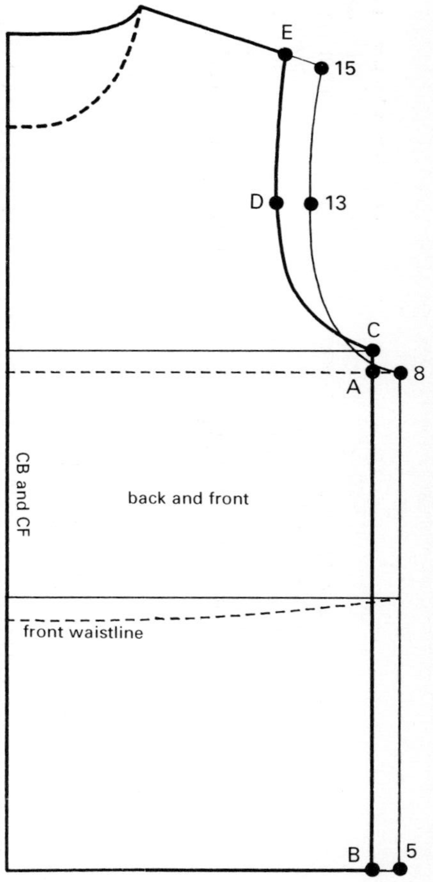

CB and CF

front waistline

back and front

pitch points

sleeve

fold line

pitch point

sleeve

fold line

pitch point

CB and CF

front waistline

back and front

The 'Flat' Overgarment Block

For boys and girls, sizes 80–164cm height
Use both blocks for all types of garments in woven and jersey fabric

MEASUREMENTS REQUIRED TO DRAFT THE BLOCKS
(e.g. 104cm height, approx. 3–4 years).
Taken from the Unisex size chart (12cm height intervals).
Refer to the size charts pages 16, 17 and 18 for standard measurements (6cm height intervals).

Chest	57cm
Across back	23.6cm
Neck size	27.5cm
Shoulder	8cm
Scye depth	13.8cm
Back neck to waist	25.4cm
Waist to hip	12.6cm
Sleeve length	37cm
Wrist	13.4cm

Back and front sections
Square down and across from 0.
0 – 1 Back neck to waist plus 3cm; square down.
1 – 2 Waist to hip: square across.
0 – 3 $1/4$ chest:
    sizes 80–116cm height   plus 6cm
          122–164cm height   plus 6.5cm;
    square down to 4 and 5.
0 – 6 2cm.
6 – 7 scye depth:
    sizes 80–116cm height   plus 4cm
          122–164cm height   plus 4.5cm;
    square across to 8.
6 – 9 $1/2$ measurement 6–7; square out.
6 –10 $1/4$ scye depth minus 2cm; square out.
0 –11 $1/5$ neck size plus 0.8cm; draw back neck curve.
7 –12 $1/2$ across back:
    sizes 80–116cm height   plus 3.5cm
          122–164cm height   plus 4cm;
    square up to 13 and 14.
14–15 sizes 80–116cm height 1.25cm
        122–164cm height 1.5cm; join 11–15.

Draw in the back armscye shape as shown in diagram to touch points 15, 13, 8.

Front section
0 –16 $1/5$ neck size plus 0.5cm; draw in front neck curve.
13–17 sizes 80–116cm height   0.6cm
        122–164cm height   0.9cm;
Draw a line below the line squared out from 10:
    sizes 80–116cm height   0.5cm
        122–164cm height   0.75cm;
11–18 The measurement 11–15; draw front shoulder line to touch the new line at point 18.
Draw in the front armscye shape as shown in diagram to touch points 18, 17, 8.

Sleeve
Square down from 0.
0 – 1 $1/2$ measurement 6–7 on body block; square across.
0 – 2 Sleeve length minus 4cm; square across.
0 – 3 The measurement of the armhole curve from 15–8.
2 – 4 $2/3$ measurement 1–3; join 3–4.
Divide 0–3 into five sections; mark points 5, 6, 7, 8.
Draw in the sleeve head:
hollow the curve 0.3cm at point 5;
raise the curve between 7 and 8;
    sizes 80–116cm height   1cm
        122–164cm height   1.25cm.

Note – Sleeve pitch points
Some sleeve adaptations require pitch points on the sleeve and body sections.
Mark point 6 on the sleeve as a pitch point with a notch.
Measure the distance 3–6.
Measure along the armhole of the body sections the same distance. Mark the pitch points with a notch.

The Kimono Block and 'Flat' Sleeve Cutting

THE BLOCK
Body sections
Trace round basic body shape of bodice, shirt, tee shirt or overgarment blocks. Mark points A, B, C, D.
B–E 1cm. Join A–E; extend the line.
A–F the measurement A–E plus the measurement 0–2 on the block sleeve used.
Square out from F to G, the measurement 2–4 on the block sleeve used plus 2cm.
C–H $1/4$ scye depth measurement.
H–I 2cm; D–J = 2cm. Join I–J and I–G.

'FLAT' SLEEVE CUTTING
The 'flat' kimono block is a good base for easy-fitting designs. Many types of easy-fitting sleeve can be drafted from the kimono block sleeve. Whilst complex cutting using the kimono block is demonstrated in Chapters 3 and 4 as part of garment adaptations, basic 'flat' raglan and dolman sleeves are shown on page 42.

Gussets are not suitable for children's wear, they are a weak construction point; however, ease can be inserted under the arm as sleeve adaptations are made.

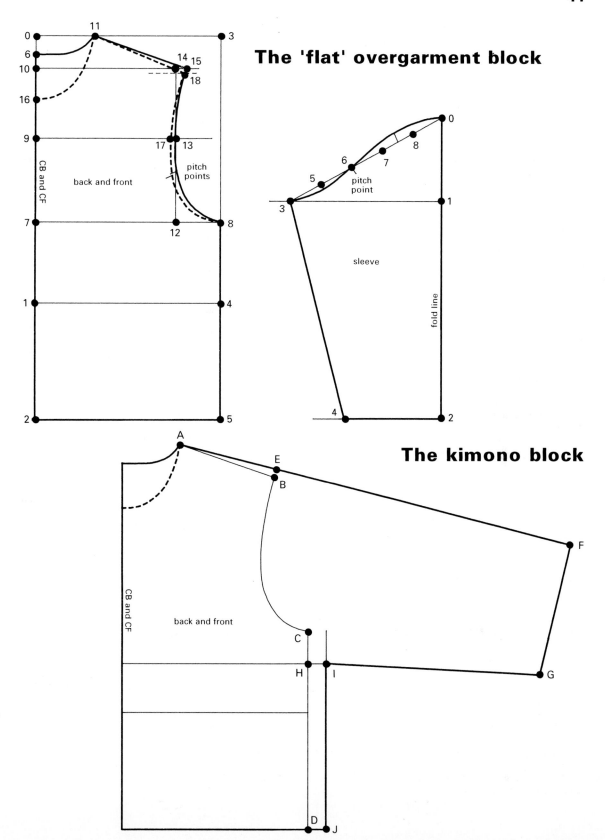

The 'flat' overgarment block

CB and CF

back and front

pitch points

sleeve

fold line

The kimono block

CB and CF

back and front

The Kimono Block – The 'Flat' Raglan Sleeve

Note   This sleeve has no underarm ease and should only be used for jersey fabrics or for very easy-fitting blocks.

Body sections
Trace round the basic kimono block.
Draw a raglan line from the underarm point to the neckline.
Trace off the body sections and mirror the front section.

Sleeve
Trace off sleeves from body section.
Mirror front sleeve.
Draw a perpendicular line.
Place sleeves to the line.

The Kimono Block – The Shaped 'Flat' Raglan Sleeve

Body sections
Trace round the basic kimono block.
Draw shaped raglan lines from underarm to neckline.
Draw in a dart: sizes up to 116cm height   1cm
                              sizes up to 164cm height   1.5cm.
Mark point A at the underarm point, B at top of the dart.
A–C   approx. 5cm, join B–C.
Trace off the body sections and mirror the front section.

Sleeve
Trace off sleeves from body section. Mirror front sleeve.
Draw a perpendicular line. Place sleeves to the line.
Cut along the line B–C, open approx. 3cm.
Re-draw the underarm sleeve seam.
Re-draw raglan lines curving the line from A–B.

The Kimono Block – The 'Flat' Dolman Sleeve

Body sections
Trace round basic kimono block. Mark points A and B.
Draw in the armhole curve as required.
B–C $^1/_2$ measurement A–B.
Draw in a dart: sizes up to 116cm height   1cm
                              sizes up to 164cm height   1.5cm.
B–D $^1/_2$ measurement B–C.
B–E $^1/_2$ measurement B–D.

Sleeve
Trace off sleeves from the body section.
Draw a perpendicular line. Place sleeves to the line.
Cut along the line D–E, open approx. 3cm.
Re-draw the sleeve seam.
Raise the sleeve head at A approx. 1cm.
Re-draw the sleeve head curving the line from B–C.

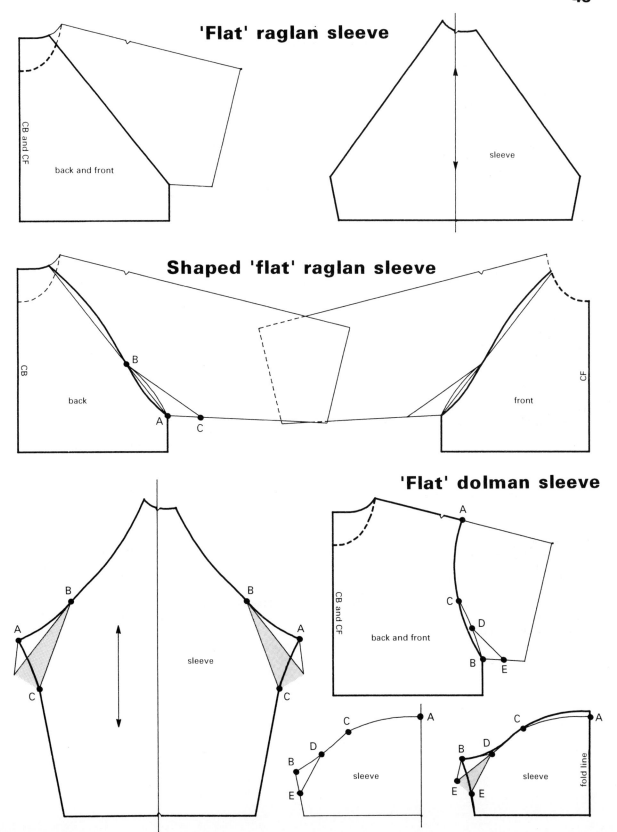

43

The Tee Shirt Blocks

For boys and girls, sizes 80–164cm height
For garments in jersey fabrics

MEASUREMENTS REQUIRED TO DRAFT THE BLOCKS
(e.g. 104cm height, approx. age 3–4 years).
Taken from the Unisex size chart (12cm height intervals).
Refer to the size charts pages 16, 17 and 18 for standard measurements (6cm height intervals).

The main figures construct a close-fitting, ribbed tee shirt; the first brackets are for a basic tee shirt, the second brackets for an easy-fitting shape.

Jersey fabric will stretch when the arm is bent; therefore, in the block instructions the sleeve length is reduced by 5cm. However, the amount of reduction will depend on the stretch and recovery of the fabric.

Chest	57cm
Across back	23.6cm
Neck size	27.5cm
Scye depth	13.8cm
Back neck to waist	25.4cm
Sleeve length	37cm
Wrist	13.4cm

Back and front sections
Square down and across from 0.
0 – 1 Back neck to waist; square across.
0 – 2 Finished length; square across.
0 – 3 Scye depth:
sizes 80–116cm height minus 1cm, plus (2.5cm) (5cm)
    122–164cm height minus 1cm, plus (3cm) (5.5cm);
    square across.
0 – 4 $\frac{1}{2}$ measurement 0–3; square across.
0 – 5 $\frac{1}{4}$ measurement 0–4; square across.

0 – 6 $\frac{1}{5}$ neck size minus 0.5cm, plus (0.2cm) (0.2cm); square up.
6 – 7 sizes 80–116cm height 1cm.
           122–164cm height 1.25cm.
Draw in the back neck curve.
3 – 8 $\frac{1}{2}$ across the back:
sizes 80–116cm height minus 1cm, plus (1cm) (2.5cm)
    122–164cm height minus 1cm, plus (1.5cm) (3cm);
    square up to 9 and 10.
10–11 0.5cm; join 7–11.
3 –12 $\frac{1}{4}$ chest:
sizes 80–116cm height minus 1.5cm, plus (2cm) (4cm)
    122–164cm height minus 1.5cm, plus (2.5cm)
    (4.5cm); square down to 13.
Draw in the armscye shape to touch points 11, 9, 12.
0 –14 $\frac{1}{5}$ neck size minus 1cm; draw in front neck.

Long sleeve
Square down to 0.
0 – 1 $\frac{1}{2}$ measurement 0–3 on body block plus 1cm, minus (1cm) (2cm); square across.
0 – 2 Sleeve length minus 3cm (5cm) (5cm); square across.
0 – 3 The measurement of the armhole curve from 11–12.
2 – 4 $\frac{1}{2}$ wrist minus 1.5cm; plus (1cm) (2cm); join 3–4.
Divide 0–3 into six sections; mark points 5, 6, 7, 8, 9.
Draw in the sleeve head:
hollow the curve 0.4cm at 5;
raise the curve at 8:
    sizes 80–116cm height 1cm.
           122–164cm height 1.25cm.

Short sleeve
1 –10 The measurement 0–1; square across to 11.
11–12 1cm; join 3–12.

Knitwear Block

Back and front sections
Trace off the body section of the easy-fitting tee shirt or overgarment block as required for the style.
Mark armhole depth line and waistline.
Remove armhole curve.
The width of the knitwear block and the armhole depth line can be adjusted for styling or to fit jacquard patterns or knitting structures.
Mark points A and B at the shoulder points.
Mark point C at the armhole.
Square up from C.

Extend the shoulder line from B to touch the line from C.
Mark point D.
D–E 1cm. Join A–E.

Sleeve
Square down from 0.
0 – 1 Sleeve length minus 5cm; square across.
0 – 2 The measurement B–D on body block; square across.
2 – 3 The measurement C–E on the body block.
1 – 4 The width required at the top of sleeve rib; square up.
4 – 5 The cuff depth; join 3–5.

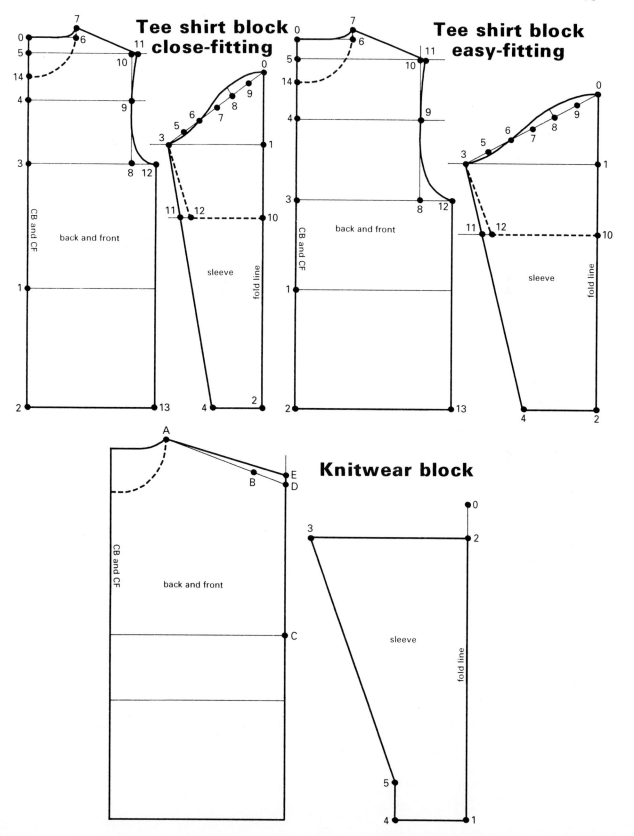

Tee shirt block close-fitting

Tee shirt block easy-fitting

Knitwear block

The Jeans Block – Close-fitting

For girls and boys, sizes 92–170cm height

The jeans block draft starts at size 92cm height. The draft is a tight-fitting shape which will not accommodate nappies. Jeans-type trousers for toddlers and for some ranges for young children are cut from the 'flat' trouser blocks (ref. pages 26 and 48) with jeans-type styling.

MEASUREMENTS REQUIRED TO DRAFT THE BLOCK
(e.g. boys, size 134cm height)
Refer to the size charts (pages 16–19 and 161) for standard measurements.

Hip/seat	73cm
Waist	64cm
Inside leg	61cm
Jeans bottom width	17cm
Waist to hip	15.6cm
Body rise	22cm
Waistband depth, e.g.	3cm

Front
Square down and across from 0.

0 – 1 Body rise minus 1.5cm and waistband depth; square across.

0 – 2 Waist to hip minus 1.5cm and waistband depth; square across.

1 – 3 Inside leg; square across.

1 – 4 $\frac{1}{2}$ measurement 1–3:
sizes 92–116cm height   minus 3cm
122–152cm height   minus 3.5cm
158–170cm height   minus 4cm;
square across.

1 – 5 $\frac{1}{12}$ hip/seat plus 1cm; square up to 6 and 7.

5 – 8 $\frac{1}{4}$ hip/seat plus 0.5cm.

5 – 9 $\frac{1}{16}$ hip/seat.

7 –10 Sizes 92–134cm height   1cm
140–170cm height   1.5cm
Join 10–6 and 6–9 with a curve touching a point:
sizes 92–116cm height   2.5cm from 5
122–152cm height   2.75cm from 5
158–170cm height   3cm from 5.

10–11 $\frac{1}{4}$ waist plus 2.5cm.

3 –12 $\frac{1}{2}$ jeans bottom width minus 0.5cm.

4 –13 The measurement 3–12 plus 1cm.

3 –14 $\frac{1}{2}$ jeans bottom width minus 0.5cm.

4 –15 The measurement 3–14 plus 1cm.
Draw side seam 11, 8, 13, 12; curve 8–11 out 0.25cm.
Draw inside leg seam 9, 15, 14. Curve in 9–15 0.5cm.

Back

5 –16 $\frac{1}{4}$ measurement 1–5; square up to 17 on hip/seat line, 18 on waistline.

16–19 $\frac{1}{2}$ measurement 16–18, 18–20 1.5cm.
20–21 1.5cm.

21–22 $\frac{1}{4}$ waist plus 2cm
sizes 92–116cm height   plus 0.75cm
122–152cm height   plus 1cm
158–170cm height   plus 1.25cm;
join 21–22 to touch the line square out from 0.

9 –23 $\frac{1}{2}$ measurement 5–9 less 0.5cm. 23–24 0.25cm.
Join 21–19 and 19–24 with a curve touching a point:
sizes 92–116cm height   3.25cm from 16
122–152cm height   3.5cm from 16
158–170cm height   3.75cm from 16.

17–25 $\frac{1}{4}$ hip/seat plus 0.5cm.

12–26 1cm. 13–27 1cm. 14–28 1cm. 15–29 1cm.
Draw side seam 22, 25, 27, 26; curve 22–25 out 0.25cm, 25–27 in 0.25cm.
Draw inside leg seam 24, 29, 28; curve 24–29 in 1cm.

21–30 $\frac{1}{2}$ measurement 21–22; square down from the line 21–22. Construct a dart on this line:
sizes 92–116cm height   length 4cm, width 0.75cm
122–152cm height   length 5cm, width 1cm
158–170cm height   length 6cm, width 1.25cm.

To complete front sections
Trace off front section; mark point 6.
Draw in curved pocket line A–B and pocket bag.
Cut off side piece along line A–B; add 3.5cm from A–B.
Draw in fly piece shape to point C 5cm below 6.
Fly piece width 3.5–4cm.
Trace off fly piece and pocket bag.

To complete back sections
Trace off back section; mark points 16, 17, 21, 22, 24, 25.
Cut along hip/seat line, open a wedge at 17:
sizes 92–116cm height   2cm
122–152cm height   2.5cm
158–170cm height   3cm

17–D 0.5cm; draw in new crotch line from 21–24.
Draw in pocket design.

21–E $\frac{1}{3}$ measurement 21–16. 22–F $\frac{1}{3}$ measurement 22–25.
Cut off yoke section along line E–F; close dart.
Join 21–22 and E–F with straight lines.

Patch pocket Trace back pocket.

Waistband G–H twice waistband depth; H–J low waist measurement; J–K fly width.
Mark centre back $\frac{1}{2}$ measurement H–J; mark fold line.

JEANS SHORTS
For jeans shorts cut across draft at length required.

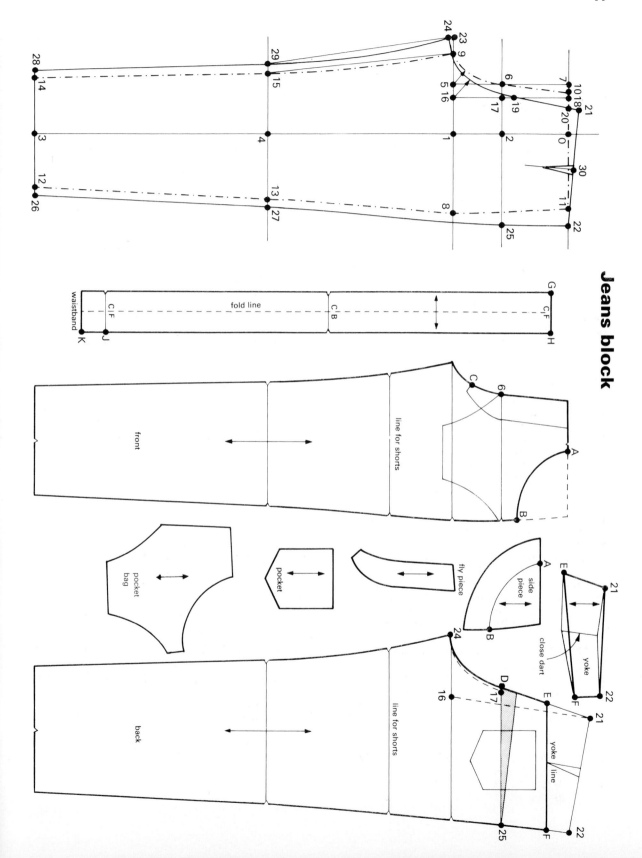

Jeans block

The Simple 'Flat' Trouser Blocks

For boys and girls, 80–164cm height
For simple trousers from leggings to very easy-fitting trousers

MEASUREMENTS REQUIRED TO DRAFT THE BLOCKS
(e.g. 104cm height, approx. age 3–4 years).
Taken from the Unisex size chart (12cm height intervals).
Refer to the size charts pages 16, 17 and 18 for standard measurements (6cm height intervals).

Hip/seat	60
Body rise	17.8
Inside leg	45

One-piece Trouser Block
The one-piece trouser block can be used as a simple shape for a wide range of simple trousers from leggings to easy-fitting sports and leisurewear. The leggings block is constructed for fabrics with good stretch and recovery.

The main figures will give the leggings shape; those in the first brackets give a basic shape; those in the second bracket will give an easy-fitting shape.

Front section
Square down and across from 0.
0 – 1 Body rise plus 1cm (1cm) (3cm); square across.
1 – 2 Inside leg measurement minus 1cm (1cm) (3cm); square across.
1 – 3 $^1/_2$ the measurement 1–2; square across.
1 – 4 $^1/_4$ hip/seat measurement:
sizes 80–116cm height minus 1cm; plus (3.5cm) (5.5cm)
122–164cm height minus 1.5cm; plus (4cm) (6cm);
square up to 5.
5 – 6 1cm.
4 – 7 $^1/_4$ the measurement 4–5.
4 – 8 $^1/_4$ the measurement 1–4 minus 0.5cm.
Join 6–7 and 7–8 with a curve touching a point 1.75cm (2cm) (2.5cm) from 4.
2 – 9 $^3/_4$ measurement 1–4 plus 1cm; square up to 10 on the knee line.
10–11 1cm (1.5cm) (2cm).
Draw inside leg seam; join 9–11 with a straight line; join 8–11 curving the line inwards 0.6cm (0.6cm) (0.8cm).

Back section
6 –12 2cm (2cm) (2.5cm); square up 2.5cm (2.5cm) (3cm) to 13. Join 13–0.
4 –14 $^1/_2$ the measurement 4–5.
8 –15 The measurement 4–8 minus 0.2cm (1cm) (0.5cm).
15–16 0.75cm (0.75cm) (1cm).
Join 13–14 and 14–16 with a curve touching a point 3.75cm (4cm) (4.5cm) from 4.

9 –17 1cm (1.5cm) (2cm).
11–18 1.5cm (2cm) (2.5cm).
Draw inside leg seam; join 18–17 with a straight line; joint 16–18 curving the line inwards 1cm (1cm) (1.2cm).

Creating a One-piece Pattern
Trace round back section (heavy line).
Trace round front section (dotted line).
Mirror the front and place the side seams together.

Two-piece Trouser Block
The two-piece block gives a better leg shape and extra back crotch rise. The main figures will give a basic shape; the figures in the brackets give an easy-fitting shape.

Front section
Square both ways from 0.
0 – 1 Body rise plus 1cm (3cm); square across.
1 – 2 Inside leg measurement minus 1cm (3cm); square across.
1 – 3 $^1/_2$ the measurement 1–2; square across.
1 – 4 $^1/_4$ hip/seat:
sizes 80–116cm height plus 3.5cm (5.5cm)
122–164cm height plus 4cm (6cm);
square up to 5.
5 – 6 1cm.
4 – 7 $^1/_4$ the measurement 4–5.
4 – 8 $^1/_4$ the measurement 1–4 minus 0.5cm.
Join 6–7 and 7–8 with a curve touching a point 2cm (2.5cm) from 4.
1 – 9 $^1/_2$ measurement 1–4; square down to 10 and 11.
11–12 $^1/_3$ measurement 1–4 plus 1cm.
11–13 = 11–12. Join 1–12; mark point 14 on the knee line.
10–15 = 10–14.
Draw inside leg seam; join 13–15 with a straight line; join 8–15 curving the line inwards 0.6cm (0.8cm).

Back section
6 –16 3cm (3.5cm); square up 2.5cm (3cm) to 17.
0 –18 2cm; join 17–18.
4 –19 $^1/_2$ the measurement 4–5.
8 –20 The measurement 4–8 minus 1cm (0.5cm).
20–21 0.75cm (1cm). Join 17–19 and 19–21 with a curve touching a point 4cm (4.5cm) from 4.
12–22 1cm. Join 18–22; mark point 23 on knee line.
13–24 1cm. 15–25 = 14–23.
Draw inside leg seam; join 24–25 with a straight line; join 21–25 curving the line inwards 1cm (1.2cm).

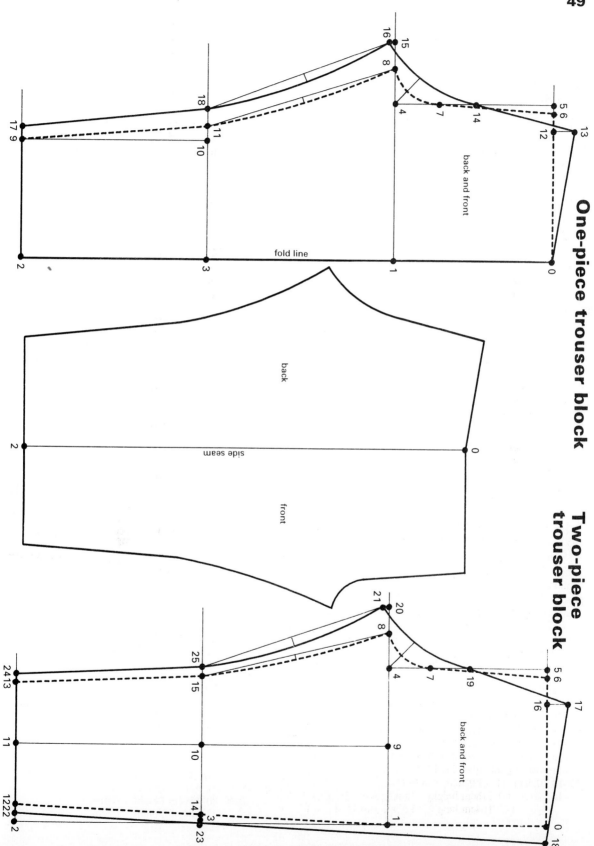

One-piece trouser block

back and front

fold line

Two-piece trouser block

back

side seam

front

back and front

The 'Flat' Underwear Blocks

For boys and girls, sizes 80–164cm height

MEASUREMENTS REQUIRED TO DRAFT THE
BLOCKS
(e.g. 104cm height, approx. age 3–4 years).
Taken from the Unisex size chart (12cm height
intervals).
Refer to the size charts pages 16, 17 and 18 for standard
measurements (6cm height intervals).

Chest	57cm
Hip/seat	60cm
Across back	23.6cm
Neck size	27.5cm
Scye depth	13.8cm
Back neck to waist	25.4cm
Waist to hip	12.6cm
Body rise	17.8cm

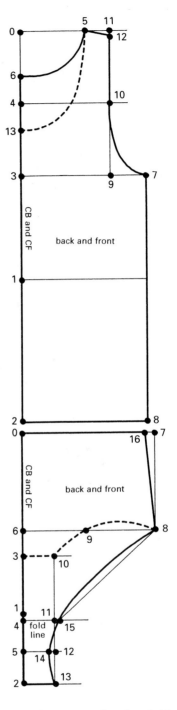

Vest

Back and front sections
Square down and across from 0.
0 – 1 Back neck to waist; square across.
0 – 2 Finished length; square across.
0 – 3 Scye depth:
sizes 80–116cm height   plus 1cm
      122–164cm height   plus 1.5cm; square across.
0 – 4 $\frac{1}{2}$ measurement 0–3; square across.
0 – 5 $\frac{1}{4}$ neck size.
0 – 6 $\frac{1}{6}$ neck size. Draw in the back neck curve.
3 – 7 $\frac{1}{4}$ chest minus 1cm; square down to 8.
3 – 9 $\frac{3}{4}$ measurement 3–7 minus 0.5cm; square up to
      10 and 11.
11–12 0.5cm; join 5–12.
Draw in the armscye shape to touch points 12, 10, 7.
0 –13 $\frac{1}{3}$ neck size plus 1cm; draw in front neck curve.

Briefs

This draft is not suitable for toddlers wearing nappies.
Square down and across from 0.
0 – 1 Body rise.
      sizes 80–116cm height   plus 1cm
            122–164cm height   plus 2cm.
1 – 2 $\frac{1}{3}$ measurement 0–1.
      sizes 80–116cm height   plus 0.5cm
            122–164cm height   plus 1cm; square out.
0 – 3 Waist to hip; square out.
3 – 4 $\frac{1}{2}$ measurement 2–3; square out.
4 – 5 $\frac{1}{2}$ measurement 2–4; square out.
3 – 6 $\frac{1}{5}$ measurement 0–3; square out.
0 – 7 $\frac{1}{4}$ hip/seat minus 1cm; square down to 8.
6 – 9 $\frac{1}{2}$ measurement 6–8.
3 –10 $\frac{1}{6}$ measurement 0–7 plus 1cm.
Square down from 10 to 11, 12, 13.
12–14 0.5cm. 11–15 0.5cm; join 8–15.
7 –16 sizes 80–116cm height   1cm
            122–164cm height   1.5cm; join 16–8.

Draw in back leg shape to touch points 8, 15, 14, 13
curving the line 8–15 inwards
      sizes 80–116cm height   0.75cm
            122–164cm height   1.25cm.
Draw in front leg shape (dotted line) to touch points 8,
9, 10 curving the line inwards from 8–9:
      sizes 80–116cm height   1cm
            122–164cm height   1.5cm.

Part One: Simple 'Flat' Pattern Cutting Boys and Girls

5 SIMPLE BASIC GARMENTS

Unisex; approximate age: birth–14 years

The following adaptations are based on the 'flat' blocks and therefore useful for basic easy-fitting flat shapes that can be used with woven or jersey fabrics. However, if jersey fabrics are used, the amount of flare or fullness inserted in designs should be moderated. The design of garments cut from 'flat' blocks relies heavily on the imaginative use of fabrics, embroidery, decorative seaming and novel pocketing. This section demonstrates very simple techniques for adapting basic body blocks into a variety of simple shapes. It also demonstrates the selection of an appropriate block and the sequence in which various adaptations of the basic blocks can take place.

The basic garments such as tee shirts, dresses and anoraks can be drafted for babies and toddlers by using the body measurements from the chart on page 16.

Dress styles, designed for woven fabrics, and which are cut with particular reference to body shape and the stance of the child are placed in Chapter 12 in Part Two: Form Cutting.

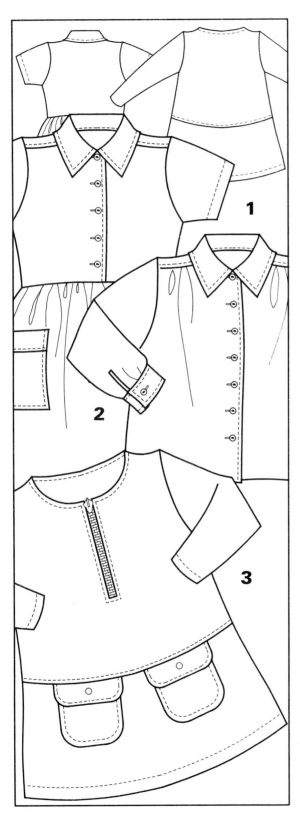

BASIC DRESSES

The basic dress shape adaptation is shown in the form of a 'schoolwear' dress, but it can be used for many different designs by the use of simple techniques e.g. seams, varied pocket shapes, collars and layered skirts.

1 BASIC SCHOOL DRESS

Body sections Trace off the 'flat' body block to the waistline. Mirror the front section. Mark points A, B, C, D on the bodice waistline.
Front Add 1.5cm buttonstand; mark buttonholes.
Add extended facing (ref. 1b, page 120).
Draw in a parallel line 2cm in from the shoulder line; cut off the top piece from the main front section.
Back Add this piece to the back along the shoulder line.
Sleeve Mirror sleeve along the centre fold line; shorten to length required.
Skirt Construct a rectangle: width = 3 × A–B + C–D on the body sections; height = length required.
Collar Construct a convertible collar (ref. 2, page 122).
Pocket Construct a rectangle to the size required; add 3cm facing to the top.

2 BASIC SCHOOL BLOUSE

Note This example demonstrates the adding of gathers by cutting pieces and inserting fullness.
Body sections Construct the bodice as for school dress, but trace off along the hipline and extend 5cm.
Front Draw a vertical line from the centre of the shoulder line to hemline; cut up the line and open approx. 3–4cm.
Short sleeve Mirror sleeve. Shorten to length required.
Long sleeve Shorten by cuff depth; construct a shirt cuff (ref. 1a, page 118).

3 FLAT 'A' LINE DRESSES

Note This example demonstrates the adding of fullness by inserting flare by the method of 'cut and spread'.
Body sections Trace off the 'flat' body block; extend body sections to the required length. Add 2.5cm flare to side seams.
Draw vertical lines from the centre of the necklines and shoulder lines to the hemline.
Draw in any low waistline seaming if required.
Widen back and front necklines and deepen front neckline.
Trace off the front and back sections; mirror the front section. Cut up the vertical lines and open approx. 3cm for a basic 'A' line.
Draw in new hemline. More flare can be added, particularly for woven fabric shapes.
Draw in patch pocket shape and pocket flap.
Back bodice Trace off back bodice along skirt seam line. Draw in facing line.
Front bodice Trace off front bodice along skirt seam line. Draw in front placket shape and facing line.
Front and back skirts Trace off front and back skirts.
Sleeve Trace off block sleeve and mirror along the fold line; narrow at wrists approx. 2cm. This amount can be increased if using jersey fabrics.
Facings Trace off back and front facings.
Pocket Trace off pocket and pocket flap.

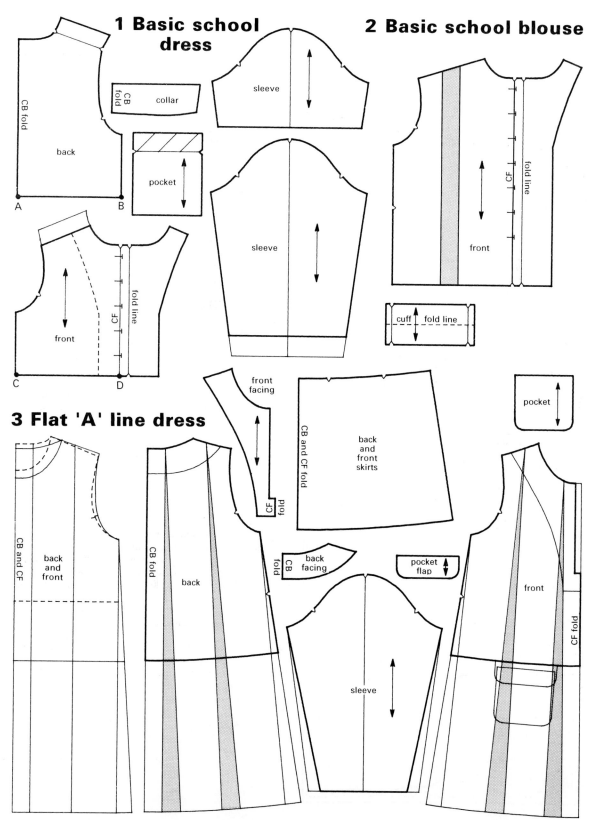

1 Basic school dress

2 Basic school blouse

3 Flat 'A' line dress

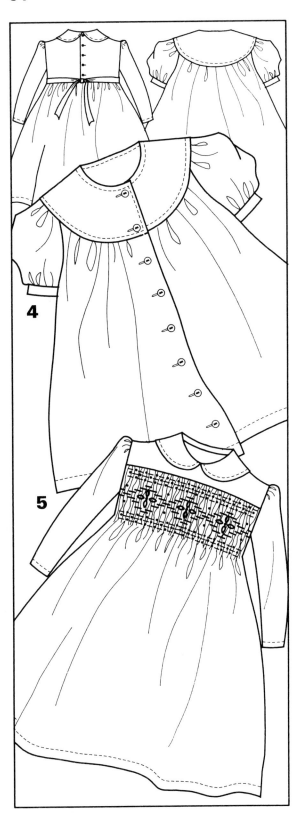

4 YOKE DRESS

Note This example demonstrates the inserting of fullness by cutting pieces, opening them and inserting flare by 'cut and spread'. This is used where the panel is curved at the top, as shown by the curved yoke design.

Body sections Trace off the 'flat' body block, extend to the length required. Mirror the front section. Mark A and B at front and back pitch points, C and D at shoulder points. Extend the shoulder, sloping it slightly downwards. Draw in yoke shapes; mark points E and F at the yoke lines, G and H at extended shoulder points.
Add 2.5cm flare to side seams.
Draw vertical lines from the yokes to the hemlines.
Back Trace off lower main section. Cut up vertical lines and open approx. 3cm at the top and 5cm at the hemline.
Note When curved pattern pieces are opened at the top, it is necessary that each section is laid on a line squared out from the line of the previous section (e.g. I–K is squared out 3cm from the line I–J; L–N is squared out 3cm from the line L–M).
Draw in new hemline.
Front Add 1.5cm buttonstand; mark buttonholes.
Add extended facing (ref. 1b, page 120).
Trace off the lower main section, cut up lines and open as for back.
Back and front yokes Trace off yoke sections.
Sleeve Mirror sleeve. Shorten to length required.
Mark O, P and Q at sleeve pitch points. O–R = A–E on back section; P–S = B–F on front section. Q–T = C–G.
Draw in a curve from R through T to S.
Drop vertical lines from the curve line. Cut up the vertical lines and open approx. 2cm.
Cuff Construct cuff: length = top arm meas. + 4cm; depth approx. 4cm.

5 SMOCKED DRESS

Body sections Trace off the 'flat' body blocks, extend the body sections to the required length.
Draw in back waistline and front yoke line.
Mark point A and B on yoke line, C at underarm point.
Drop a vertical line from A. Draw two vertical lines in the section from A–C; mark points D and E at the armhole.
Mark points F and G on back waistline, H at the hemline.
Back bodice Trace off back bodice section. Add 1.5cm buttonstand; mark buttonholes.
Add extended facing (ref. 1b, page 120).
Front Trace off main front section and mirror. Cut up the vertical lines and open the section A–C to 3 times its original width as shown. Redraw the curve through points D and E. Extend A–B to 3 times its original width.
Front yoke Trace off yoke section.
Back skirt Construct a rectangle: width = 3 × F–G; height = F–H.
Sleeve Mirror sleeve; construct a gathered sleeve head (ref. 8, page 112). Shorten if required.
Collar Construct a two-piece flat collar (ref. 4, page 124).
Tie Construct tie: length = 2 × F–G; depth approx. 4cm.

4 Yoke dress

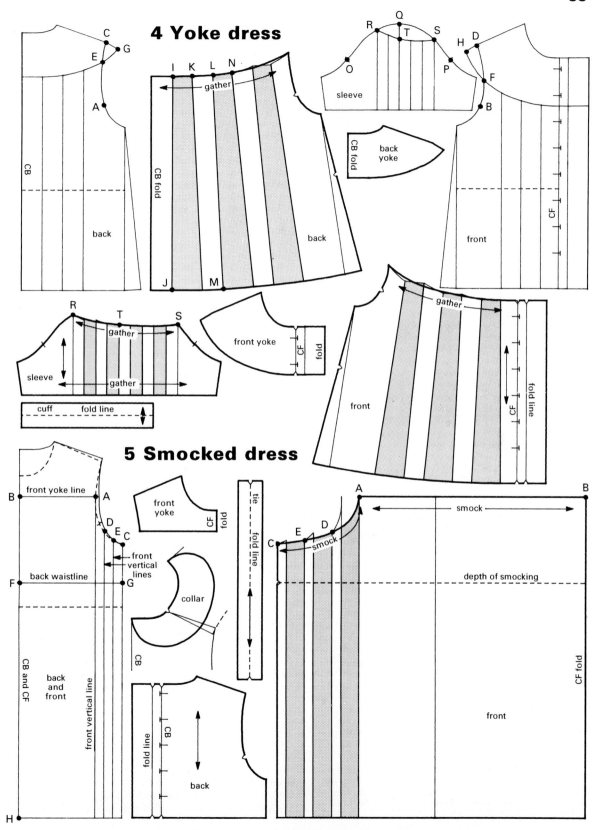

CB

back

C
E
G
A

I K L N
gather
CB fold
back
J M

back yoke
CB fold

sleeve
R Q T S
O P

H D
F
B
front
CF

R T S
gather
sleeve
gather

front yoke
CF fold

cuff   fold line

gather
front
CF
fold line

5 Smocked dress

front yoke line
B   A
D
E C
front vertical lines
back waistline
F   G

CB and CF
back and front
front vertical line

H

front yoke
CF fold

collar
CB

back
CB
fold line

tie
fold line

A   B
smock
C
E D
smock
depth of smocking

front
CF fold

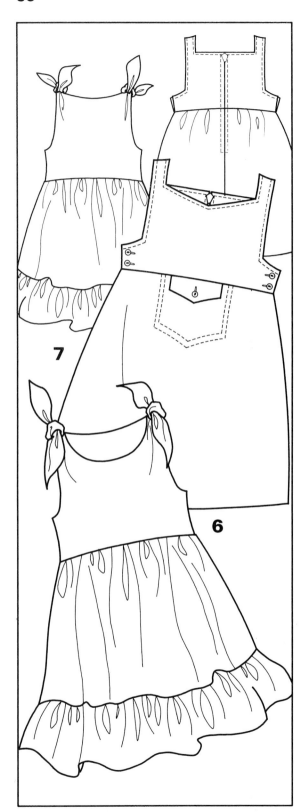

The back and front armhole of many sleeveless adaptations are the same. When this is the case, the style lines for the back and front can be drawn on one basic draft. This is a speedy way of working for designers in industry; however, if students find this too confusing, the front can be mirrored to enable the style lines to be drawn on separate sections as shown in the previous adaptations.

6 SLEEVELESS DRESS
Note This example demonstrates the adding of fullness in simple rectangular pieces by constructing rectangles and then adding flare by 'cut and spread'.
Body sections Trace off the 'flat' body block, extend to the length required. If a close-fitting shape is required use the sleeveless adaptation (page 38).
Draw in lowered necklines and new armhole shapes.
Draw in a high waistline and a lower skirt line.
Mark points A, B, C, D, E.
Back and front bodices Trace off both bodices, mirror the front bodice. Mark the centre of the shoulder line, square up approx 16cm. Draw in the type of tie shape required.
Back and front top skirts Construct a rectangle: height = A–C; width = 2 × A–B. Divide into 4 sections; draw in vertical lines. Cut up the lines and open at the base approx. 2cm. Redraw the waistline and hemline with smooth curves. Mirror the front section.
Back and front lower skirts Construct a rectangle: height = C–E; width = 3 × C–D. Divide into 8 sections, draw in vertical lines. Cut up the lines and open approx. 2.5cm; complete as top section.

7 PINAFORE
Body sections Trace off the 'flat' body block, extend to the length required. If a wider fitting shape for over thick sweater is required extend the side seam approx. 1–2cm.
Draw in lowered necklines and new armhole shapes.
Draw in a high waistline. Draw in pocket flap and pocket bag. Add 2cm flare to hemline.
Mark points A and B. Drop a vertical line from midway A–B.
Back bodice Trace off back bodice, add about 3.5cm extension to the side seam, extending the armhole shape; mark button positions.
Front bodice Trace off front bodices, mirror the front bodice, mark buttonholes.
Front skirt Trace off front skirt, cut up vertical line and open approx. 3cm–4cm.
Construct placket facing at B on the waistline; width approx. 3.5cm; length approx. 7.5cm. Fold back when cutting along the waistline to ensure a correct line extension at B.
Back skirt Trace off back skirt, cut up vertical line and open approx. 3.5cm.
Extend centre back at A by approx. 6cm–8cm.
Construct a placket extension, approx. 3.5m at B on the waistline. Place side seams together to ensure that the placket lies correctly under the front placket facing.
Construct a facing for the back placket extension.
Pocket Trace off the pocket flap and pocket bags.

6 Sleeveless dress

7 Pinafore

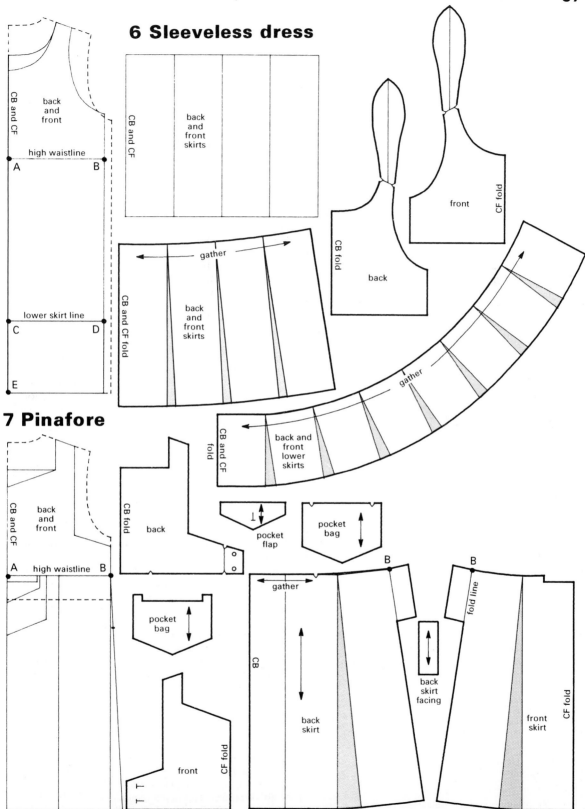

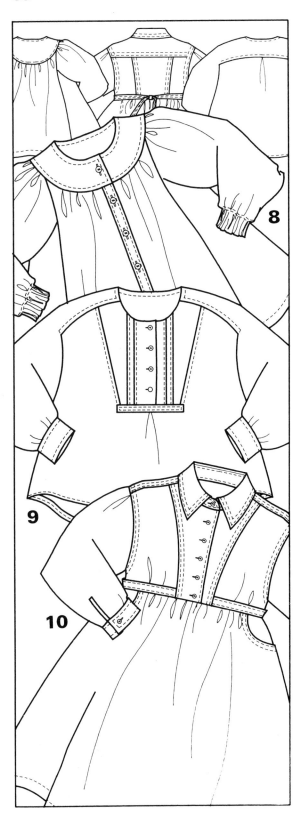

EASY-FITTING (KIMONO BASE) DRESSES AND TOPS

Select either the 'flat' body block or the 'flat' shirt block for the kimono adaptation (this depends on the level of easy-fit required). Extend to dress length if required. The back and front armhole of the kimono block are the same; therefore, the style lines for the back and front are drawn on one draft.

8 KIMONO SHAPE 1

Body sections Trace off the kimono shape (body block); extend to length required. Draw in back and front yoke lines.

Mark point A at the shoulder point, B at the underarm. Draw in back and front panel lines. Mark points C and D on the panel line. Draw in a slightly curved armhole shape; mark point E. Construct a dart of approx. 1cm. B–F is half the distance B–E. B–G is the measurement B–F; join F–G. Draw vertical lines through centre of back and front panels. Draw 2 lines parallel to sleeve line midway A–C and C–E. Add buttonholes and buttonstand.

Back and front Trace off back and front; cut up vertical lines, open approx. 5cm. Add approx. 3cm flare to seam.

Front strap Trace off front strap; mark buttonholes.

Back and front side panels Trace off side panels and add approx. 3–4cm flare to each panel seam.

Back and front yoke Trace off back and front yokes; join at the shoulder seam.

Sleeve Trace off sleeve. Cut and open the lines at the top edge the required amount as shown.

Cut up the line F–G and open approx. 3cm. Re-draw the curve along the top edge; curve the underarm seam.

Draw in facing for an elasticated sleeve hem. Trace off. Mirror front sleeve.

9 KIMONO SHAPE 2

Body sections Trace off the kimono shape (shirt block); extend to the length required. Add 2cm–3cm flare to hemline.

Draw in curved hemlines for back and front sections. Mark points A, B and C.

B–D is $\frac{1}{2}$ the distance B–C; B–E = B–D. Draw in curve from D through E to the hem.

Draw in a slightly curved armhole shape to centre of the armhole curve, mark point F. A–G is $\frac{2}{3}$ the distance A–F. Construct 1cm dart. F–H is half the distance F–G; join E–H. Shorten sleeve by cuff depth.

Draw in back and front yoke lines; front panel line vertical tuck lines and front strap.

Back Trace off back. Add 2cm tuck to centre back.

Front Trace off front and mirror. Add 2cm to centre front.

Front panel Trace off front panel. Add buttonholes, buttonstand, mirror along fold line for double panel. Cut up tuck lines and open 0–5cm.

Sleeve Trace off back and front sleeves with yoke sections; join at centre line. Cut up lines H–E and open approx. 3cm.

Re-draw sleeve heads and underarm seams with curves.

Back and front yoke facing Trace off back and front yokes; join at the shoulder seam.

Cuff Construct cuff depth required length = base of the sleeve minus tuck measurements.

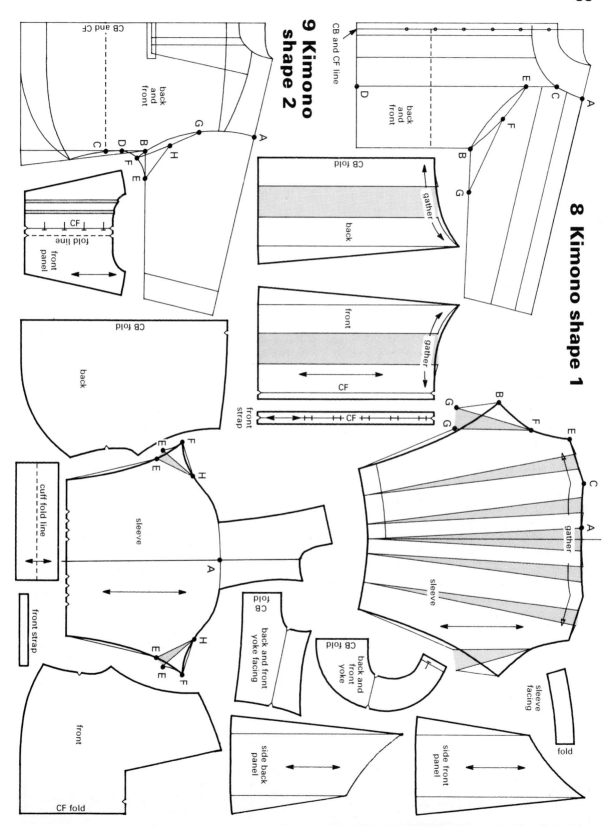

8 Kimono shape 1

9 Kimono shape 2

10 Shirt style dresses and tops

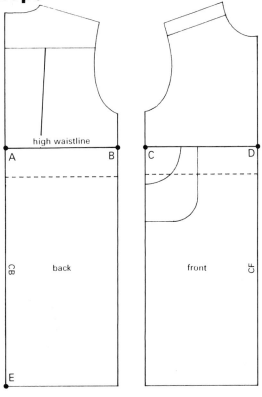

10 SHIRT STYLE DRESSES AND TOPS

Body sections Trace off the 'flat' shirt block, extend the body sections to the required length. Mirror front section. Draw in a slightly higher waistline. Mark points A, B, C, D, E.

Draw in back and front yoke lines, back panel line, pocket opening and pocket bag.

Back sections Trace off centre back and side panels.

Back yoke Trace off front and back yoke sections; place front yoke to back yoke along the shoulder line.

Front Trace off front section. Lower front neckline 1cm. Add 1.5cm buttonstand; mark buttonholes. Construct a standard facing (ref. 1a, page 120).

Back skirt Construct a rectangle: height = A–E; width = 3 × A–B.

Front skirt Trace off front skirt along the pocket line; extend the front until the skirt hem width = 3 × width C–D.

Collar Construct a shirt collar (ref. 3, page 122).

Sleeve Shorten sleeve by cuff depth.

Mark point F at sleeve head G at inverted tuck position. Square down to H approx. 6cm; square across to centre line.

Draw a vertical line. Place top section to line. Place main section with base of sleeve touching the line and the top point G opened out to required tuck width.

Mark the centre of the opening point I; fold the inverted tuck into position before cutting sleeve head. Mirror sleeve. Square across from the base of the sleeve to centre line.

Cuff Construct a shirt cuff (ref. 1a, page 118).

Pocket bag Trace off pocket bags.

Tie Construct tie: length = 2 × A–B + 10cm; width = approx. 4cm.

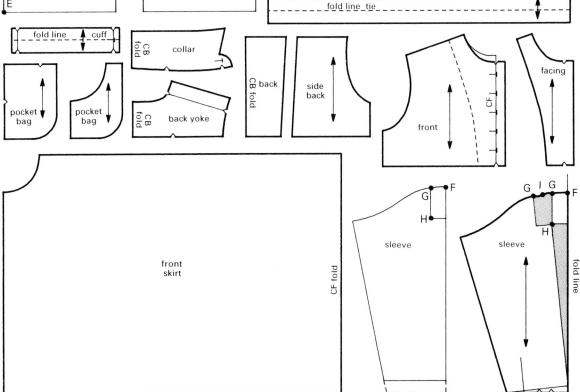

Part One: Simple 'Flat' Pattern Cutting Boys and Girls

6 OVERGARMENTS

Unisex; approximate age: birth–14 years

Overgarments are categorised in this chapter as being easy-fitting garments that fit over other clothes: this covers garments as different as overalls and duffle coats. The adaptations in Chapters 6 and 7 demonstrate the importance of selecting the appropriate blocks for creating different shapes.

Tailored types of overgarment, which are cut with particular reference to body shape and the stance of the child, are placed in Chapter 12 in Part Two: Form Cutting.

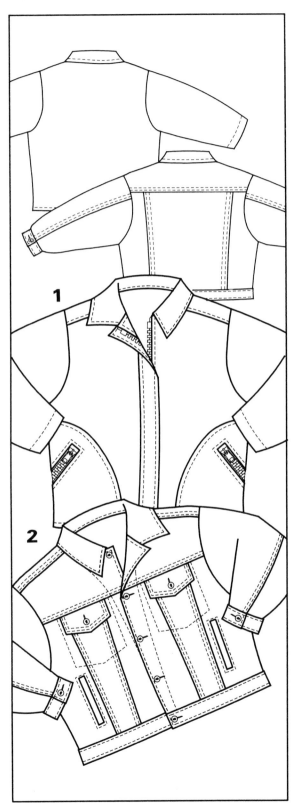

1 BASIC JACKET

This type of jacket can be adapted in many different ways with different seams, front fastenings, collars and pockets.

Body sections Trace off the 'flat' overgarment block; extend to the length required. Mirror the front block. Draw a parallel line 2cm from front shoulder line; cut off top piece from the main section. Add this piece to the back along the shoulder line.

Front Construct the standard zip front (ref. 3, page 120).

Draw in pocket line with zip opening and facing.

Collar Construct a convertible collar (ref. 2, page 122).

Sleeve Trace off sleeve block and mirror.

Pockets Trace off the pocket and pocket facing.

2 JEANS JACKET

Body sections Trace off the kimono shape adapted from the 'flat' shirt block; extend to length required. Mark point A at the underarm, B at the hemline, C and D at the sleeve hem.

A–E = 2cm; E–F = 1.5cm; B–G = 0.5cm. Joint F–G and F–D.

Draw in armhole. Mark point H at the shoulder; H–I = $\frac{1}{2}$ meas. H–F. Draw in 1cm dart.

F–J = $\frac{1}{2}$ meas. F–I; F–K = F–J. Join J–K.

Draw in cuff line approx. 3.5cm from the hemline. Trace off front section and mirror.

Back Draw in back yoke line and back panel line. Mark point L. Trace off back, back panel and back yoke.

Front Draw a parallel line 2cm from front shoulder line; cut off top piece from main section. Add this piece to the back yoke along the shoulder line.

Draw in front yoke line. Mark point M at centre of the yoke line.

Draw in panel lines using point M as the centre.

Draw in top pocket flap and pocket bag.

Draw in side pocket and pocket bag.

Add 1.5cm buttonstand. To distribute the buttonhole markings evenly, draw in a small length of waistband. Draw in facing line as shown.

Trace off front, centre and side panels, front yoke.

Facing Trace off front facing.

Collar Construct a convertible collar (ref. 2, page 122).

Sleeves Trace off sleeve; cut up line J–K and open approx. 2.5cm. Re-draw underarm seam and sleeve head. Mirror sleeve. H–N = H–L on back armhole line plus 1cm.

C–O = $\frac{1}{2}$ distance C–D. Mark a 2cm tuck on sleeve hem. Trace off front sleeve. Trace off back sleeve, add 1cm underwrap at point O; length = approx. 6cm.

Pockets Trace off the pocket flap, welt and pocket bags.

Waistband Construct a rectangle: width = 3.5cm; length = the measurement of the base of the traced off body pieces.

Cuff Construct a rectangle: width = 3.5cm; length = base of the sleeve sections, minus tuck.

Tab Construct tab: width = 3cm; length approx. 8cm–10cm.

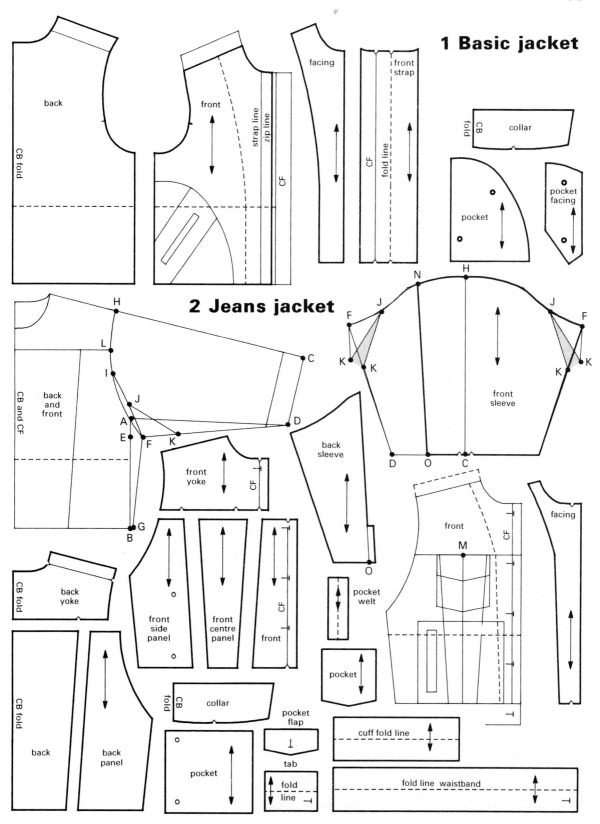

1 Basic jacket

back

CB fold

front

strap line

zip line

CF

facing

front strap

CF

fold line

fold

CB

collar

pocket

pocket facing

2 Jeans jacket

H

L

I

J

A

E

F

K

G

B

CB and CF

back and front

front yoke

CF

back sleeve

O

N

H

J

F

K

K

J

F

K

K

front sleeve

D

O

C

front

M

CF

facing

CB fold

back yoke

CB fold

back

back panel

front side panel

front centre panel

CF

front

fold

CB

collar

pocket

pocket flap

tab

fold line

pocket welt

pocket

cuff fold line

fold line waistband

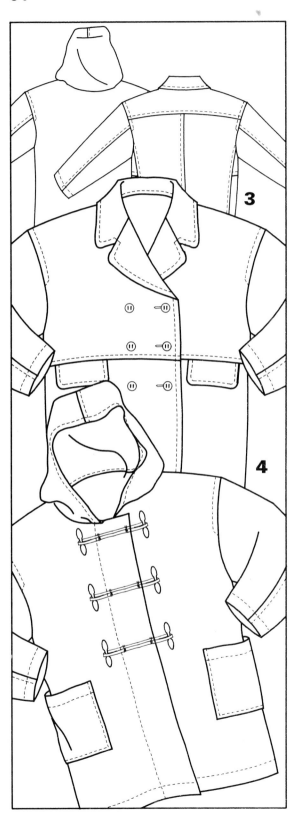

3 OVERJACKET

Extra ease can be added to the overgarment block to give a very easy-fitting shape.

Body sections Trace off 'flat' overgarment block to length required. Mirror the front block and sleeve. Construct the lowered armhole adaptation (ref. page 108).

Draw in back yoke line.

Mark point A at the armhole; square down to B at the waistline. B–C = 1cm; draw in back panel line.

Construct a double breasted front (ref. 2, page 120).

Draw in facing line.

Draw in front lowered waistline; draw in pocket flap and pocket bag.

Back Trace off back and yoke.

Front Trace off front and lower front.

Facing Trace off facing.

Collar Construct a convertible collar (ref. 2, page 122).

Sleeves Mark point D at the sleeve head; E and F on the hemline. Mark point G at back pitch point.

E–H = $\frac{1}{2}$ meas. E–F minus 1cm. H–I = 1cm; join to G–H at elbow point.

Trace off front sleeve and back sleeve; curve the back seam line on both sleeves.

Pockets Trace off the pocket flap and pocket bag.

4 DUFFLE COAT

The duffle coat is shown with an attached hood; however, the coat can be constructed with a collar and detachable hood.

Body sections Trace off the 'flat' overgarment block; extend to the length required. Mirror the front block. Construct the lowered armhole adaptation (ref. page 108).

Extend the front edge approx. 3cm. Mark duffle fastenings approx. 5cm from front edge.

Construct an extended facing (ref. 1b, page 120).

Draw in patch pocket.

Hood Construct an attached version of hood 1 (ref. 1, page 128).

Sleeves Construct top and under sleeve as above.

Pockets Trace off the patch pocket; add 3cm extension.

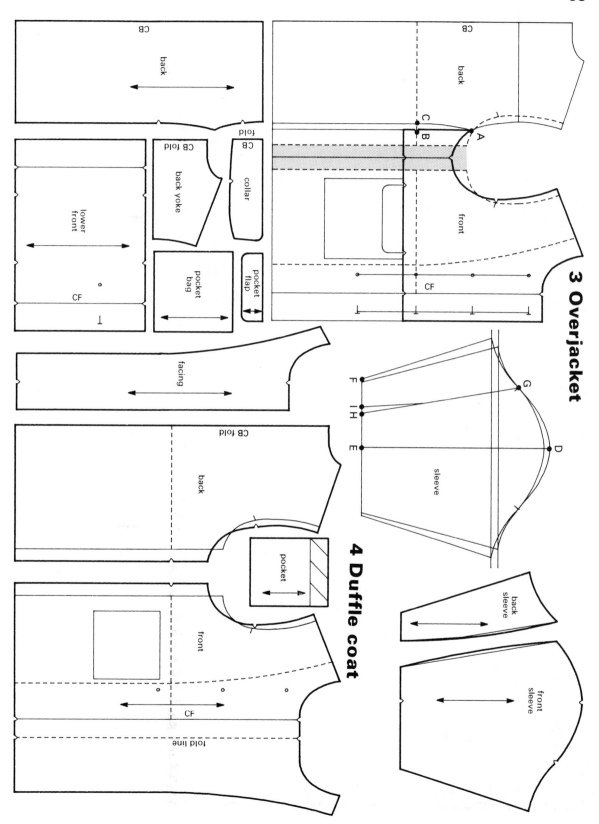

3 Overjacket

CB
back

CB
back

C B
A

collar
CB fold
CB
fold

back yoke
CB fold

front
CF

lower
front
CF

pocket
bag

pocket
flap

facing

CF

4 Duffle coat

CB fold
back

pocket

front
CF
fold line

sleeve
F
I H
E
G
D

back
sleeve

front
sleeve

66

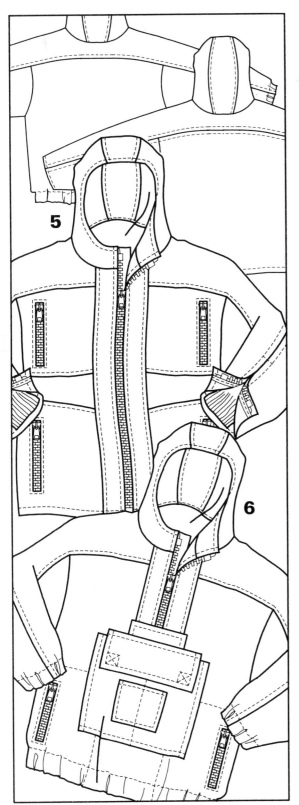

Many 'flat' easy-fitting overgarments are adapted from the kimono block. Some incorporate detachable inner garments. The anoraks are shown with an attached hood. The anoraks can be constructed with a standing straight collar or convertible collar (ref. 1 and 2, page 122), but with a separate hood (ref. page 128).

5 ANORAK 1

Body sections Trace off the kimono block (adapted from the overgarment block); extend to length required. Lower neckline for the attached hood 2 (ref. 2, page 128).
Draw in front panel line and zip line; this is $^1/_2$ the meas. of the zip from the centre front line.
Draw in back and front yoke line; extend down the sleeve.
Draw in lower sleeve shaping and under sleeve line.
Draw in armhole line. Mark A at yoke line; B at underarm.
Draw in a 1cm dart. B–C = $^1/_2$ meas. A–B, B–D = B–C.
Mirror the front block.
Front Draw in pocket lines and pocket facings.
Front panel Trace off front panel and mirror.
Fly Construct an inner fly piece; length = meas. of zip; width approx. 5cm; mark fold line through centre.
Back Trace off back.
Sleeve/yoke Trace off back and front sleeve/yoke sections; join along the outer sleeve line.
Back and front sleeves Trace off sleeve; cut up line C–D; open approx. 3cm–4cm. Re-draw the top curve and the underarm seam curve.
Under sleeve Trace off under sleeve; shorten by ribbed cuff depth.
Pockets Trace off the pockets and pocket facings.
Hood Construct hood 2 (ref. 2, page 128).

6 ANORAK 2

This example shows the anorak with elasticated cuff and hem, shortened zip opening and alternative front pockets.
Body sections Construct the anorak as above without the under sleeve.
Front Trace off front along shortened zip line.
Draw in front strap, patch pockets, pocket flap, side zip pocket with pocket bag and pocket facing.
Front panel Trace off front panel and mirror.
Fly Construct an inner fly piece; length = meas. of zip; width approx. 5cm; mark fold line through centre.
Pockets Trace off all the pocket sections.
Strap Trace off strap.
Complete the remainder of the anorak as above.

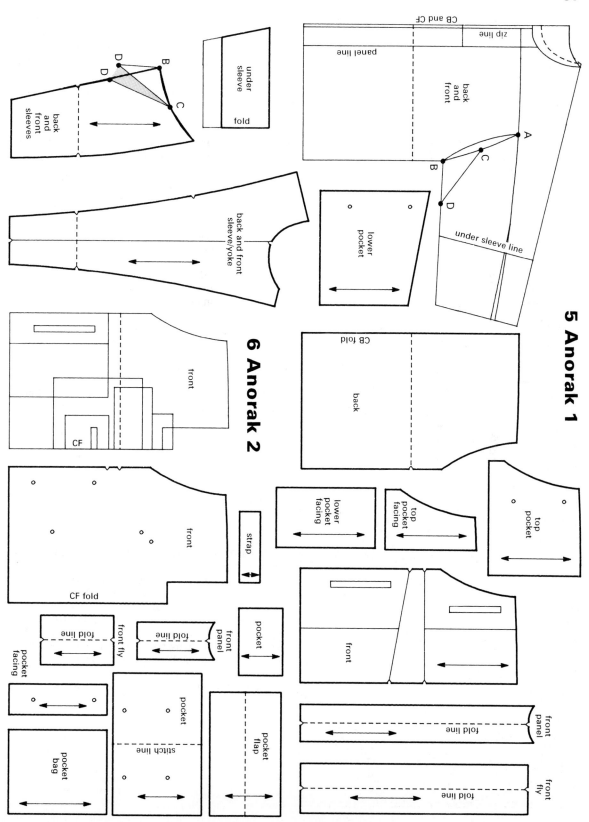

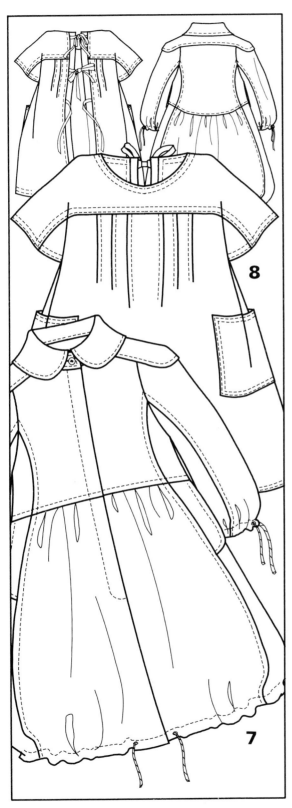

7 STYLED WEATHERCOAT

Body sections Trace off the kimono shape adapted from the 'flat' overgarment block; extend to length required. Draw in armhole line. Mark point A at shoulder line; B at underarm; C at waistline. Join A–B, B–D = ½ meas. A–B. Draw in a 1cm dart. B–E = ½ meas. B–D. B–F = B–E. Draw in sleeve panel lines and side panel lines. Draw in lower sleeve shaping. Mirror front. Draw in back and front yoke shapes. Draw a line approx. 4cm from the outside sleeve seam. Draw in low waistlines on back and front; curve down at centre back; curve up at centre front. Draw a vertical line down centre of both skirt side panels. Draw 3 vertical lines through both main skirt panels. Lower neckline 1.5cm. Add buttonstand; draw in fly front strap line. Create separate facing (ref. 1a, page 120). Draw in pocket welt and pocket bag.

Back and front bodices Trace off back and front bodices; trace off back and front side panels.

Back and front skirts Trace off back and front skirts. Trace off back and front skirt panels. Cut up vertical lines; open to twice original width (this depends on fabric type).

Back and front yoke Trace yokes, joint at shoulder line.

Collar Construct shirt collar with band (ref. 3a, page 122). Cut and spread the outer edge of the collar approx. 1cm.

Fly strap Trace off front fly strap and mirror. Mark vertical buttonholes on the centre front line.

Back and front under sleeve Trace off under sleeve; cut up line E–F; open approx. 3cm. Re-draw underarm seam.

Top sleeve Trace off top sleeves and mirror. Cut up vertical lines and open approx. 3cm at the top and 1.5cm at the sleeve hem as shown. Draw in sleeve facing on top sleeve and under sleeve.

Sleeve facing Trace off sleeve facings and join together.

Pockets Trace off the pocket welt and pocket bag.

8 OVERALLS

The overgarment block can be used for an easy fit, the shirt block can be used if a closer fit is required.

Body sections Trace off kimono shape of block required; extend length, lower neck, shorten sleeve required amounts. Mark point A at the neckline, B at the underarm, C at waistline. Join A–B, B–D = ½ meas. B–C; B–E = B–D. Add 2cm flare to hemline. Mirror front section. Draw in back tie panel line; mark tie positions. Draw in back and front yokes. Mark point F on line A–B. Draw vertical tuck lines on the back and front sections at approx. 3cm intervals. Draw in front pocket.

Back and front Trace off sections; cut up vertical lines and open twice the width of tuck required. Cut up lines B–F; open approx. 3cm–4cm. Re-draw the top curve and the underarm seam curve from D–E.

Back tie panel Trace off back tie panel and mirror.

Sleeve/yoke Trace off back and front sleeve/yoke; join along outer sleeve line. Draw in neck facing line.

Neck facing Trace off back and front neck facing.

Pockets Trace off pocket.

Tie Construct rectangle approx. 15cm × 2cm.

7 Styled weathercoat

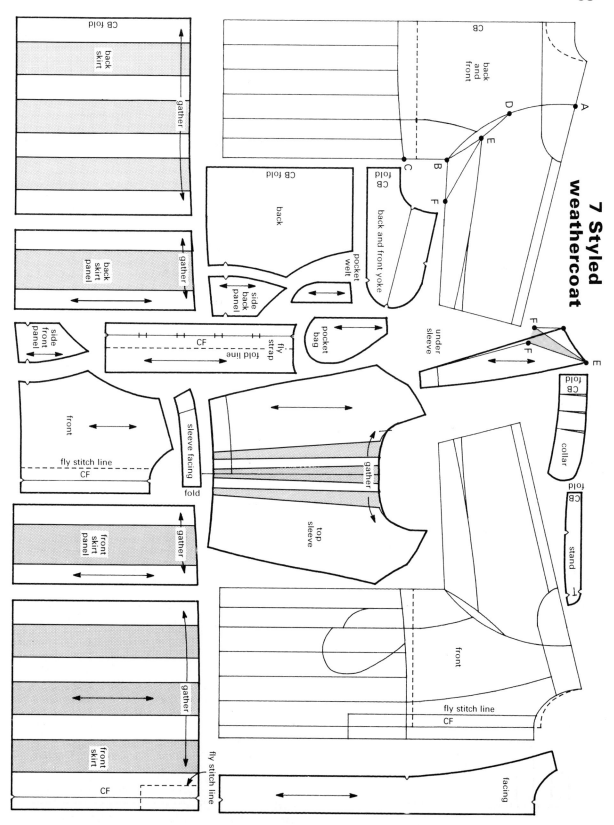

8 Overalls

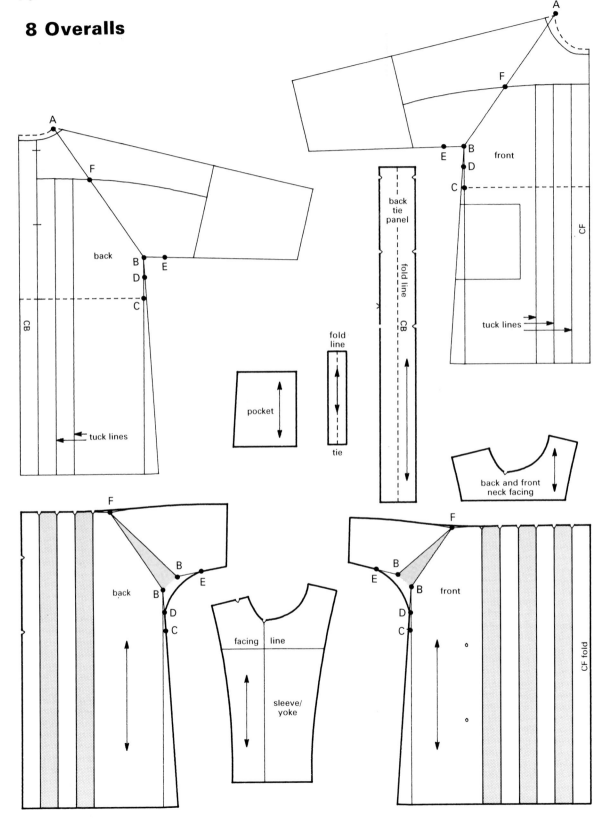

Part One: Simple 'Flat' Pattern Cutting Boys and Girls

7   LEISUREWEAR

Unisex; approximate age: birth–14 years

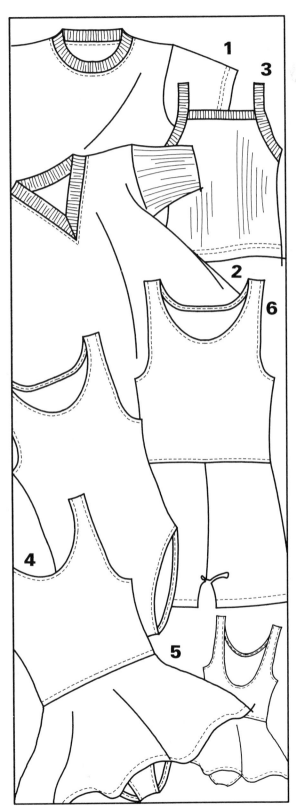

1 BASIC TEE SHIRTS

Basic tee shirts in a variety of fittings can be constructed by tracing of appropriate blocks (ref. page 44).

2 'TEE' DRESSES

An increasing number of dresses are cut in jersey fabric. They can be cut from the basic body block; however, if a 'tee' shirt look is required, use the tee shirt blocks. Dresses can be straight or flared as shown. If a mix of jersey fabrics is used, e.g. plain and ribbed, as shown, then modifications to the blocks are needed.

Body sections Trace off the basic tee shirt block, extend to the length required. Draw in V neck shape.
Raise the armhole approx. 2cm. Re-draw armhole curve.
Draw vertical lines from the centre of the neckline and the centre of the shoulder to the hemline.
Trace off back and front sections; mirror the front block.
Cut up the lines and open at hemline the required amount.
Sleeve Construct a new close-fitting tee shirt sleeve (ref. page 44) using the measurement of new armhole shape.

3 BODY FITTING TOPS

Many simple shapes can be constructed. Ribbed and elasticated edges provide the best fit.
Body sections Trace off the close-fitting tee shirt block. Mirror the front section and join at the side seam.
Draw in front and back top shaping and ribbing line.
Mark points A, B, C, D, E and F.
The garment can be in one piece with a centre back seam or with a side seam and a centre back fold.
Ribbing The strap, back and front edging = F–B–A + D–E minus approx. 4–6cm. Front edging = B–C minus 2cm.

4 SWIMWEAR 1

This adaptation creates a basic shape from which a range of necklines and other adaptations can be constructed.
Body sections Trace off the pants block and the vest blocks to the waistline (ref. page 50). Add 2.5cm to waistline. Join pants to vest top along the new waistline. Shape side seam at waist. Trace front section and mirror.

5 SWIMWEAR 2

Body sections Construct the basic shape as above.
Draw in a low waistline. Draw in skirt lines.
Back bodice Trace off back. Draw in new low neckline.
Front Trace off front section and mirror.
Pants Trace off back and front pants sections.
Back and front skirts Trace off skirt section; draw two vertical lines from waistline to the hem.
Cut up the lines and open at hemline the required amount.

6 SWIMWEAR 3

Body sections Trace the vest block to 4cm below the waistline (ref. page 50). Mirror front section.
Trouser sections Trace off leggings block 4cm below waistline and with 4cm inside leg seam.
Mirror front section.
Shape centre seams to ensure that the measurements of bodice waistline and trouser waistline are identical.

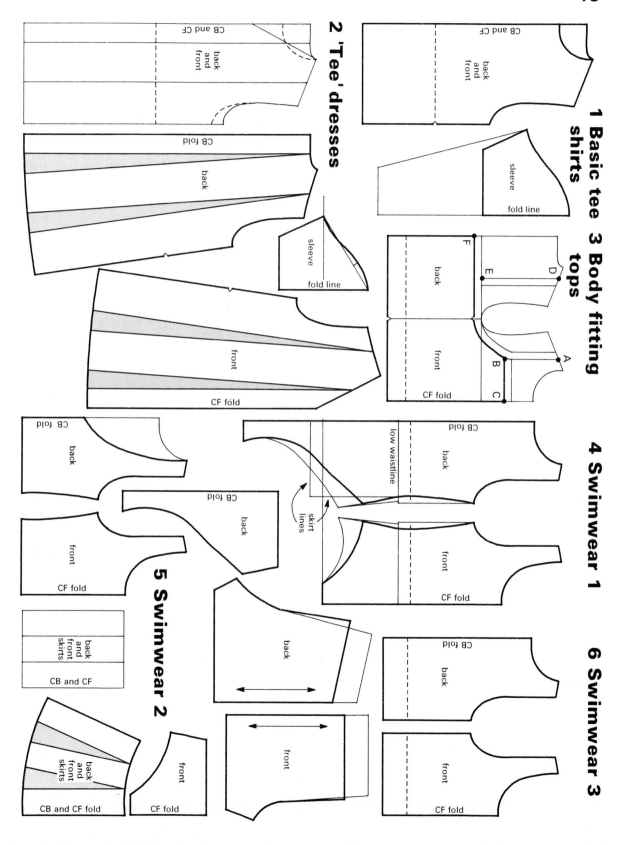

1 Basic tee shirts
2 'Tee' dresses
3 Body fitting tops
4 Swimwear 1
5 Swimwear 2
6 Swimwear 3

74

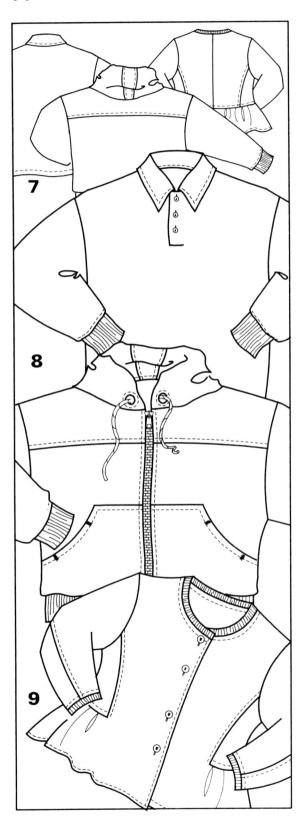

The styles illustrated are examples of selecting different blocks for different easy-fitting jersey styles; e.g. sports shirts are often cut with a straight sleeve head using the knitwear block; very easy-fitting shapes can be cut from the kimono block adapted from the easy-fitting tee shirt block; the easy-fitting tee shirt blocks is also a good base for many different fashion styles.

7 EASY-FITTING SPORTS SHIRT

Body sections Trace off the knitwear block; extend to length required.
Back Trace off back section.
Front Trace off front section. Mirror front block down centre front line. Mark depth of front fly opening. Add buttonstand; mark buttonholes. Draw in right front placket line. Draw in left and right front facing lines.
Left front facing Trace off facing.
Right front placket Trace off placket; add facing.
Sleeve Trace off sleeve; shorten by ribbed cuff depth.
Collar Construct convertible collar (ref. 2, page 122).

8 EASY-FITTING JERSEY WEAR

Body sections Trace off kimono block (easy-fitting tee shirt block); extend to length required minus ribbing. Draw in armhole line. Mark point A at shoulder, B at underarm. A–C = $^1/_2$ A–B. Draw in dart approx. 1cm. Lower neckline for an attached hood (page 128). Draw in zip line; this is $^1/_2$ the meas. of the zip from the centre front line. Draw in facing line. Draw in back and front yoke line. Draw in patch pocket. Mark pocket opening and facing. Shorten sleeve by ribbed cuff depth.
Back sections Trace off back section and back yoke.
Front sections Mirror the front block. Trace off front section, front yoke and facing.
Sleeve Trace off sleeve.
Pockets Trace off the pocket and pocket facing.
Hood Construct hood 2 (ref. 2, page 128).
Hem and cuff ribs Construct ribs of required depth.

9 STYLED JERSEY WEAR

Body sections Trace off the easy-fitting tee shirt block; extend to length required. Mirror front block. Join back and front sections along the side seam. Draw in waistline and panel lines on back and front. Draw in slight waist shaping on panel lines and at the centre back. Mark points A, B, C and D.
Back Trace off back section along the waistline.
Front Trace off front section, continue along back waistline. E–F = 2 × measurement A–B; F–G = 2 × measurement C–D. Mark buttonholes, add 1.5cm buttonstand. Construct an extended facing (ref. 1b, page 120).
Side panel Trace off front and back panel; join at side seam.
Sleeve Trace off sleeve; shorten by ribbed cuff depth. Shape wrist in 1.5cm at centre line. (This seam allows the sleeve to be sewn on the flat before the shoulder is joined.)
Neck and cuff ribs Construct ribs.

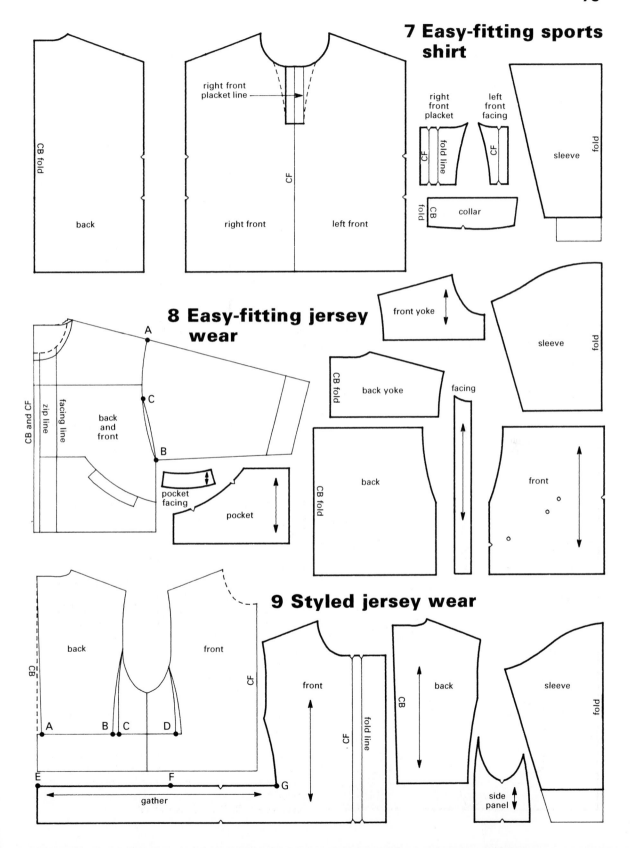

7 Easy-fitting sports shirt

CB fold

back

right front placket line

CF

right front

left front

right front placket

left front facing

CF

fold line

CF

sleeve

fold

fold

CB

collar

8 Easy-fitting jersey wear

CB and CF

zip line

facing line

back and front

A

C

B

pocket facing

pocket

front yoke

sleeve

fold

CB fold

back yoke

facing

CB fold

back

front

9 Styled jersey wear

CB

back

front

CF

A B C D

E F G

gather

front

CF

fold line

CB

back

sleeve

fold

CF

side panel

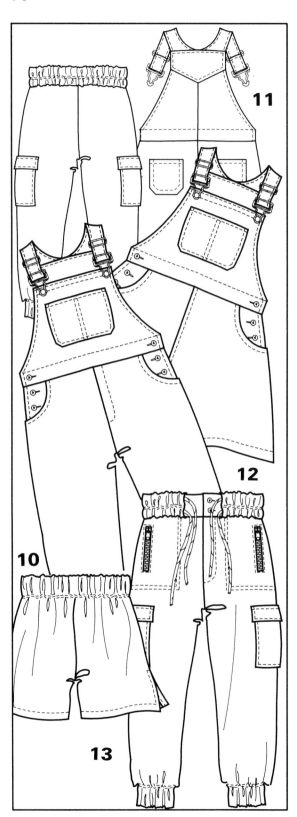

10 DUNGAREE TROUSERS

Body sections Trace off the 'flat' trouser block and body block. If a very 'baggy' look is required use the easy-fitting 'flat' trouser block and the overgarment block.

Adjust the back and front waistline of the trousers at centre front and back to the same measurement as bib waistline.

Front bib Trace off front block and mirror.

Add 3cm to waistline. Draw in bib, pocket and strap. Mark buttonhole on waist extension.

Trace off front, add 2cm facing to top edge.

Back bib Trace off back block. Add 3cm to waistline. Draw in bib; draw in yoke and back strap. Place front strap to back strap leaving 1cm gap at outer shoulder; extend strap 10cm. Mark point A at strap edge. Joint point A to B on yoke back with a straight line. Trace off back strap and back yoke.

Back and front facings Trace off facings along the original waistline.

Back trousers Draw in patch pocket.

Front trousers Mirror front trousers.

Draw in pocket line and pocket bag line.

Draw in mock fly line; mirror on centre front line.

Draw in button facing line; mark buttonholes.

Trace off trousers along the pocket line.

Pockets, pocket bags Trace off bib pocket, back trouser pocket and pocket bags.

Button facings Trace off front button facing. To create back facing, trace off and mirror front facing and add a 3cm waist extension. Mark button placings.

ONE-PIECE BACK

Join back bib to back trousers along the waistline.

11 DUNGAREE SKIRTS

Body sections Construct the body sections as for the dungaree trousers.

Back skirt Construct a rectangle: width = width of bib; length = length required.

Draw two vertical lines from waistline to the hemline. Cut up the lines and open at hemline the required amount.

Front skirt Mirror front skirt. Draw in buttonholes, facing line, pocket line and pocket bag line.

Trace off skirt along the pocket line.

Pockets, pocket bags and button facings Construct as trouser sections above.

12 EASY-FITTING TROUSERS

See page 78.

13 SPORTS SHORTS

See page 78.

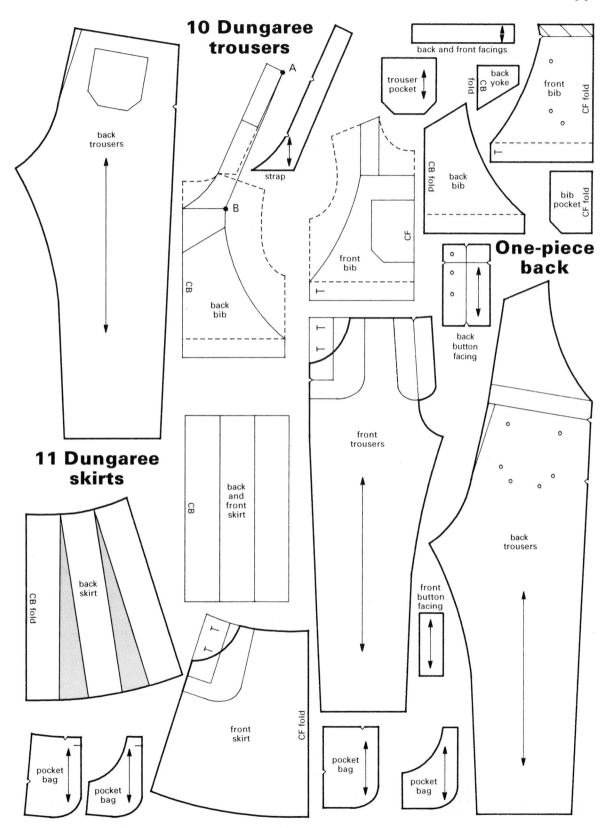

10 Dungaree trousers

One-piece back

11 Dungaree skirts

back trousers

strap

A

B

CB

back bib

CF

front bib

back and front facings

trouser pocket

CB fold

back yoke

front bib

CF fold

CB fold

back bib

bib pocket

CF fold

back button facing

front trousers

front button facing

back trousers

back and front skirt

CB

CB fold

back skirt

front skirt

CF fold

pocket bag

pocket bag

pocket bag

pocket bag

T

78

12 EASY-FITTING TROUSERS

Trace off the easy-fitting two-piece 'flat' trouser block.
Add 5cm extension to hem line.
Front trousers   Mirror front trousers.
Draw zip pocket position and pocket bag line.
Draw in patch pocket and flap. Draw in fly line.
Mark A at centre front, B at position of gathering cords.
Back trousers   Mark patch pocket position.
Fly   Trace off fly facing. Construct fly extension: trace
fly facing, mirror, and add waistband depth.
Waistband   Construct rectangle: length = waistline
measurement of front and back; depth = 3.5cm–4cm.
C–D = A–B on front waistline; mark cord positions.
Mark buttonholes.
Pockets, pocket bags   Trace off patch pocket, pocket
flap and pocket bags.

13   SPORTS SHORTS

Trace off the basic one-piece 'flat' trouser block to leg
length required. Separate the side seam for a side slit.
Add a 2cm extension for the slit.
Add 5cm extension to the waistline.
Add 1.5cm to the inside leg seams at the hem.

13 Sports shorts

12 Easy-fitting trousers

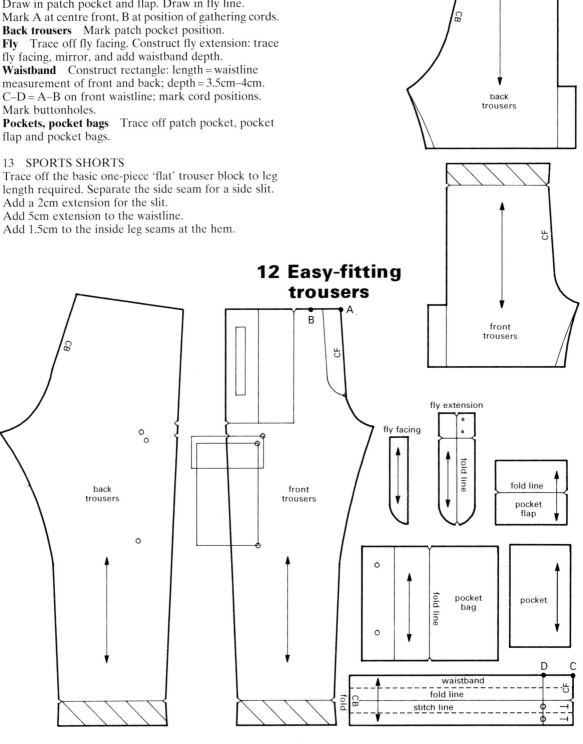

Part One: Simple 'Flat' Pattern Cutting Boys and Girls

8 NIGHTWEAR

Unisex; approximate age: birth–14 years

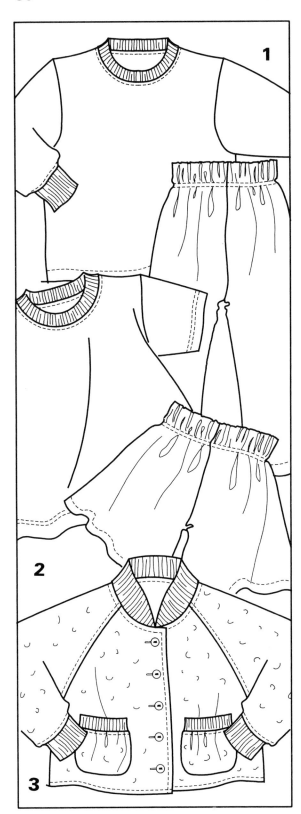

JERSEY NIGHTWEAR

The majority of nightwear is cut in jersey fabrics with a tee shirt look. Many designs are based on easy-fitting sport and leisurewear; the main differences are the printed fabric designs used and the soft textures created on some of the jersey fabrics.

1 SIMPLE PYJAMA SHAPE (JERSEY)

Body sections   Trace off the easy-fitting tee shirt block. Extend the body sections to the required length. Mirror the front section.

If a neck ribbing of more than 1.5cm is used, widen the back and front neck and deepen the front neck accordingly.

Sleeves   Mirror sleeve. Shorten sleeve by cuff depth.

Trousers   Trace off the basic shape of the 'flat' trouser block. Construct as a one-piece shape (ref. page 48). Add a 5cm casing for elastic to the top of the trousers.

Neck and cuff ribs   Create ribs – required length and depth. A summer version can be adapted by using short sleeves and short trousers.

2 'A' LINE PYJAMAS (JERSEY)

Body sections   Trace off the easy-fitting tee shirt block. Extend the body sections to the required length.

Drop vertical lines from the centre of the necklines and shoulder lines to the hemline.

If a neck ribbing of more than 1.5cm is used, widen the back and front neck and deepen the front neck accordingly.

Mirror the front section. Cut up the vertical lines and open approx. 2.5cm. Add 2cm flare to side seams. Draw in new hemline.

Sleeve   Mirror sleeve. Shorten sleeve to required length.

Trousers   Trace off basic shape of the 'flat' trouser block, construct as a one-piece shape (ref. page 48). Shorten to the length required.

Drop vertical lines from waistline and crotch line to the hemline. Cut up the vertical lines and open approx. 2.5cm.

Draw in new hemline. Add 5cm casing to waistline.

Neck and cuff ribs   Create ribs – required length and depth. A winter version can be adapted by using long sleeves and the basic shape of the 'flat' trouser block.

3 FLEECY NIGHT JACKET (JERSEY)

Body sections   Trace off the kimono block. Extend the body sections to required length. Mirror the front section. Widen back and front neck 1cm; deepen front neck 2cm. Draw in raglan lines.

Front   Add 1.5cm buttonstand; mark buttonholes. Add extended facing (ref. 1b, page 120). Draw in pocket shape.

Sleeves   Complete the construction of the shaped 'flat' raglan sleeve (ref. page 42). Shorten sleeve by cuff depth.

Collar   Construct standing straight collar $A–B = {}^{3}/_{4}$ neck measurement plus buttonstand; $B–C = 5cm$. $B–D = {}^{2}/_{3}$ $A–B$; join $D–C$ with a curve.

Pocket   Trace off pocket shape minus rib depth.

Pocket and cuff ribs   Create ribs – required length and depth.

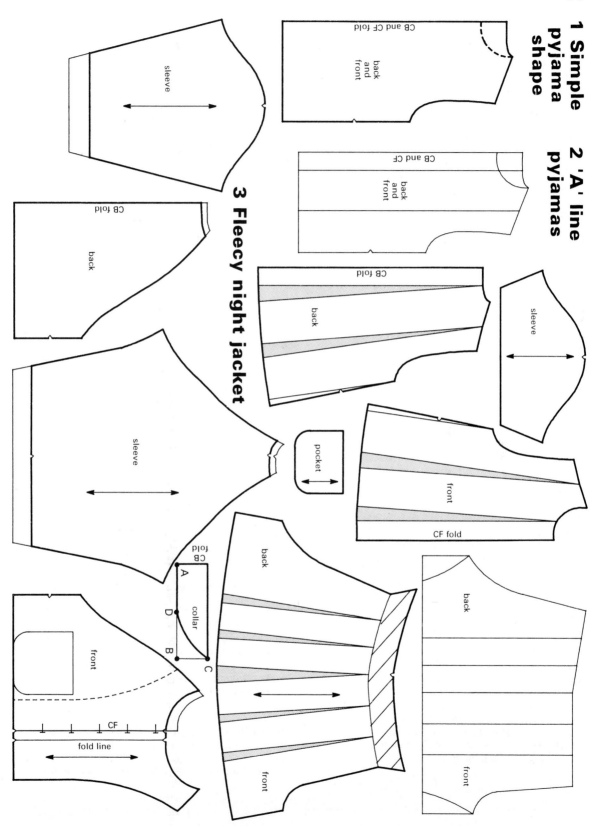

1 Simple pyjama shape

sleeve

back and front

CB and CF fold

2 'A' line pyjamas

back and front

CB and CF

sleeve

3 Fleecy night jacket

CB fold

back

back

CB fold

sleeve

pocket

front

CF fold

collar

A

D

B

C

CB fold

back

back

front

CF

fold line

front

front

The 'Flat' Pyjama Block

For boys and girls, sizes 80–164cm height

MEASUREMENTS REQUIRED TO DRAFT THE BLOCKS
(e.g. 104cm height, approx. age 7–8 years).
Taken from the Unisex chart (12cm height intervals).
Refer to the size charts on pages 16, 17 and 18 for standard measurements (6m height intervals).

Chest	67cm
Across back	27.6cm
Neck size	30cm
Shoulder	9.8cm
Scye depth	16.4cm
Back neck to waist	30.2cm
Sleeve length	47cm
Wrist	14.6cm

PYJAMA JACKET BLOCK
Back and front sections
Square down and across from 0.

0 – 1 1.25cm

1 – 2 Length required; square across.

1 – 3 Back neck to waist; square down.

0 – 4 $\frac{1}{4}$ chest:
  sizes 80–116cm height   plus 4.5cm
       122–164cm height   plus 5cm;
  square down to 5 and 6.

1 – 7 Scye depth:
  sizes 80–116cm height   plus 3.5cm
       122–164cm height   plus 4cm;
  square across to 8.

1 – 9 $\frac{1}{2}$ measurement 1–7; square out.

1 – 10 $\frac{1}{4}$ scye depth minus 2cm; square out.

0 – 11 $\frac{1}{5}$ neck size plus 0.5cm; draw back neck curve.

7 – 12 $\frac{1}{2}$ across back:
  sizes 80–116cm height   plus 2.5cm
       122–164cm height   plus 3cm;
  square up to 13 and 14.

14–15 sizes 80–116cm height   plus 1cm
       122–164cm height   plus 1.25cm.

Draw in the back armscye shape to touch points 15, 13, 8.

Front section
0 –16 $\frac{1}{5}$ neck size; draw in the front neck curve.

13–17 sizes 80–116cm height   0.6cm
       122–164cm height   0.9cm;

Draw a line below the line squared out from 10:
  sizes 80–116cm height   0.5cm
       122–164cm height   0.75cm.

11–18 The measurement 11–15; draw front shoulder line to touch the new line.

Draw in the front armscye shape as shown in diagram to touch points 18, 17, 8.

Sleeve
Square down from 0.

0 – 1 $\frac{1}{2}$ measurement 1–7 on body block; square across.

0 – 2 Sleeve length minus 2cm; square across.

0 – 3 The measurement of the armhole curve from 15–8.

2 – 4 $\frac{2}{3}$ measurement 1–3; join 3–4.

Divide 0–3 into six sections; mark points 5, 6, 7, 8, 9.
Draw in the sleeve head:
hollow the curve 0.4cm at 5;
raise the curve at 8; sizes 80–116cm height   1.25cm
                    122–164cm height   1.5cm.

Sleeve pitch points
Mark point 6 on the sleeve as a pitch point with a notch.
Measure the distance 3–6.
Measure along the armhole of the body sections the same distance. Mark the pitch points with a notch.

PYJAMA JACKET ADAPTATION
Back Trace off back section.

Front Trace off front section and mirror.
Add buttonstand, mark buttonholes. Construct an extended facing (ref. 1b, page 120). Mark fold line. Draw in pocket shape.

Collar Construct a convertible collar (ref. 2, page 122).

Pocket Add 3cm facing to top of pocket.

PYJAMA TROUSERS
Construct the basic shape of the 'flat' trouser block as a one-piece shape (ref. page 48).
Add a 5cm casing for elastic to the top of the trousers.

ADAPTATION FOR OLDER BOYS
Pyjamas designed for older boys can be adapted to give a longer back length for the boy's developing figure.

Jacket back Cut across back along the line 9–13; insert:
        sizes 128–140cm height   1cm
             152–164cm height   1.5cm.

Sleeve Mirror the front sleeve. Insert the same amount that was inserted in the back section at the line 0–2.
Mark pitch point for the shoulder on the forward line.

Trouser fly opening Mark points 6 and 7 from the trouser block. Mark A at top of casing. 6–B = 6–A.
Add a 4cm–5cm extension down to point 7.
Construct a fly piece the same size as the extension.

Pyjama jacket block

Pyjama jacket adaptation

Adaptation for older boys

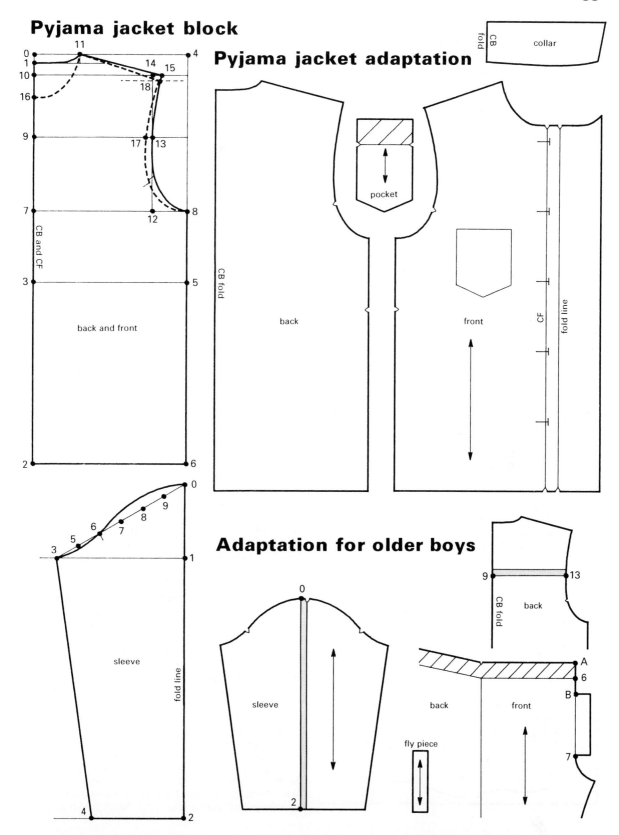

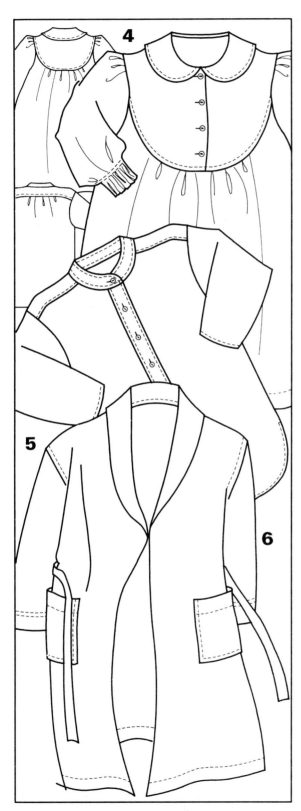

While the majority of nightwear is cut in jersey fabrics some styles are based on dress designs. If woven fabrics are used, include extra fullness in the body; e.g. by using gathers from yokes, see examples 4 and 5.

4 NIGHTDRESS

Trace off the 'flat' bodice and sleeve block with sleeve pitch points; mirror the front body section and the sleeve. Extend the body sections to the required length. Mark points A and B at sleeve pitch points on armhole, mark C and D at the position of sleeve gathers.
Add approx. 5cm flare to hemline on both side seams.
Back   Draw in the back yoke shape; mark E at the centre back, F at gather position. E–G is the measurement E–F; square down to the hemline. Trace off back section.
Front   Draw in the front yoke shape; mark H at the centre front, I at gather position. H–J is the measurement H–I; square down to the hemline. Trace off front section.
Yokes   Trace off both yokes. Front yoke (self faced) – add buttonstand, mark buttonholes. Mark fold.
Sleeve   Mark K and L at pitch points on sleeve.
K–M   The measurement A–C on back body section.
L–N   The measurement B–D on front body section.
Cut up centre line of sleeve and open 4cm–6cm at sleeve head, 2cm–3cm at hemline. Raise sleeve head 1cm.
Trace round pattern. Add 4 cm to the hem for casing.
Collar   Construct a flat collar (ref. 4, page 124).

5 NIGHTSHIRT

Trace off the 'flat' shirt and sleeve block; mirror the front body section and the sleeve. Lower front neckline 1cm. Extend the body sections to the required length. Mark in positions of side shaping, draw curves to hemline.
Back   Draw in back yoke; mark A at centre back, B at gather position. A–C is the measurement A–B; square down to the hemline. Trace off back section.
Front   Draw in front yoke. Add 1.5cm buttonstand; mark strap line 3cm from front edge; mark buttonholes on centre front line. Trace off front section.
Yokes   Trace off both yokes; join at the shoulder line.
Sleeve   Use the traced off shirt sleeve.
Front strap   Trace off front strap.
Collar   Construct standing straight collar 2.5cm depth (ref. 1, page 122). Curve top edge parallel to lower edge.

6 BATHROBE OR DRESSING GOWN

Trace off the back and front of the kimono block; mirror the front section. Draw in the finished length. Curve the front hemline down to 1cm at the centre front.
Back and front   Construct the 'flat' dolman sleeve (page 42). A–B for the gusset point is $\frac{1}{3}$ the underarm meas. Add 2.5cm flare to the hem on both side seams. Draw in pocket shape on front body section.
Facing and collar   Add 5cm to the centre front line for wrap over front. Mark C at the break point.
Construct a simple roll collar (ref. 9, page 124).
Pocket   Trace off pocket; add 3cm facing to top edge.
Belt   Construct a belt; D–E is twice width required; D–F $\frac{1}{2}$ waist measurement plus 35cm. Mark fold line.

4 Nightdress

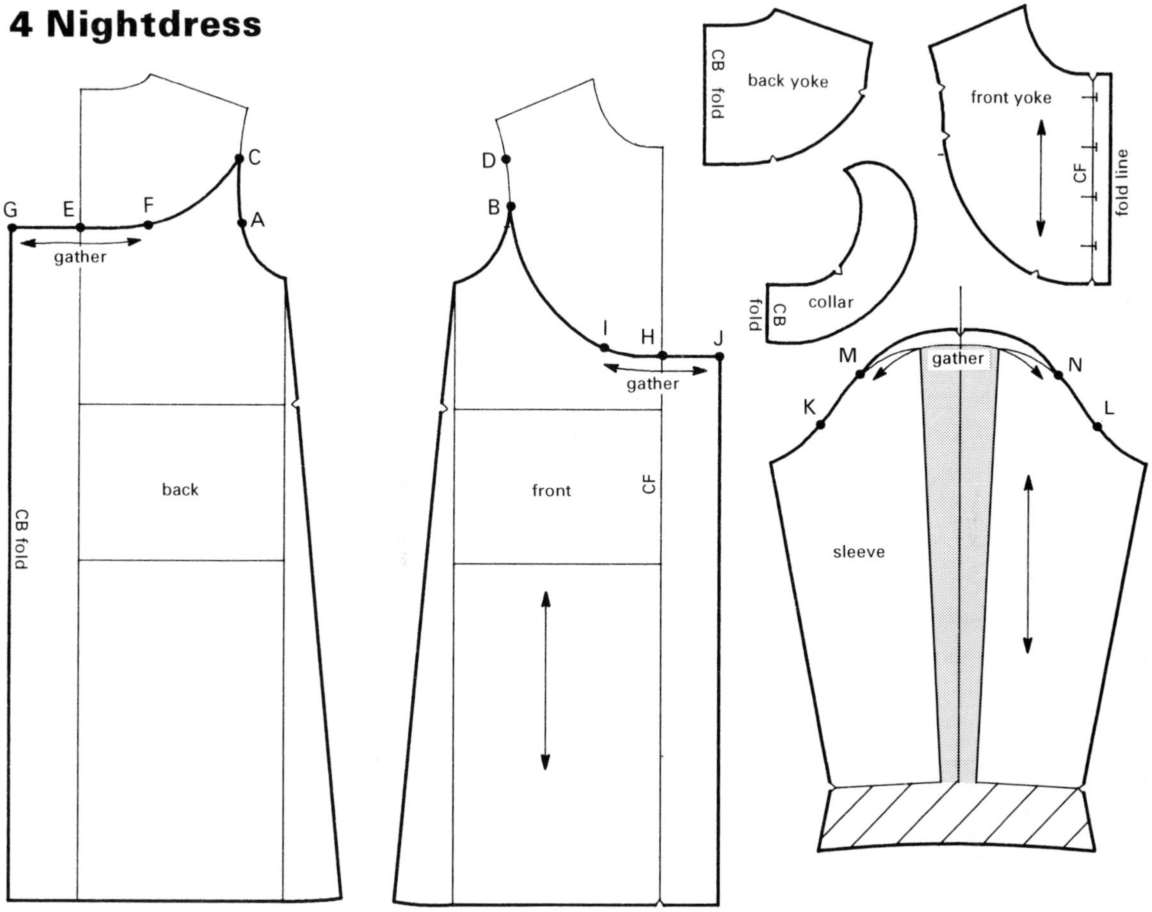

CB back yoke
fold

front yoke

CF
fold line

CB collar
fold

G E F
gather

C

A

back

CB fold

D
B

I H J
gather

front

CF

M gather N

K L

sleeve

5 Nightshirt

C A B
gather

back

CB fold

front

CF
strap line

strap

CB yoke
fold

CB collar
fold

sleeve

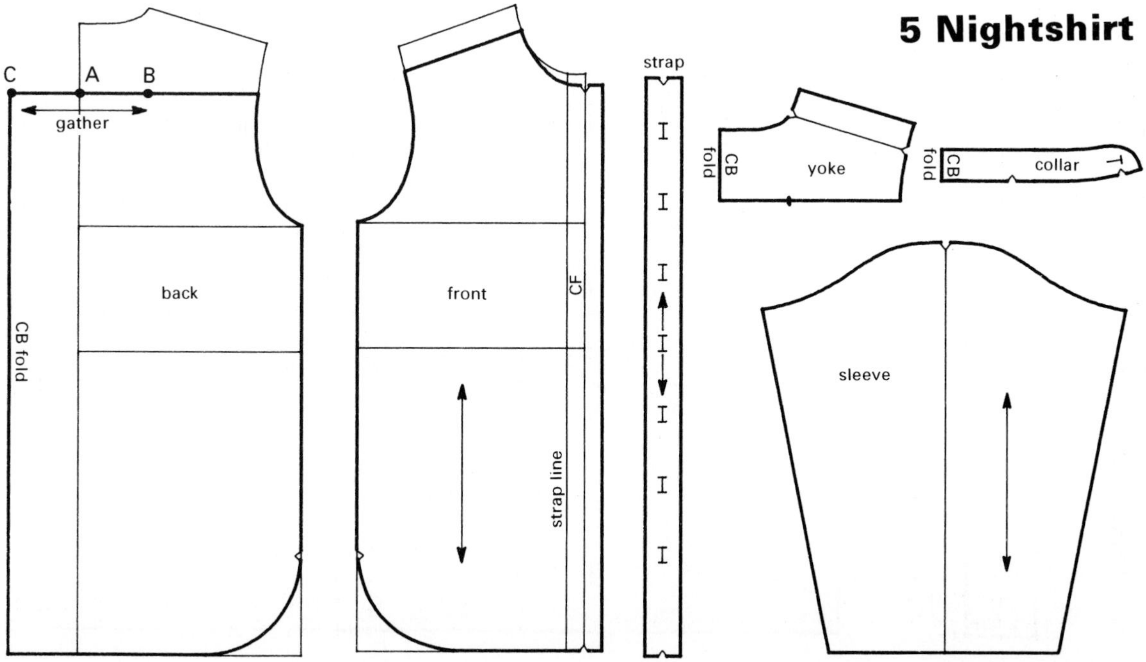

6 Bathrobe or dressing gown

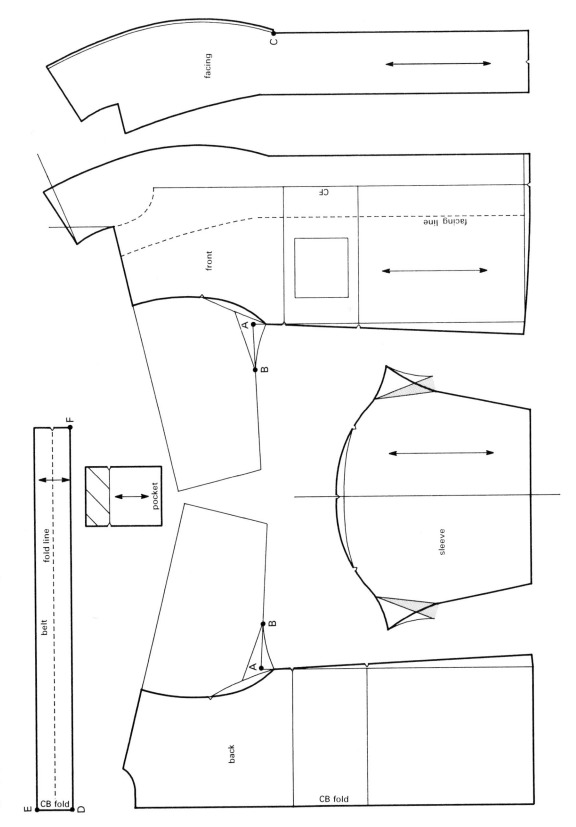

Part Two: Classic 'Form' Pattern Cutting Boys and Girls

9   THE BASIC BODY BLOCKS

Boys and girls; approximate age: 1–3 years (80–98cm)
Girls (undeveloped figures); approximate age 4–12 years (104–152cm)
Boys; approximate age: 4–14 years (104–170cm)

CLASSIC 'FORM' PATTERN CUTTING
Classic 'form' pattern cutting is used for garments which have a close relationship with the body shape. This is required mainly when working with fabrics without stretch characteristics or for cutting garments for traditional masculine and feminine shapes. Usually, the size charts on pages 16–18 are used to construct the blocks. These are based on 6cm height intervals and separated into different charts for boys and girls after the 98cm height interval (approximate age 3 years).

In most cases, easier fitting garments or garments made in stretch fabrics are constructed by using the 'flat' blocks and 'flat' methods of pattern cutting in the section Simple 'Flat' Pattern Cutting.

The Classic Bodice Block – Infants

For boys and girls, sizes 80–98cm height: approximate age 1–3 years
The blocks are for close-fitting formal garments; for easier fitting garments use the 'flat' blocks on page 23

MEASUREMENTS REQUIRED TO DRAFT THE
BLOCK
(e.g. size 92cm height)
Refer to the size chart (page 16) for standard
measurements.

Chest	53cm
Across back	22cm
Neck size	26.5cm
Shoulder	7cm
Scye depth	12.6cm
Back neck to waist	23cm

Body sections

0 – 1 Neck to waist plus 1cm; square across.
0 – 2 $\frac{1}{2}$ chest plus 4cm; square down to 3.
  e.g. 92cm height: $(53 \div 2) + 4cm = 30.5cm$
0 – 4 1cm.
4 – 5 Scye depth plus 1cm; square across to 6.
4 – 7 $\frac{1}{2}$ measurement 4–5; square out.
4 – 8 $\frac{1}{4}$ scye depth minus 2cm; square out.

0 – 9 $\frac{1}{5}$ neck size plus 0.3cm; draw in neck curve.
5 –10 $\frac{1}{2}$ across the back plus 0.5cm; square up.
Mark point 11 on the line from 7.
9 –12 Shoulder measurement.
Draw back shoulder line to touch the line from 8.
2 –13 $\frac{1}{5}$ neck size.
2 –14 $\frac{1}{5}$ neck size; draw in neck curve.
12–15 0.4cm; square across.
13–16 shoulder measurement; draw in front shoulder
  line to touch the line from 15.
14–17 $\frac{1}{2}$ measurement 6–14 plus 1cm; square across.
6 –18 The measurement 5–10 minus 0.7cm; square up
  to 19. Join 19 to 16.
5 –20 $\frac{1}{2}$ measurement 5–6; square down to 21.
10–22 1.8cm; 18–23 1.5cm.
Draw in the armscye shape as shown in diagram to
touch points 12, 11, 22, 20, 23, 19, 16.
3 –24 1.5cm; join 1–24 with a curve.

Sleeve Draft a one-piece sleeve (page 98) or two-piece
sleeve (page 100) to fit armscye measurement.

The Classic Bodice Block – Girls

For girls (undeveloped figures), sizes 104–152cm height: approximate age 4–12 years

MEASUREMENTS REQUIRED TO DRAFT THE
BLOCK
(e.g. size 110cm height)
Refer to the size chart (page 16 for standard
measurements.

Chest	59cm
Across back	24.4cm
Neck size	28cm
Shoulder	8.2cm
Scye depth	14.4cm
Back neck to waist	26.6cm

Body sections

0 – 1 Neck to waist plus 1.25cm; square across.
0 – 2 $\frac{1}{2}$ chest.
  sizes 104–116cm height   plus 4.5cm
    122–152cm height   plus 5cm;
  square down to 3.
  e.g. 110cm height: $(59 \div 2) + 4.5cm = 34cm$.
0 – 4 1.25cm.
4 – 5 Scye depth plus 1cm; square across to 6.
4 – 7 $\frac{1}{2}$ measurement 4–5; square out.
4 – 8 $\frac{1}{4}$ scye depth minus 2cm; square out.
0 – 9 $\frac{1}{5}$ neck size plus 0.3cm; draw in neck curve.
5 –10 $\frac{1}{2}$ across the back plus 0.5cm; square up;

Mark point 11 on the line from 7.
9 –12 Shoulder measurement.
Draw back shoulder line to touch the line from 8.
2 –13 $\frac{1}{5}$ neck size.
2 –14 $\frac{1}{5}$ neck size; draw in neck curve.
12–15 sizes 104–116cm height   0.5cm
      122–152cm height   0.6cm;
  square across.
13–16 shoulder measurement; draw in front shoulder
  line to touch the line from 15.
6 –17 The measurement 5–10 minus 0.7cm; square up.
17–18 $\frac{1}{4}$ measurement 4–5.
17–19 $\frac{1}{2}$ measurement 10–17 plus 0.5cm; square down
  to 20.
10–21 sizes 104–116cm height   2cm
      122–152cm height   2.25cm.
17–22 sizes 104–116cm height   1.75cm
      122–152cm height   2cm.
Draw in the armscye shape as shown in diagram to
touch points 12, 11, 21, 19, 22, 18, 16.
3 –23 sizes 104–116cm height   1cm
      122–152cm height   0.5cm;
  join 1–23 with a curve.

Sleeve Draft a one-piece sleeve (page 98) or two-piece
sleeve (page 100) to fit armscye measurement.

The classic bodice block – infants

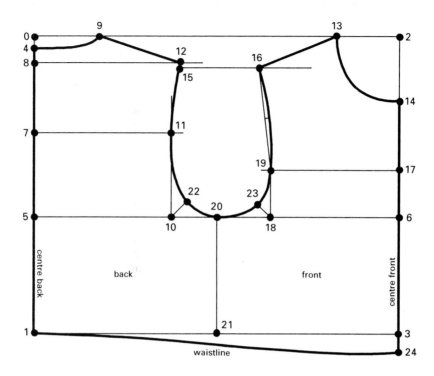

The classic bodice block – girls

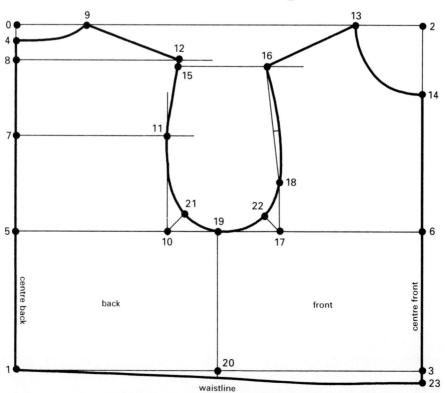

The Classic Dress Block

For girls, sizes 80–152cm height

The dress block is constructed to knee length; this provides a consistent guide. Final length is marked at the pattern cutting stage.

A one-piece dress block for children is usually cut to avoid shaping directly in the waist area. Fitted dresses are not very suitable for small children as they tend to have rather large stomachs. The block is adapted to give high waist shaping as this flatters the figure.

Separate front and back bodice block.
Trace round bodice block; use the line 1–21 and 21–3 as the waistline to begin the draft.
Mark points 1, 3, 13, 20, 21.

Back
Square down from 1 and 21.
1–A   Waist to knee measurement; square across to B.
B–C   5cm; join 21–C.
21–D   The measurement 21–B, shape hem with a curve to D.

Curve in bodice side seam 20–21 0.75cm.
1–E   Waist to hip measurement; square across.

Front
Square down from 3 and 21.
3–F   Waist to knee measurement; square across to G.
G–H   5cm; join 21–H.
21–J   The measurement 21–G.
F–K   The measurement 3–23 on original bodice block; shape hem with a curve from K–J.
3–L   The measurement F–K; join L to 21 with a curve.
3–M   Waist to hip measurement; square across.

Sizes 80–116cm height
Young children have a forward stance; this means that extra fullness is required in the front block.

Square down from 13 to N: cut up the line and open block at hem line.
N–P   Sizes 80–104cm height   2.5cm
            110–116cm height   1.5cm.
Trace round new block shape; re-mark waistline, scye depth line and hip line.

The Sleeveless Dress Block

Back and front
Trace round dress block.
Mark point A at underarm point.
Raise scye depth line 1cm.
A–B   1cm; square up to C on new scye depth line.
Mark point D at shoulder point.

D–E   0.75cm; draw in new armscye shape from E–C as shown.
Mark point F at waistline. G at hemline.
F–H   0.75cm; draw in new side seam, join H–G; join C–H with a curve.

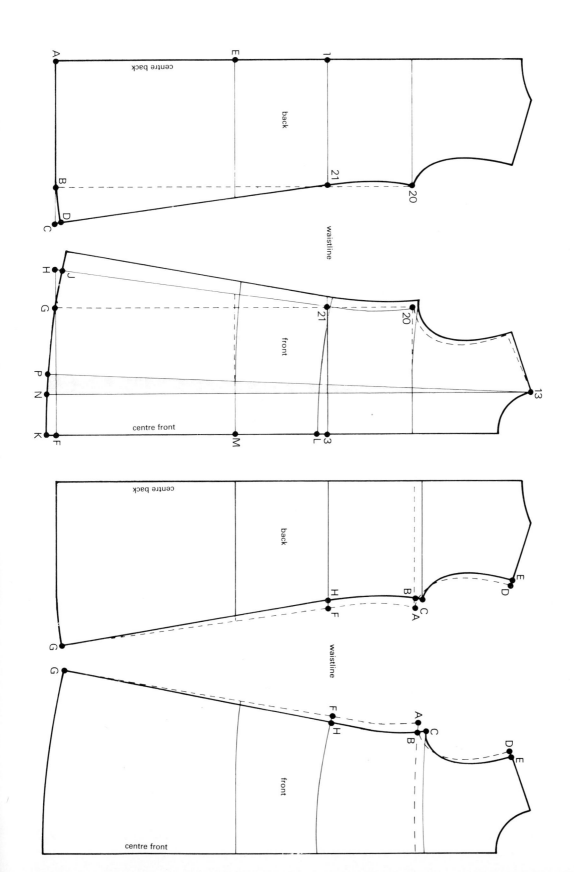

The Formal Coat Block – Infants and Girls

For boys and girls, sizes 80–98cm height
For girls (undeveloped figures), sizes 104–152cm height

This coat block is developed from the Classic Dress Block to give a classic, slightly flared, full length shape. It is especially suitable for girls and infants.

Back and front
Mark points A and B at shoulder, points C at underarm.
C–D   2cm, mark new scye depth line 2cm below previous scye depth line.
D–E   2.5cm
Raise the shoulder line 0.5cm.
Square up from A to touch new shoulder line at F.

F–G   0.5cm. Correct neck curve.
Extend armscye line from B–11 and B–19 1cm.
Re-draw armscye line as shown.
Mark H at waistline, J at hipline, K at hemline.
Extend H, K, J 1.5cm; draw in new side seam.
Shape in line from underarm to waistline 0.5cm.

Sleeve
Draft one-piece sleeve (page 98) or two-piece sleeve (page 100) to fit new armscye measurement.

The Classic Overgarment Block – Infants

For boys and girls, sizes 80–98cm height: approximate age 1–3 years

A simple version of the classic straight overgarment block can be made for infants by adding extra ease to the bodice block. This can give a 'tailored' look by using the two-piece sleeve block. For easy-fitting overgarments (i.e. anoraks or duffle coats) use the 'flat' block on page 40.

Body sections
Cut out the basic bodice block, cut up side seam.
Draw round back block with a dotted line.
Mark points 1, 4, 9, 11, 12.
4–A   Final length square across.
Extend scye depth line, waistline and hemline.
Mark B at underarm point.
B–C   5cm.
Square down from C to D, place front block correctly on extended lines to touch the line C–D; trace round.
Square down to E on hemline.

Mark points 3, 13, 16, 19.
F midway B–C; square down to G to make new side seam.
F–H   2cm; draw in new scye depth line.
Raise shoulder line 0.5cm.
Square up from 9 and 13 to touch new shoulder lines at J and K.
J–L and K–M 5cm; correct neck curves.
Extend armscye line from 11–12 and 16–19 1.25cm.
Re-draw armhole to touch new scye depth line.
Lower waistline 1–3 0.5cm.
E–N   The measurement 3–24 on original bodice block.
Join G–N with a curve.

Sleeve
Draft one-piece sleeve (page 98) or a two-piece sleeve (page 100) to fit new armscye measurement.

The formal coat block

The classic overgarment block 1–3 years

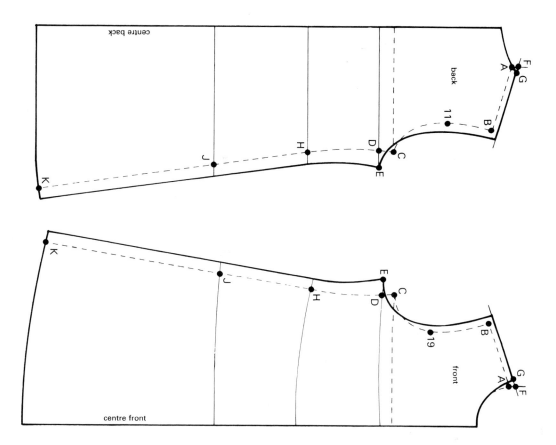

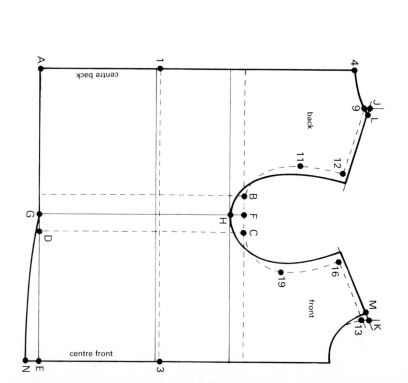

The Classic Overgarment Blocks

For boys, sizes 104–170cm height: approximate age 4–14 years
For girls (undeveloped figures), sizes 104–152cm height; approximate age 4–12 years

The blocks are constructed to reflect the changing shape of boys and girls from age 7. The boy's back section is longer in proportion to the front section. The blocks are used for garments with classic one-piece or two-piece set-in sleeves.

MEASUREMENTS REQUIRED TO DRAFT THE BLOCK
(e.g. boy or girl size 134cm height)
Refer to the size charts (pages 17 and 18) for standard measurements.

	Girls	Boys
Chest	69cm	70cm
Across back	28.4cm	29.2cm
Neck size	31cm	31cm
Shoulder	10cm	10.5cm
Neck to waist	31.4cm	32.2cm
Scye depth	16.8cm	17.2cm
Waist to hip	15.6cm	15.6cm

Body sections
Square both ways from 0.
0 – 1 Neck to waist:
  sizes 104–152cm height   plus 2.25cm.
  158–170cm height   plus 2.5cm.
0 – 2 $1/2$ chest plus 10cm; square down, mark point 3 on waistline.
0 – 4 Sizes 104–152cm height   1.75cm
  158–170cm height   2cm.
4 – 5 Scye depth:
  sizes 104–152cm height   plus 3cm
  158–170cm height   plus 3.5cm;
  square across to 6.
4 – 7 $1/2$ measurement 4–5; square out.
4 – 8 $1/4$ scye depth; square out.
5 – 9 $1/2$ across back plus 2.5cm; square up to 10 and 11.
11–12 2cm; square out.
0 –13 $1/5$ neck size plus 0.8cm; draw in neck curve.
12–14 Sizes 104–152cm height   1.5cm
  158–170cm height 2cm; join 13–14.
The back shoulder measurement includes 0.5cm ease.

Girls
Point 2 now becomes point 15.
15–16 $1/5$ neck size plus 0.8cm.
16–17 $1/2$ measurement 16–6 plus 2cm; square across.
6 –18 The measurement 5–9 minus 0.8cm; square up to 19.

Boys (up to 122cm height follow the girl's instructions above).
2 –15 Sizes 122–134cm height   0.5cm
  140–152cm height   1cm
  158–170cm height   1.5cm;
  square across.
15–16 $1/5$ neck size plus 0.8cm.
16–17 $1/2$ measurement 16–6 plus 2cm; square across.
6 –18 The measurement 5–9;
  sizes 122–152cm height   minus 1cm
  158–170cm height   minus 1.25cm;
  square up to 19.

15–20 $1/5$ neck size plus 0.5cm; draw in neck curve.
Join 20 to point 11 with a straight line.
20–21 The measurement 13–14 minus 0.5cm.
21–22 Sizes 104–152cm height   1cm
  158–170cm height   1.25cm.
18–23 $1/2$ measurement 9–18 plus 0.5cm; square down; mark point 24 on waistline.
Draw in armscye shape as shown, measurement of curve:
  sizes 104–152cm height   from 9 and 18 2.25cm
  158–170cm height   from 9 and 18 2.5cm.
4 –25 Finished length; square across to 26 and 27.
27–28 1cm; join 26–28 with a curved line.
1 –29 Waist to hip; square across.

Sleeve
Draft a one-piece sleeve (page 98) or a two-piece sleeve (page 100) to fit armscye measurement.

Note Separate instructions are required for the different sexes because a boy is developing a longer back length and wider back width than a girl at this period of his growth.

Boys' classic overgarment block

Girls' classic overgarment block

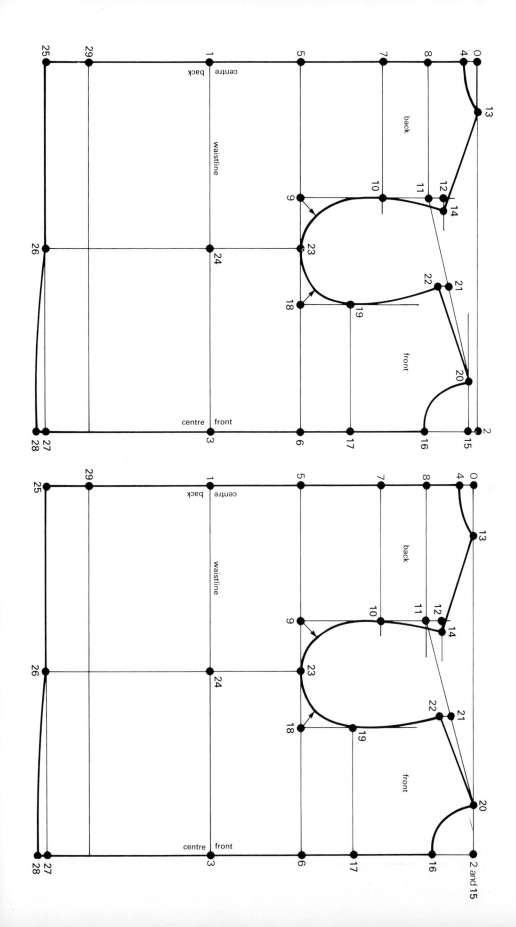

The Classic Blazer Block

For boys, sizes 122–170cm height
For girls (undeveloped figures), sizes 122–152cm height
Approximate age 7–14 years

MEASUREMENTS REQUIRED TO DRAFT THE BLOCK
(e.g. boy or girl size 134cm height)
refer to the size charts (pages 17 and 18) for standard measurements.

	Girls	Boys
Chest	69cm	70cm
Across back	28.4cm	29.2cm
Neck size	31cm	31cm
Shoulder	10cm	10.5cm
Neck to waist	31.4cm	32.2cm
Scye depth	16.8cm	17.2cm
Waist to hip	15.6cm	15.6cm

Body sections
Square both ways from 0.

0 – 1 Sizes 122–152cm height   1.75cm
       58–170cm height   2cm.

1 – 2 Neck to waist; square across.

1 – 3 Finished length; square across.

2 – 4 Waist to hip; square across.

1 – 5 Scye depth:
     sizes 122–152cm height   plus 2.5cm
       158–170cm height   plus 3cm;
     square across.

1 – 6 $\frac{1}{2}$ measurement 1–5; square across.

1 – 7 $\frac{1}{4}$ scye depth; square across.

5 – 8 $\frac{1}{2}$ across back plus 1.25cm; square up to 9 and 10.

10–11 2cm; square out.

0 –12 $\frac{1}{5}$ neck size plus 0.5cm; draw in neck curve.

12–13 Shoulder length plus 1.5cm.

2 –14 1cm; square down to 15 and 16. Join 6–14.

0 –17 $\frac{1}{2}$ chest plus 8cm; square down to 18, 19 and 20.

18–21 The measurement 5–8 minus 0.5cm; square up.

21–22 $\frac{1}{2}$ measurement 5–7 minus 2cm.

21–23 $\frac{1}{2}$ measurement 21–18 minus 0.3cm; square up to 24 and down to hem line.

Girls
Point 24 and 25 are the same point.

Boys
24–25 Sizes 122–134cm height   0.5cm
       140–152cm height   1cm
       158–170cm height 1.5cm.

Join 25 to point 10; extend the line past point 25.

25–26 Sizes 122–134cm height   1.5cm
       140–152cm height   1.75cm
       158–170cm height   2cm.

25–27 The measurement 12–13 minus 0.5cm; square down 1cm to 28. Join 25–28 with slight curve.

21–29 $\frac{1}{2}$ measurement 8–21. Mark 29 underarm point.

Draw in armscye shape as shown; measurement of curve:
Sizes 122–134cm height from 8 2.5cm; from 21 2cm
     140–152cm height from 8 2.8cm; from 21 2.3cm
     158–170cm height from 8 3cm;   from 21 2.5cm.

29–30 $\frac{1}{3}$ measurement 29–21; square down to 31 on waistline, 32 on hip/seat line.

31–33 $\frac{2}{3}$ measurement 31–32; construct a 1cm dart on the line 30–33.

8 –34 $\frac{1}{4}$ scye depth minus 1cm; square across to 35 on armscye line. Square down to 36 on waistline.

8 –37 Sizes 122–152cm height   2cm
       158–170cm height   2.5cm;
     square down to 38, 39 and 40.

40–41 $\frac{1}{6}$ measurement 5–8; draw in back seam line through points 35, 38, 41 and points 35, 36, 40.

18–42 $\frac{1}{2}$ measurement 18–19 minus 2cm. 19–43 1.5cm.

43–44 The measurement 42–43. Mark points 42, 43 and 44 as buttonholes.

42–45 2cm; square up and down. Join 45 to point 26 and extend the line.

20–46 1.5cm; join 46 to 40 on back seam line.

46–47 $\frac{1}{5}$ measurement 3–40 plus 1cm. Draw in front line of blazer from 45–47 as shown.

25–48 $\frac{1}{8}$ neck size plus 0.5cm; square across to 49 on centre front line.

48–50 1.5cm; join 50–49 and extend the line.

49–51 1.5cm; draw in neckline with a curve to break line as shown. Draw in rever edge from 51–45 with a curve.

Pockets
23–52 $\frac{1}{3}$ measurement 23–18.

52–53 Size 122cm height 7.5cm (add 0.5cm each size up).

53–54 1cm; size 122cm height square down 7.5cm from 52 and 54 (add 0.7cm each size up).

Draw in lower edge of pocket; curve the corners at bottom edge of pocket.
On the line from 24 mark point 55 on the waistline, 56 on hip/seat line.

55–57 $\frac{1}{2}$ measurement 55–56 minus 2cm.

57–58 Size 122cm height 13.5cm (add 0.7cm each size up).

Draw two parallel lines from 57 and 58 parallel to the hemline.

57–59 Size 122cm height 12.5cm (add 0.5cm each size up).

Square down from 59 using the line 57–59 to complete pocket. Curve the corners at bottom edge of pocket.

Sleeve
Draft a two-piece sleeve (page 100) to fit armscye measurements.

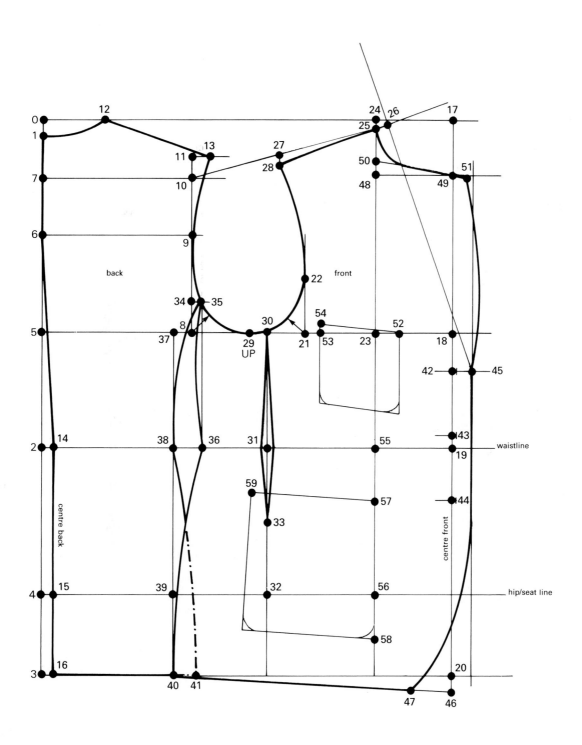

The One-piece Sleeve Block

To be used with all body blocks: boys and girls – all sizes

MEASUREMENTS REQUIRED TO DRAFT THE
BLOCK
(e.g. size 110cm height)
Refer to the size charts (pages 16–19 and 161) for
standard measurements.

Armscye girth   (measure the armscye)
Sleeve length   39.5cm
(For coats and overgarments add 1.25cm to sleeve
length.)

Mark basic points on body block
(If the dress or formal coat block is used, draw a scye
depth line and place armhole points together at A.)
Mark point A at underarm, B and C at shoulder points.
Square up from scye depth line to touch back and front
armscye lines.
Mark points D and E on scye depth line.

Sleeve
Square up and across from 0.
0 – 1 $^1/_3$ armscye girth: square across.
0 – 2 $^1/_2$ measurement 0–1; square across.
0 – 3 $^1/_2$ measurement 0–2.
On body block: E–F equals the measurement 0–3 on
sleeve block.
Square out to FP (front pitch point) on armscye.
D–BP (back pitch point) equals the measurement 0–2
on sleeve block.
On sleeve:
3 – 4 The measurement C–FP measured in a curve:
    sizes 80–116cm height   plus 0.4cm
          122–152cm height   plus 0.6cm
          158–170cm height   plus 0.8cm; join 3–4.
4 – 5 The measurement B–BP measured in a curve:
    sizes 80–116cm height   plus 0.3cm
          122–152cm height   plus 0.5cm
          158–170cm height   plus 0.7cm; join 4–5.
3 – 6 The measurement FP–A measured in a curve;
    join 3–6.

5 – 7 The measurement BP–A measured in a curve;
    join 5–7.
4 – 8 Sleeve length from shoulder; square across to 9
    and 10.
Draw in outline of the sleeve head.
7 – 5 Hollow the curve:
    sizes 80–116cm height   0.3cm
          122–152cm height   0.4cm
          158–170cm height   0.5cm.
5 – 4 Raise the curve:
    sizes 80–116cm height   0.7cm
          122–152cm height   0.8cm
          158–170cm height   0.9cm.
4 – 3 Raise the curve at 11, $^1/_3$ measurement 4–3:
    sizes 80–116cm height   1.2cm
          122–152cm height   1.3cm
          158–170cm height   1.4cm.
3 – 6 Hollow the curve:
    sizes 80–116cm height   0.5cm
          122–152cm height   0.6cm
          158–170cm height   0.7cm.
9 –12 $^1/_2$ measurement 6–9; square across.
To shape side seams:
9 –13 $^1/_6$ measurement 8–9.
10–14 $^1/_6$ measurement 8–10.
Join 6–13 and 7–14.
If wrist curve is required:
14– 8 Lower the curve:
    sizes 80–116cm height   0.5cm
          122–152cm height   0.7cm
          158–170cm height   0.9cm.
    Hollow the curve:
    sizes 80–116cm height   0.5cm
          122–152cm height   0.7cm
          158–170cm height   0.9cm.

Note It is important that all curved measurements are
measured very accurately along the curved line, with the
tape upright (see diagram)

Body block

Measuring a curve

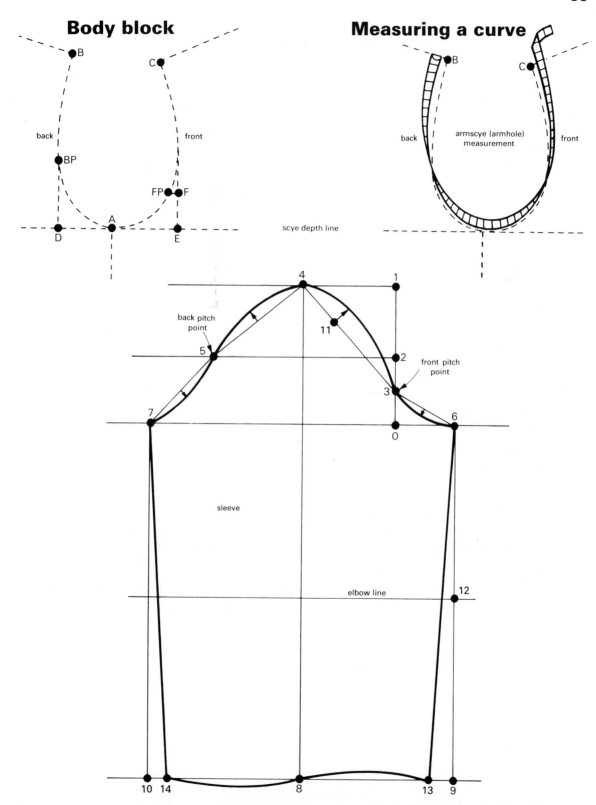

back

front

BP

FP F

A

D E

scye depth line

back

armscye (armhole)
measurement

front

back pitch
point

front pitch
point

sleeve

elbow line

The Two-piece Sleeve Block

To be used with all body blocks: boys and girls – all sizes

MEASUREMENTS REQUIRED TO DRAFT THE BLOCK
(e.g. size 110cm height)
Refer to the size charts (pages 16–19 and 161) for standard measurements.

Armscye girth   (measure the armscye)
Sleeve length   39.5cm
(For coats and overgarments add 1.25cm to sleeve length.)
Cuff size for two-piece sleeve.

Mark basic points on body block
(If the dress or formal coat block is used draw a scye depth line and place armhole points together at A.)
Mark points A at underarm, B and C at shoulder points.
Square up from scye depth line to touch back and front armscye lines.
Mark points D and E on scye depth line.

Sleeve
Square up and across from 0.
0 – 1 $\frac{1}{3}$ armscye girth plus 0.25cm; square across.
1 – 2 $\frac{1}{3}$ measurement 0–1 plus 1cm; square across.
0 – 3 $\frac{1}{4}$ measurement 0–1.
On body block: E–F equals the measurement 0–3 on sleeve block.
Square out to FP (front pitch point) on armscye.
D–BP (back pitch point) equals the measurement 0–2 on sleeve block.
On sleeve:
3 – 4   The measurement C–FP measured in a curve:
   sizes 80–116cm height   plus 0.5cm
           122–152cm height   plus 0.8cm
           158–170cm height   plus 1cm; join 3–4.
4 – 5   The measurement B–BP measured in a curve:
   sizes 80–116cm height   plus 0.4cm
           122–152cm height   plus 0.6cm
           158–170cm height   plus 0.8cm; join 4–5.

0 – 6   The measurement A–E on body block:
0 – 7   sizes 80–116cm height   1.5cm
           122–152cm height   1.75cm
           158–170cm height   2cm; square across.
7 – 8 and 7 – 9
   sizes 80–116cm height   1.25cm
           122–152cm height   1.5cm
           158–170cm height   1.75cm; square down.
1 –10   Sleeve length from shoulder; square across to 11 and 12.
10–13   Sizes 80–116cm height   2cm
           122–152cm height   2.5cm
           158–170cm height   3cm; square across.
10–14   Cuff size for two-piece sleeve; join 10–14 and 10–11.
7 –15 $\frac{1}{2}$ measurement 7–10; square across (elbow line). Curve inner sleeve seams inwards at elbow line, the measurement 7–8.
Draw in sleeve head.
5 – 4   Raise the curve:
   sizes 80–116cm height   0.7cm
           122–152cm height   0.8cm
           158–170cm height   0.9cm.
Mark point 16, 4–16 is $\frac{1}{3}$ measurement 4–3.
4 – 3   Raise the curve at 16:
   sizes 80–116cm height   1.25cm
           122–152cm height   1.5cm
           158–170cm height   1.75cm; join 3–8.
6 –17   The measurement A–BP on body block, measured straight plus 0.5cm.
Join 6–17, draw a curve hollowed 1.25cm.
Check the measurement of the curve 6–17 on the sleeve equals the curve A–BP on the body block.
Join 6–9 with a slight curve.
Join 17–14 and 5–14.
Mark points 18 and 19 on elbow line.
Curve outer sleeve seams outwards, the measurement 7–8 at points 18 and 19.

Note   It is important that all curved measurements are measured very accurately along the curved line, with the tape upright (see diagram).

Body block

Measuring a curve

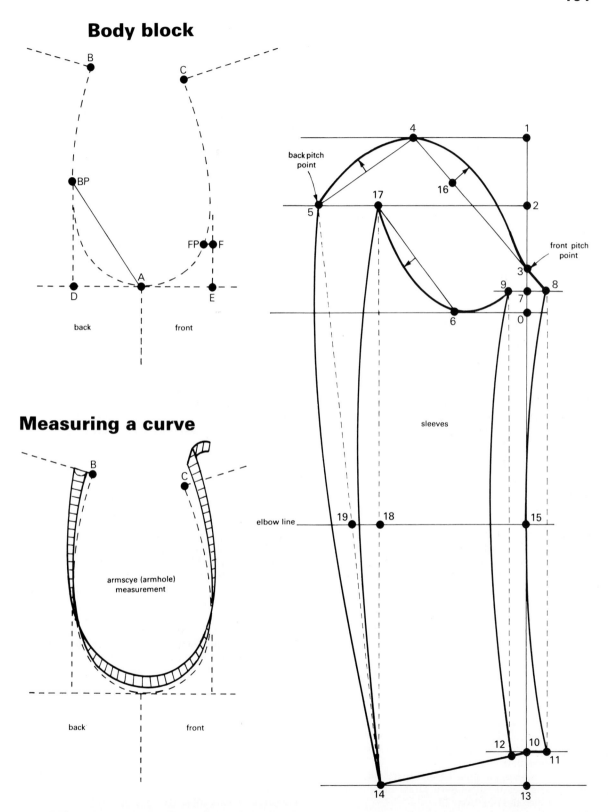

back pitch
point

front pitch
point

back

front

armscye (armhole)
measurement

back

front

elbow line

sleeves

The Classic Shirt Block – Infants and Girls

For infants, sizes 80–116cm height
For girls, sizes 122–164cm height

MEASUREMENTS REQUIRED TO DRAFT THE
BLOCK
(e.g. size 110cm height)
Refer to size charts (pages 16–19 and 161) for standard
measurements.

Chest	59cm	Neck size	28cm
Scye depth	14.4cm	Sleeve length	39.5cm
Neck to waist	26.6cm	Cuff size	16.2cm
Across back	24.4cm		

Body sections
Square up and down from 0; square across approx.
10cm.
0 – 1 Scye depth plus 2cm; square across.
0 – 2 Neck to waist; square across.
0 – 3 Shirt length required; square across.
1 – 4 $^1/_2$ chest:
  sizes 80–116cm height   plus 8cm
      122–152cm height   plus 8.5cm
      158–164cm height   plus 9.5cm;
  square up, square down to 5.
0 – 6 sizes 80–116cm height   plus 3cm
      122–152cm height   plus 3.25cm
      158–164cm height   plus 3.5cm;
  square across to 7.
6 – 8 $^1/_5$ neck plus 0.2cm; square down to 9.
0 –10 $^1/_3$ measurement 0.9; draw a curve from 8–10.
6 –11 $^1/_5$ scye depth minus 0.5cm; square out.
0 –12 $^1/_5$ measurement 0–1 plus 1cm; square half-way
  across the block.
1 –13 $^1/_2$ across back:
  sizes 80–116cm height   plus 2cm
      122–152cm height   plus 2.25cm
      158–164cm height   plus 2.5cm;
  square up to 14 and 15.
15–16 0.75cm; join 8–16.
14–17 $^1/_2$ measurement 12–14 minus 1.5cm.
14–18 0.5cm; join 17–18 with a curve.
7 –19 Sizes 80–116cm height   plus 3.5cm
      122–152cm height   plus 4cm
      158–164cm height   plus 5cm;
  square across.
19–20 $^1/_5$ neck size minus 0.8cm.
19–21 $^1/_5$ neck size:
  sizes 80–116cm height   minus 1.2cm
      122–152cm height   minus 1.4cm
      158–164cm height   minus 1.6cm;
  draw in neck curve.
19–22 $^1/_5$ scye depth plus 0.5cm; square out.
20–23 The measurement 8–16. Draw a line from 20 to
  touch the line from 22.
21–24 $^1/_2$ measurement 4–21 plus 1cm; square across.

4 –25 The measurement 1–13:
  sizes 80–116cm height   minus 1cm
      122–152cm height   minus 0.8cm
      158–164cm height   minus 0.2cm;
  square up to 26.
25–27 $^1/_2$ measurement 13–25 plus 0.5cm; square down
  to 28 and 29. Draw armscye curve 16, 18, 27, 26,
  23.
29–30 $^1/_4$ measurement 28–29.
29–31 $^1/_3$ measurement 5–29, 29–32 $^1/_3$ measurement
  3–29. Join 30–31 and 30–32 with curves.
Curve both side seams in 0.75cm at 28.
21–33 1.5cm buttonstand; square down.
33–34 3.5cm facing; square down. Shape neckline.
12–35 2cm (back pleat); square down.

Sleeve
Square down from 0.
0 – 1 $^1/_4$ armscye measurement (see measuring a
  curve on page 99); square across.
0 – 2 Sleeve length minus cuff depth plus 2cm ease;
  square across.
1 – 3 $^1/_2$ measurement 1–2; square across.
0 – 4 $^1/_2$ armscye measurement; square down to 5.
0 – 6 $^1/_2$ armscye measurement; square down to 7.
Divide 0–4 into four sections, mark points 8, 9, 10.
Divide 0–6 into four sections, mark points 11, 12, 13.
8 – 0 Raise the curve:
sizes 80–116cm height 0.5cm at 9; 0.75cm at 10
    122–152cm height 0.75cm at 9; 1.25cm at 10
    158–164cm height 1cm   at 9; 1.75cm at 10.
Raise the curve at 11:
    sizes 80–116cm height   0.5cm
      122–152cm height   0.75cm
      158–164cm height   1cm.
Hollow the curve at 13:
    sizes 80–116cm height   0.5cm
      122–152cm height   0.75cm
      158–164cm height   1cm.
5 –14 $^1/_4$ measurement 2–5 minus 0.5cm; join 4–14.
7 –15 $^1/_4$ measurement 2–7 minus 0.5cm; join 6–15.
Mark points 16 and 17 on the line from 3.
14–18 1cm; join 16–18 with a curve.
15–19 1cm; join 17–19 with a curve.
20 Midway 2–18; square up to 21.
21–22 $^1/_3$ measurement 20–21.
20–23 0.75cm; join 18–2 with a curve.
Cuff
Cuff length – cuff size plus 2cm.
Cuff depth – approx. size 4.5cm–7cm (ref. 1, page 118).
Collar
Construct a shirt collar (ref. 3, page 122).
Depth of shirt collar and stand approx. 6cm–8cm.

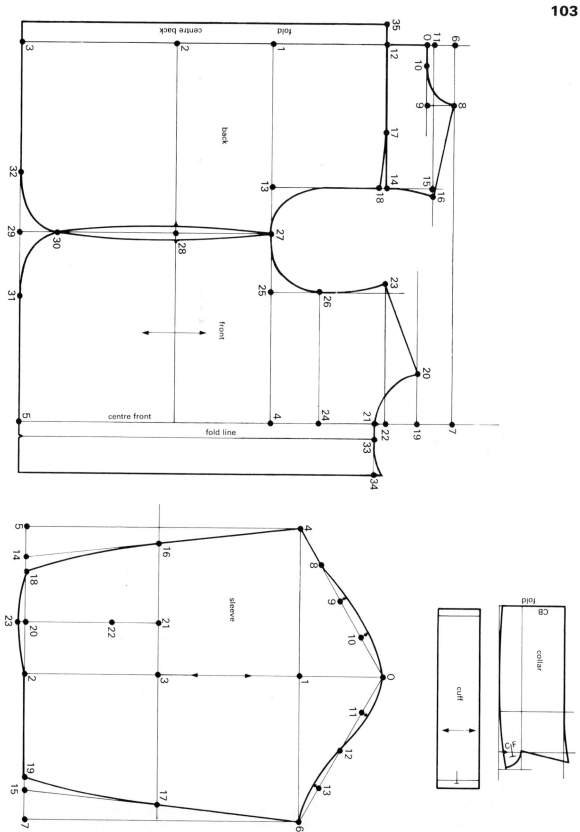

The Classic Shirt Block – Boys

Approximate age 7–14 years
For boys, size 122–170cm height

MEASUREMENTS REQUIRED TO DRAFT THE BLOCK
(e.g. size 134cm height)
Refer to size chart (pages 17 and 18) for standard measurements.

Chest	70cm
Scye depth	17.2cm
Neck to waist	32.2cm
Across back	29.2cm
Neck size	31cm
Sleeve length	49.5cm
Cuff size	18cm

Body sections
Square down from 0; square across approx. 10cm.
0 – 1 Scye depth plus 2cm; square across.
0 – 2 Neck to waist; square across.
0 – 3 Shirt length required; square across.
1 – 4 $^{1}/_{2}$ chest:
sizes 122–152cm height   plus 9cm
158–170cm height   plus 10cm;
square up, square down to 5.
0 – 6 Sizes 122–152cm height   3.5cm
158–170cm height   3.75cm;
square across to 7.
6 – 8 $^{1}/_{5}$ neck plus 0.2cm; square down to 9.
0 –10 $^{1}/_{3}$ measurement 0–9; draw a curve from 8–10.
6 –11 $^{1}/_{5}$ scye depth minus 0.5cm; square half-way across the block.
0 –12 $^{1}/_{5}$ measurement 0–1 plus 1cm; square half-way across block.
1 –13 $^{1}/_{2}$ across back:
sizes 122–152cm height   plus 2.25cm
158–170cm height   plus 2.5cm;
square up to 14 and 15.
15–16 0.75cm; join 8–16.
14–17 $^{1}/_{2}$ measurement 14–12 minus 1.5cm.
14–18 0.5cm; join 17–18 with a curve.
7 –19 Sizes 122–152cm height   5cm
158–170cm height   5.8cm.
19–20 $^{1}/_{5}$ neck size minus 0.8cm.
19–21 $^{1}/_{5}$ neck size:
sizes 122–152cm height   minus 1.5cm
158–170cm height   minus 1.2cm;
draw neck curve.
19–22 $^{1}/_{5}$ scye depth plus 0.5cm; square out.
20–23 The measurement 8–16. Draw the line from 20 to touch the line from 22.
21–24 $^{1}/_{2}$ measurement 4–21 plus 1cm; square across.

4 –25 The measurement 1–13:
sizes 122–152cm height   minus 1cm
158–170cm height   minus 1.5cm;
square up to 26.
25–27 $^{1}/_{2}$ measurement 13–25 plus 0.5cm; square down to 28 and 29. Draw armhole curve 16, 18, 27, 26, 23.
29–30 $^{1}/_{4}$ measurement 28–29.
29–31 $^{1}/_{3}$ measurement 5–29.
29–32 $^{1}/_{3}$ measurement 3–29;
join 30–31 and 30–32 with a curve.
Curve both side seams inwards 0.75cm at 28.
21–33 1.5cm buttonstand; square down.
33–34 3.5cm facing; square down. Shape neckline.
12–35 2cm (back pleat); square down.
Sleeve
Square down from 0.
0 – 1 $^{1}/_{4}$ armscye measurement (see 'measuring a curve' on page 99); square across.
0 – 2 Sleeve length minus cuff depth plus 2cm ease; square down.
1 – 3 $^{1}/_{2}$ measurement 1–2; square across.
0 – 4 $^{1}/_{2}$ armscye measurement; square down to 5.
0 – 6 $^{1}/_{2}$ armscye measurement; square down to 7.
Divide 0–4 into four sections, mark points 8, 9, 10.
Divide 0–6 into four sections, mark points 11, 12, 13.
8 – 0 Raise the curve:
sizes 122–152cm height   0.75cm at 9; 1.25 at 10
158–170cm height   1cm   at 9; 1.75cm at 10.
Raise the curve at 11:
sizes 122–152cm height   0.75cm
158–170cm height   1cm.
Hollow the curve at 13:
sizes 122–152cm height   0.75cm
158–170cm height   1cm.
5 –14 $^{1}/_{4}$ measurement 2–5 minus 0.5cm; join 4–14.
7 –15 $^{1}/_{4}$ measurement 2–7 minus 0.5cm; join 6–15.
Mark points 16 and 17 on the line from 3.
14–18 1cm; join 16–18 with a curve.
15–19 1cm; join 17–19 with a curve.
20 is mid-way 2–18; square up to 21.
21–22 $^{1}/_{3}$ measurement 20–21.
20–23 0.5cm; join 18–2 with a curve.
Cuff
Cuff length – cuff size plus 2cm.
Cuff depth – approx. size 5.5cm–8cm (ref. 1, page 118).
Collar
Construct a shirt collar, one-piece or collar with band (ref. 3, page 122).
Depth of classic shirt collar and stand:
sizes 122–152cm height   7cm
158–170cm height   8cm.

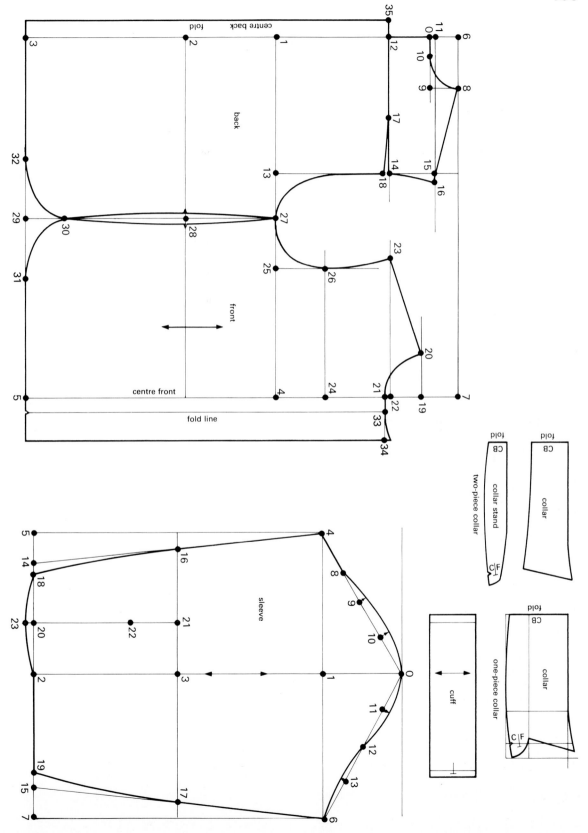

Shaping the Bodice Block

For some designs the bodice may require some shape. Waist shaping without darts is used for sizes up to 116cm height. Designs have only side seam shaping or no waist shaping where elasticated waists or belts provide a waist fit for a wide range of children. The standard ease allowance on a shaped waistline is approx. 6cm.

Skirts on waisted dresses are usually gathered, tucked or pleated; the controlling measurement for this type of skirt is the waist measurement of the completed bodice pattern.

BODICE SHAPING WITHOUT DARTS

Always used for sizes up to 116cm height.
Mark points 1, 20, 22 on bodice block.
1–A and 22–B $\frac{1}{4}$ waist plus 1.5cm.
Draw in curved side seams 20–A and 20–B.
Adjust the line of the waistline at A and B to ensure that the lines 20–A and 20–B are the same length.

BODICE SHAPING WITH DARTS

Mark points 1, 5, 6, 10, 18, 20, 22 on bodice block.
5–A $\frac{1}{2}$ measurement 5–10; square down to B.
6–C $\frac{1}{2}$ measurement 6–18; square down to D.
A–E and C–F 2cm.
1–G $\frac{1}{4}$ waist:
        122–134cm height   plus 2.25cm
        140–152cm height   plus 2.75cm.
22–H $\frac{1}{4}$ waist:
        122–134cm height   plus 2.75cm
        140–152cm height   plus 3.75cm.
Draw in curved side seams 20–G and 20–H.
Construct back and front darts on lines E–B and F–D:
        122–134cm height both darts 1cm
        140–152cm height back dart 1.5cm
                        front dart 2cm.
Adjust the line at waistline to ensure that the lines 20–G and 20–H and the dart lines are the same length.

Shaping the classic bodice blocks

Bodice shaping without darts

Bodice shaping with darts

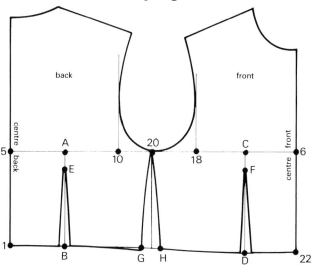

Part Two: Classic 'Form' Pattern Cutting Boys and Girls

10   CLASSIC SLEEVE CUTTING

SPECIAL NOTE

The classic body blocks produce a very basic fit for the garment at the body and at the armhole. If slightly more ease is required in the body and armhole shape, the adaptation for a lowered armhole (page 108) must be completed before proceeding with the styling. For more easy-fitting styles use the 'flat' blocks in the section Simple 'Flat' Pattern Cutting. The kimono block (pages 40 and 42) can be used to construct very adaptable armhole shapes, including 'flat' raglan and dolman sleeves.

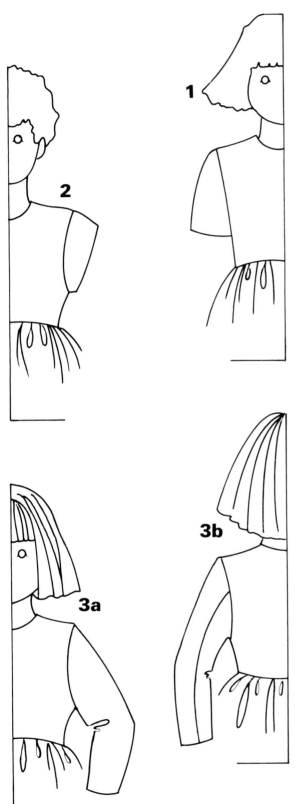

LOWERED ARMHOLES

For easier fitting armhole shapes use the 'flat' block adaptations (pages 40 and 42); however, if the armhole needs to be lowered a small amount when using the Classic Blocks, the following adaptation can be made. This is done before starting further adaptations. Note that when an armhole is lowered, extra ease in the body is also required.

Body section Trace body section of block required; cut up side seam, open 2.4cm. Mark points A and B. Draw new side seam down the centre. Mark point C. C–D is $^2/_3$ of the measurement A–B (1.6cm). Square out both ways to construct new scye depth line.
Extend shoulder lines at E and F $^1/_2$ meas. A–C (0.6cm). Draw in new armhole shape as shown.
Mark G and H at new front and back pitch points.
Sleeve Trace one-piece sleeve block; draw a parallel line below armhole depth $^1/_2$ measurement C–D.
Mark I and J at front and back pitch points, K at the top.
Draw the curve I–L to the new armhole depth line. The curve should equal the curve G–D on the back body block. Draw the curve J–M to equal H–D on front body block.
Draw in underarm seams, narrow at wrist if required.
K–N is the measurement the shoulder is extended.
Draw in the new top curve of the sleeve I, N, J as shown.
Note The amount the armhole is lowered can vary but the proportions to other measurements should remain the same.

1 SHORT SLEEVE

Trace round one-piece sleeve block to short sleeve length required. Shape in 1.5cm at the bottom of each side seam.
Sleeve facings Add 3cm to lower edge for facing. Fold along this line, wheel off the shape of the side seam line to complete the facing.

2 CAP SLEEVE

Square down from 0.
0–1 $^1/_4$ scye depth plus 0.5cm; square across.
1–2   3cm–4cm; square across.
0–3 and 0–5 $^1/_2$ armscye measurement plus 0.5cm; square down to 4 and 6.
7 and 8 are midway between 0–3 and 0–5.
0–7 and 0–8 raise the curve 0.75cm
3–7 and 8–5 hollow the curve 0.5cm.
4–9 and 6–10 1.5cm; join 3–9 and 5–10.
2–11   1.5cm; draw curve 9, 11, 10.

3a SEMI-SHAPED SLEEVE WITH DART

Cut from back elbow line to point A and from point A to wrist line. Pivot this section forward 2.5cm. Halve the length of the dart made at back elbow.

3b SEMI-SHAPED SLEEVE WITH SEAM

Complete adaptation for 3a. Mark A and B on wristline, D at back pitch point, E at dart point.
A–C $^1/_4$ measurement A–B. Join D–E and E–C, cut along line.
Close dart in back sleeve.
Curve both underarm seams as shown. Curve back and front sleeves outwards 0.5cm from D–E.

Lowered armhole

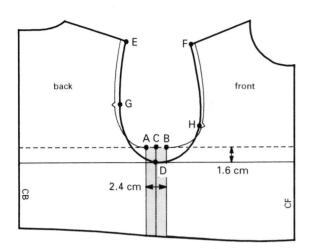

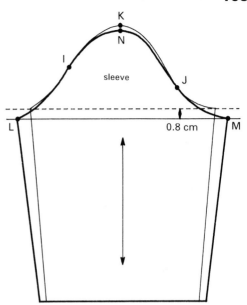

1 Short sleeve

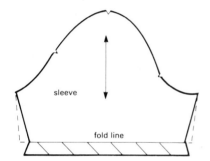

2 Cap sleeve

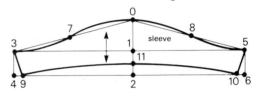

3 Semi-shaped sleeves

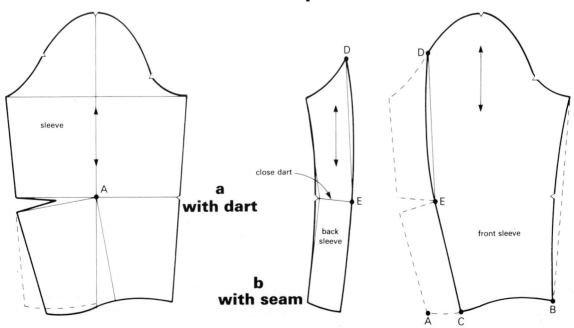

a with dart

close dart

b with seam

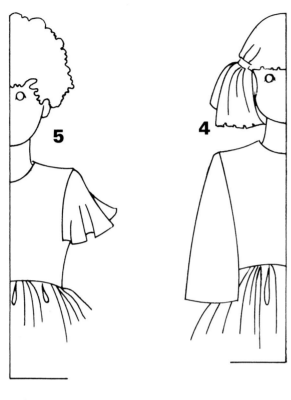

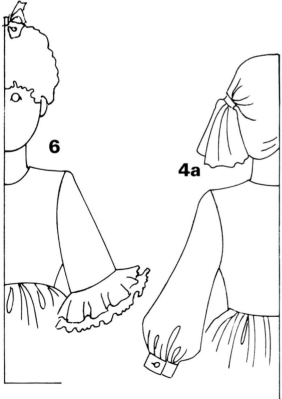

4 FLARED SLEEVES

Trace round one-piece sleeve block with straight hem to length required. Square down from front and back pitch points. Divide centre section into six.
Cut up lines, open approx. 1cm–2cm at the hem.
Grain line is in centre of the middle opening.
Trace round pattern.

4a FLARED SLEEVE WITH CUFFS

Flared sleeves of many different lengths can be gathered onto cuffs.
Trace off one-piece sleeve block with shaped hem.
Shorten sleeve the measurement of cuff depth.
Complete flare adaptation.
Draft relevant cuff (ref. 1a, page 118).

5 SLEEVE WITH EXTRA FLARE

Extra flare can be inserted between the sections.
Short sleeves Shape hem 1cm up at outer edges as shown.

6 SLEEVE WITH FLARED SECTIONS

Trace round flared sleeve to length required, mark points A and B.
Draw in section line; mark C and D. Draw in frill line; mark E and F.
Divide lower sleeve into eight sections.
Lower sleeve Cut away lower sleeve. Cut up lines, open for the required amount of flare (design shows 2cm).
Frill Measure the section line C–D.
Construct a circle; the circumference is the measurement C–D (see 'constructing a circle', page 10).
G–H The measurement C–E.
Draw an outer circle from H.

4 Flared sleeves

6 Sleeve with flared sections

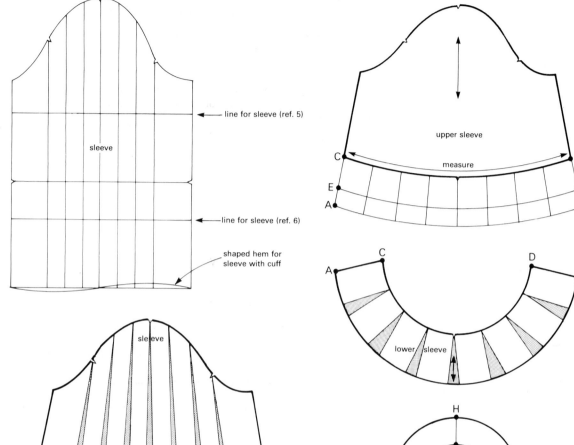

line for sleeve (ref. 5)

sleeve

line for sleeve (ref. 6)

shaped hem for
sleeve with cuff

upper sleeve

C measure D

E F
A B

A C D B

lower sleeve

H
G

frill

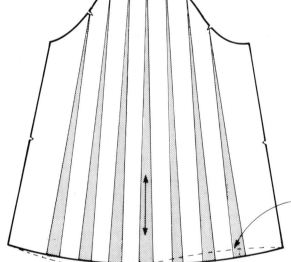

sleeve

shaped hem for
sleeve with cuff

5 Sleeve with
extra flare

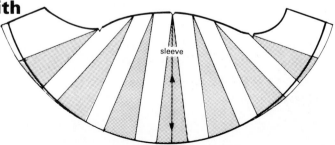

sleeve

Note It is useful to number sections that are to be detached from the main pattern. This means that they can be placed in the correct order (e.g. ref. 7, gathered sleeve).

7 GATHERED (PUFF) SLEEVE
Trace round short sleeve. Square down from back and front pitch points. Divide centre section into six. Open sections the amount required (examples shows 2.5cm). Add approx. 2cm extra depth to sleeve head and hem as shown.
Trace round pattern.

8 GATHERED SLEEVE HEAD
Trace round short sleeve. Square across from back pitch point. Divide sleeve head into six sections.
Mark balance points for gathers at points A and B.
Cut up the sections and open out the amount required (example shows 2cm).
Trace round pattern.

9 GATHERED AND FLARED SLEEVE
Trace round one-piece sleeve with straight side seams to the required length.
Square down from back and front pitch points.
Divide centre section into six. Open sections 1.5cm at sleeve head 3cm at hem (extra may be inserted).
Trace round pattern.
This sleeve can also be gathered onto a cuff.

Note It is necessary to make sure that when the pattern sections are opened at the sleeve head each section is laid on a line squared out from the line of previous section (e.g. line A–B).

10 GATHERED OR FLARED AND GATHERED SECTIONS (FRILLS)
Trace round one-piece sleeve block with shaping.
Draw in section line. Mark points A, B and C.
Square down from A, B and C.
A–D Depth of frill; square across to E and F.
Trace off top sleeve section.
10a Gathered section Measure the lengths A–C and C–B.
Construct the section, G–H and H–J are twice the measurements A–C and C–B; square down.
G–K The measurement A–D; square across to L.
10b Flared and gathered section Construct a half circle, the circumference of the whole circle is four times the measurement A–B (see 'constructing a circle', page 10). Mark points G and H.
G–J Twice measurement A–C.
G–K and H–L are the measurement A–D.
Complete outer sleeve line.

7 Gathered (puff) sleeve

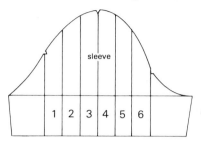

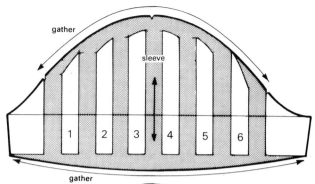

8 Gathered sleeve head

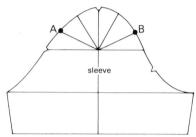

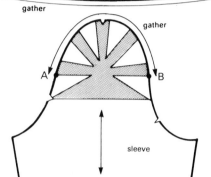

9 Gathered and flared sleeve

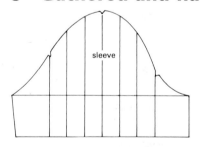

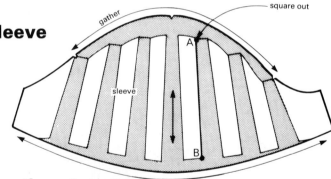

a gathered section

10 Gathered or flared and gathered sections

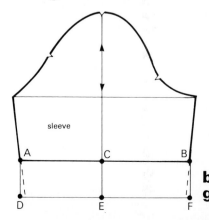

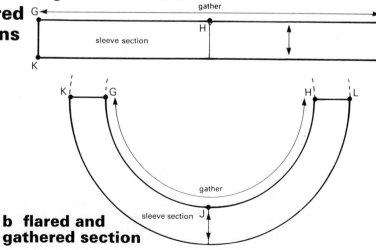

b flared and gathered section

11 EXTENDED SLEEVE WITH YOKE

Body section   Trace body section of block required.
Mark points A and B at pitch points on body block.
Draw in yoke lines; mark points C and D at armhole
edge. Trace off yoke sections.

Sleeve   Trace one-piece sleeve, cut up centre line.
Mark points E and F at pitch points on sleeve block.

E–G   The measurement A–C on back body section.

F–H   The measurement B–D on front body section.

Back yoke   Place sleeve to yoke matching point C to G.

Front yoke   Place sleeve to yoke with point H opposite
D and sleeve head touching shoulder point.

The top of the sleeve head will rise above the shoulder
on both yokes, raise shoulder line at armhole edge to
make a smooth continuous line at sleeve head.

Front bodice   D–J the measurement D–H on yoke,
draw new armhole shape.

Note   For deep yokes use 'flat' kimono block (pages 40
and 42) as placing deep yokes to a sleeve head creates
problems.

12 DROPPED SHOULDER

Body section   Trace body section of block required.
Mark points A and B at pitch points on body block.
Extend shoulder to shape required.
Mark points C and D at base of extended shoulder.

Sleeve   Trace one-piece sleeve block. Mark points E
and F at pitch points on sleeve block, G at sleeve head.

E–H   The measurement A–C on back body section.

F–J   The measurement B–D on front body section.

G–K   The measurement the shoulder has been
extended.

Draw new sleeve head H, K, J.

12a WITH FLARED SLEEVE

The new sleeve shape can be flared (ref. 4, page 110) or
gathered (ref. 7, page 112) or gathered and flared (ref. 9,
page 112) to create different styles.

13 TULIP SLEEVE

Sleeve   Trace one-piece sleeve block.
Shorten sleeve the required amount.
Mark points A, B, C at pitch points.
Drop perpendicular lines from points A, B, C.
Divide back section A–B into three further sections.
Divide front section A–C into three further sections.
Mark adjacent points D and E for position of the 'tulip'
lines.
Mark points F and G at underarm points.
Draw in curved 'tulip' lines from points H and I at the
hem of the sleeve to points D and E.
Cut out sleeve along the lines as shown.
Cut up vertical lines and open the required amount.
Trace off back section F, B, D, A, E, H.
Trace off front section G, C, E, A, D, I.
For a sleeve without an underarm seam: draw a vertical
line, place the underarm seams to touch the line.

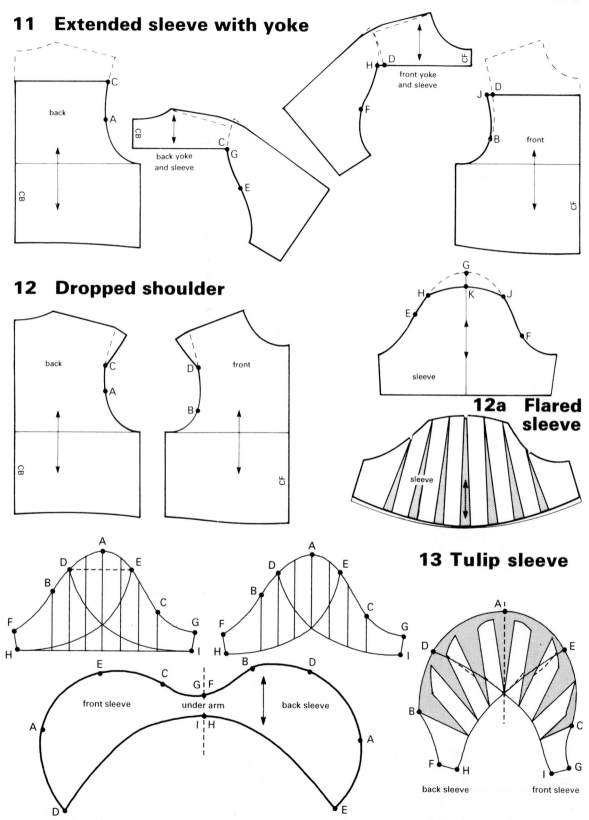

11 Extended sleeve with yoke

back

CB

back yoke and sleeve

CB

C

A

C

G

E

front yoke and sleeve

H D CF

F

J D

B

front

CF

G

H K J

E F

sleeve

12a Flared sleeve

sleeve

12 Dropped shoulder

back

CB

C

A

D

B

front

CF

A

D E

B

C

F G

H I

E C

front sleeve

G F

under arm

B D

back sleeve

A

I H

A

D

E

13 Tulip sleeve

A

D E

B

C

F H

I G

back sleeve

front sleeve

14   RAGLAN SLEEVE
Body section   Trace body section of block required.
Add to back shoulder line:

      80–116cm height   0.3cm
      122–152cm height   0.6cm
      158–170cm height   0.9cm.

Remove the above amount from front shoulder line.
Mark A and B at new shoulder points.
A–C and B–D   80–116cm height   2.25cm
              122–152cm height   2.5cm
              158–170cm height   2.75cm.

Mark E and F at pitch points on body block. E–G 1cm.
Mark H on front armhole directly opposite point G.
Draw curved lines from C–G and D–H; draw dart on
back shoulder, size is amount of shoulder ease
(overgarments only).
Cut off shaded sections. Close back shoulder dart.
Sleeve   Trace one-piece sleeve block; draw centre line
of sleeve. Mark J at sleeve head; J–K is the amount
added to the back shoulder; square down from K.
Mark L and M at pitch points.
L–N   The measurement E–G on back body block.
M–P   The measurement F–H on front body block.
Cut up line from K.
Place back body section to back sleeve; place G to touch
N, place shoulder point to touch sleeve head.
Place front body section to front sleeve; place H to
touch P, place shoulder point to touch sleeve head.
Add 0.5cm to the centre line of each sleeve.
Mark point Q 5cm down from the top of the sleeve
head.
Draw shoulder lines to Q with curved lines as shown.

15   FLARED RAGLAN SLEEVE
Mark points A and B at the centre of the neckline on the
back and front sleeve. Draw curved lines to the hem
line. Cut up the lines. Place back and front sleeve
together; open approx. 4cm at the hem line.
Open the curved lines approx. 4cm at the hem line.
Shorten neck dart 3cm. Shape up hem 1cm at outer
edge.

Note   The sleeve can be gathered onto a cuff.

16   EASY-FITTING RAGLAN SLEEVE
Complete adaptation for lowered armhole (page 108).
Body section   Adapt shoulders as for raglan sleeve.
Mark points A, B, C, D.
Mark E at back pitch point, F at front pitch point.
Mark G on back armhole directly opposite point F.
Draw curved lines from C–G and D–F; draw in dart on
back shoulder, size is amount of shoulder ease.
Cut off shaded sections. Close back shoulder dart.
Sleeve   Adapt centre line of sleeve as raglan sleeve.
Mark H at sleeve head, J and K at sleeve pitch points.
J–L   The measurement E–G on body block.
Complete the adaptation for the classic raglan placing G
to L on back sleeve and F to K on front sleeve.

14 Raglan sleeve

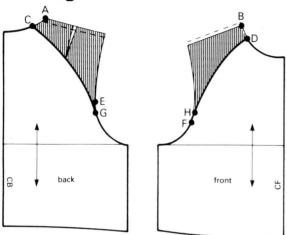
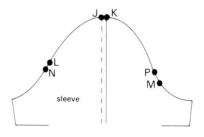
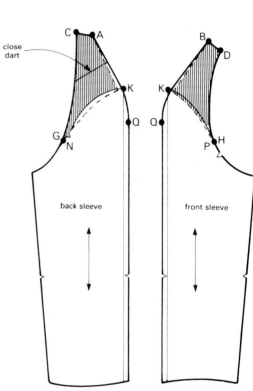

15 Flared raglan sleeve

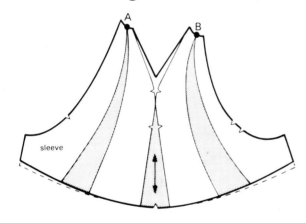

16 Easy-fitting raglan sleeve

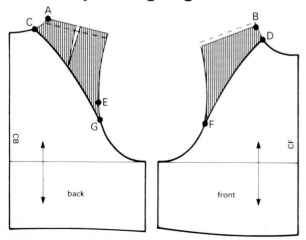
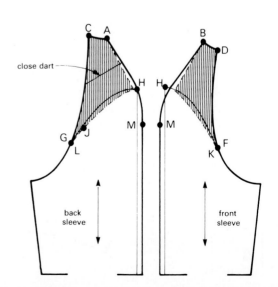

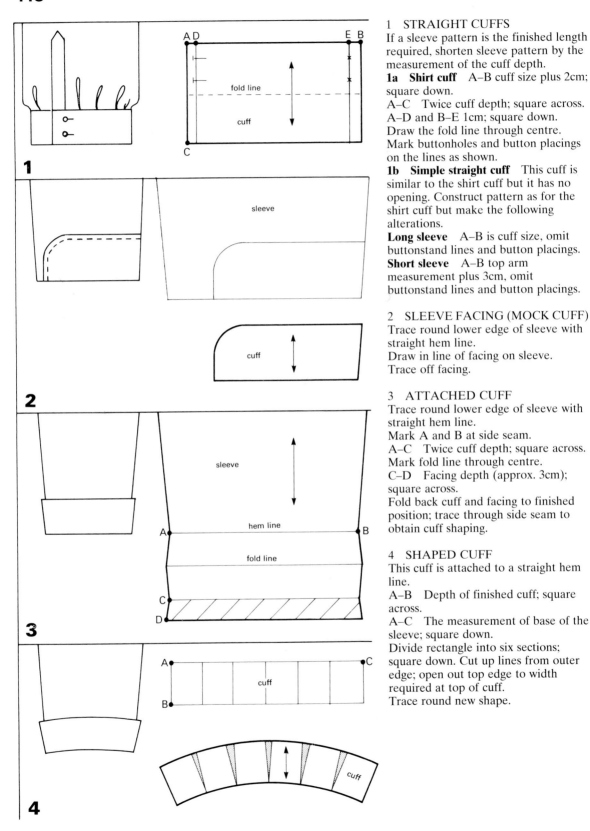

1 STRAIGHT CUFFS

If a sleeve pattern is the finished length required, shorten sleeve pattern by the measurement of the cuff depth.

1a Shirt cuff A–B cuff size plus 2cm; square down.
A–C Twice cuff depth; square across.
A–D and B–E 1cm; square down.
Draw the fold line through centre.
Mark buttonholes and button placings on the lines as shown.

1b Simple straight cuff This cuff is similar to the shirt cuff but it has no opening. Construct pattern as for the shirt cuff but make the following alterations.

Long sleeve A–B is cuff size, omit buttonstand lines and button placings.

Short sleeve A–B top arm measurement plus 3cm, omit buttonstand lines and button placings.

2 SLEEVE FACING (MOCK CUFF)

Trace round lower edge of sleeve with straight hem line.
Draw in line of facing on sleeve.
Trace off facing.

3 ATTACHED CUFF

Trace round lower edge of sleeve with straight hem line.
Mark A and B at side seam.
A–C Twice cuff depth; square across.
Mark fold line through centre.
C–D Facing depth (approx. 3cm); square across.
Fold back cuff and facing to finished position; trace through side seam to obtain cuff shaping.

4 SHAPED CUFF

This cuff is attached to a straight hem line.
A–B Depth of finished cuff; square across.
A–C The measurement of base of the sleeve; square down.
Divide rectangle into six sections; square down. Cut up lines from outer edge; open out top edge to width required at top of cuff.
Trace round new shape.

Part Two: Classic 'Form' Pattern Cutting Boys and Girls

11   OPENINGS – COLLARS – HOODS

FRONT OPENINGS

When drafting designs with front openings it is necessary to be aware that the centre front is a stable position and cannot be moved. Any movement will alter the fit of the garment; therefore, care must be taken when adding straps and facings. It is the convention that the front of girls' garments overlap towards the left, while boys' garments overlap towards the right. Garments designed for both sexes often have centre openings.

If the neckline requires widening or lowering, this must be done before working the instructions for front openings. Note that garments in the smaller sizes are often designed to have lowered and widened necklines as they offer easier dressing for toddlers.

1a STANDARD FRONT
Mark buttonholes on centre front line (buttonholes overlap the line by 0.2cm). Add buttonstand approx. 2cm (varies with sizes of button).
Draw in back and front facings, trace round neck edges, front edge of pattern and facing lines to construct facings.

1b EXTENDED FACING
Mark buttonholes; add buttonstand.
Fold front edge line, trace through facing line and neckline to construct an extended facing.

2 DOUBLE BREASTED FRONT
Draw two button lines at equal distances each side of centre front. Mark buttonholes, button placings; add buttonstand. Construct facing as for standard front.

3 STANDARD ZIP FRONT (ZIP EXPOSED)
Measure width of zip to be exposed. Mark in from centre front half this distance and mark this zip line, front edge line. Rub out centre front line.
Construct facing as for standard front.

3a STRAP FOR ZIP FRONT
Mark strap line on front section. Mark A at top of strap line, B at centre front.
Construct strap twice the measurement A–B. Mark fold line at outer edge. Mark centre front.

CONCEALED ZIP
Construct front and facing as for standard zip front but work to centre front line. Add 2cm seam allowance to centre front line of front and facing.
Place zip between front and facing and top-stitch.

4 SIMPLE FLY FRONT
Fly front Add button stand to centre front, mark stitch line. Add extension to front edge 2cm below top edge to 5cm below stitch line. The extension must be 1.5cm wider than width of stitch line.
Trace off facing with the same extension. Mark vertical buttonholes on centre front line of facing.
Buttoned front Construct as a standard front.

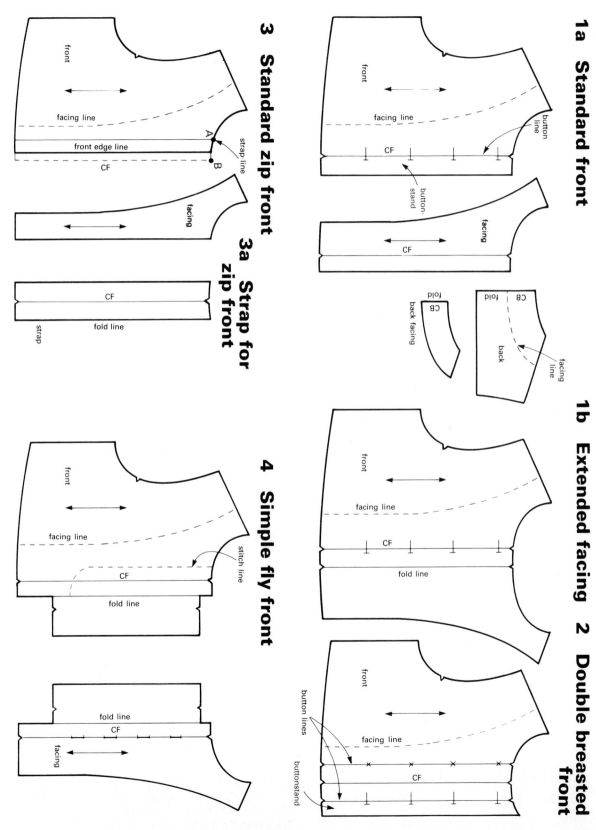

1a Standard front

front

facing line

button line

CF

button-stand

facing

CF

1b Extended facing

fold

CB

back facing

fold   fold

CB

back

facing line

front

facing line

CF

fold line

facing

2 Double breasted front

front

button lines

facing line

CF

buttonstand

3 Standard zip front

front

facing line

front edge line

A

strap line

B

CF

facing

3a Strap for zip front

CF

fold line

strap

4 Simple fly front

front

facing line

stitch line

CF

fold line

fold line

CF

facing

TERMS USED FOR COLLAR CONSTRUCTION
Neckline   Line where the collar is joined to the neck.
Style line   Outer edge of collar and rever.
Roll line   The line where the collar rolls over.
Stand   Rise of the collar from neckline to roll line.
Fall   Depth of the collar from roll line to style line.
Break point   Where the rever turns back.
Break line   Line along which the rever rolls back.

Note   The break line and the roll line are sometimes referred to as crease lines.

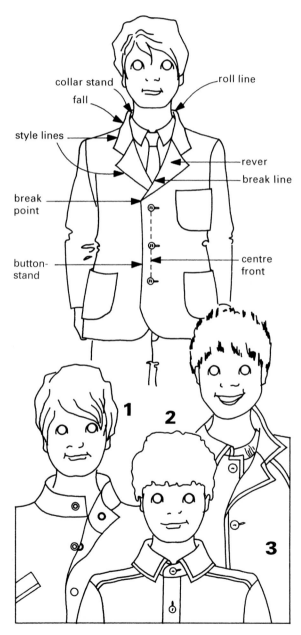

Before drafting a collar
Alter neckline if required, mark any button lines, buttonholes and buttonstands.
Collar shapes   ·
Although the style line determines the shape of the outer edge of the collar, the length of the outer edge determines where it sits on the body. If the outer edge of a collar is tightened it sits higher in the neck, increasing the stand. If it is widened it reduces the stand (see diagram).
Top collars
Add approx 0.25cm (depending on thickness of fabric) to outer edge of top collars from A–B. Some collar designs require 0.25cm on back neckline from C–D.

STANDING COLLARS
Measuring the neckline
If the neckline is to be lowered, complete this first. Place back shoulder to front shoulder, measure the neckline accurately from centre back to centre front with the tape measure upright (see diagram); this gives $\frac{1}{2}$ *neckline measurement*. This measurement is not $\frac{1}{2}$ the neck size body measurement as the neckline measurement is drafted to include the ease required for the garment.

1   STANDING STRAIGHT COLLAR
0–1 $\frac{1}{2}$ neckline measurement; 1–2 buttonstand; square up from 0 and 2.
0–3   Collar depth; square across to 4.
4–5   1.25cm; 5–6 equals 1–2; 0–7$\frac{1}{2}$ measurement 0–1.
2–8   1cm; join 5–8 and 6–1.
Join 7–8 with a curve. Mark any buttonholes.

2   CONVERTIBLE COLLAR
0–1 $\frac{1}{2}$ neckline measurement; square up from 0 and 1.
0–2 $\frac{3}{4}$ measurement 0–1 minus 1cm; square up.
0–3   Collar depth; square across to 4 and 5.
0–6   0.5cm; 1–7 0.8cm; shape neckline of collar from 6–7. Draw style line of collar from 4–7.

Note   If depth of collar exceeds 7cm, the outer edge from 3–4 is cut and spread to sit lower on shoulder.

3   SHIRT COLLAR
0–1 $\frac{1}{2}$ neckline measurement; square up from 0 and 1.
0–2   Collar and stand depth (approx. 6cm–8cm); square across.
0–3 $\frac{3}{4}$ measurement 0–1; square up to 4.
0–5 $\frac{1}{2}$ measurement 0–2 minus 1cm; square across to 6.
1–7   Buttonstand measurement; square up.
0–8   0.25cm; 7–9 0.75cm; join 8–3 and 3–9 with a curve.
6–10   0.5cm. Draw outline of collar as shown.

3a   SHIRT COLLAR WITH BAND
Trace round collar. Mark points 5, 9, 10.
5–11   0.5cm; 10–12 0.25cm. Join 11–12–9.
Trace round collar and stand as shown.

Collar shapes

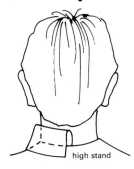

high stand

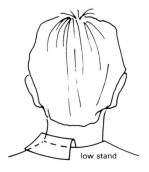

low stand

Measuring the neckline

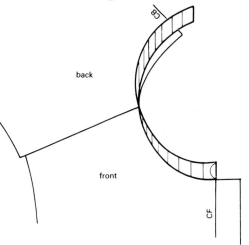

CB

back

front

CF

Top collars

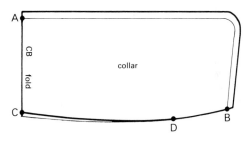

A

CB

fold

collar

C

D

B

1 Standing straight collar

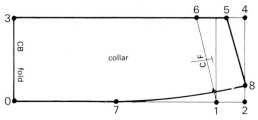

3

CB

fold

collar

6 5 4

C F

8

0

7 1 2

2 Convertible collar

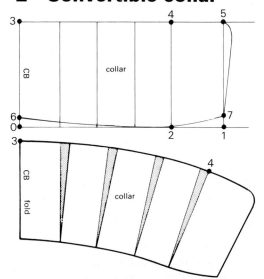

3

CB

collar

4 5

6

0

7

2 1

3

CB

fold

collar

4

3 Shirt collar

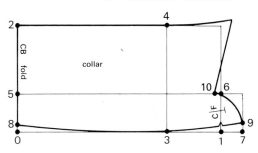

2

CB

fold

collar

4

5

8

10 6

C F

9

0

3 1 7

3a Shirt collar with band

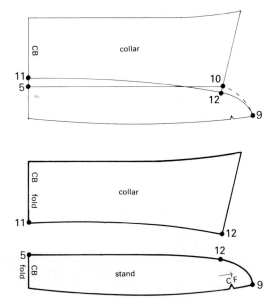

CB

collar

11

5

10

12

9

CB

fold

collar

11

12

5

fold

CB

stand

12

C F

9

4 BASIC FLAT COLLAR (PETER PAN)

Many shapes of flat collar can be drafted from this adaptation by changing the style line (example shows classic peter pan shape).
Dotted line shows two-piece collar for back opening.
Place shoulder of back bodice to shoulder of front bodice, neck points touching.

Overlap outer shoulders: 80–116cm height 1cm
                          122–152cm height 1.5cm
                          158–170cm height 2cm.
Draw in collar shape. Trace off collar.

5 ETON COLLAR

Construct a peter pan collar.
Divide the collar into six sections as shown.
Cut up the lines, overlap the outer edge 0.5cm.
Trace round new collar shape with a smooth line.

6 LOWERING THE NECKLINE

Draw in new neckline on front and back bodice.
Place shoulder of back bodice to shoulder of front bodice, neck points touching.
Overlap shoulders amount given for peter pan collar.
Draw in collar shape.
Trace collar; trace bodice sections with new neckline.

7 SAILOR COLLAR

Place shoulder of back bodice to shoulder of front bodice, neck points touching.
Overlap shoulders amount given for peter pan collar.
Draw in 'V' neckline. Draw in collar as shown.
The collar is 1cm wider than the shoulder line.
Trace off collar pattern. The collar can be cut in one piece or have a join at the shoulder.

8 FRILLED COLLAR

Measure the total neckline. Construct a circle, the circumference is twice the measurement of the neckline (see 'constructing a circle', page 10).
Mark point A at top of circle. A–B is depth of frill. Draw outer circle.
Mark points C and D 1.5cm each side of A; square up.
Mark balance points E and F. C–E and D–F are twice the measurement of back neckline.

Note For extra frilling construct a circle with a greater circumference.

9 SIMPLE ROLL COLLAR

Trace round front bodice. Mark buttonholes, add buttonstand. Mark point 1 at break point. Mark point 2 at neckline; square up from 2.
2–3 back neck measurement.
3–4   80–116cm height 2.5cm
      122–152cm height 3cm
      158–170cm height 3.5cm.
2–4 The measurement 2–3. Join 2–4 with a slight curve.
Square out from the line 2–4.
4–5 6cm–9cm approx.
5–6 1cm. Draw in style line of collar as shown.
Draw in facing line. Trace off facing.
Add 0.5cm (depending on the thickness of fabric) to rever edge from 6–1.

125

4 Basic flat collar (peter pan)

5 Eton collar

6 Lowering the neckline

7 Sailor collar

8 Frilled collar

9 Simple roll collar

10 STANDARD BLAZER COLLAR

Trace round front section of the blazer block; extend the shoulder line. Draw in facing line, break line, centre front. Extend the break line.

Mark point 1 at break point, 2 at neckline, square down from 2. Re-mark point 26 point 3.

3–4 Back neck measurement plus 0.5cm.

4–5 1.5cm; make 3–5 the same measurement as 3–4.

 80–116cm height 5–6 2cm; 5–7 3cm
122–152cm height 5–6 2.25cm; 5–7 3.25cm
158–170cm height 5–6 2.5cm; 5–7 3.5cm.

Draw a line from 6 parallel to the line 5–3 to touch the line squared down from 2. Mark point 8.

Mark point 9 where break line crosses neckline, draw a curve from 8–9.

Mark collar point 10 1cm from centre front line.

10–11 80–116cm height 2cm
122–152cm height 2.5cm
158–170cm height 3cm.

Draw style line of collar; curve outer edge inwards. Trace off facing and collar.

Note 1 Add 0.5cm (depending on thickness of the fabric) to rever from point 1–10. Draw in roll line on collar as shown.

Note 2 Under-collars of tailored garments are cut on the cross. The grain line of the rever is placed parallel to the rever edge.

11 STANDARD REVER COLLAR FOR BODICE, COAT AND OVERGARMENT BLOCKS

Trace round block required. Extend shoulder line.
Raise front neckline 1cm. Re-draw neck curve.
Mark buttonholes, buttonstand. Draw in facing line.
Square down from 2.

2–3 80–116cm height 1.5cm
122–152cm height 1.75cm
158–170cm height 2cm.

Draw in break line from 1–3; extend line.

3–4 Back neck measurement plus 0.5cm.

4–5 1.5cm; make 3–5 the same measurement as 3–4.

 80–116cm height 5–6 2.5cm 5–7 3.5cm
122–152cm height 5–6 2.75cm 5–7 3.75cm
158–170cm height 5–6 3cm 5–7 4cm.

Draw a line from 6 parallel to the line 5–3 to touch the line squared down from 2. Mark point 8.

Mark point 9 where break line crosses neckline, draw a curve from 8–9. Mark point 10 on centre front line.

Draw in style line of collar from 7–10. Draw in style line of rever from 10–1. Trace off facing and collar.

See Notes 1 and 2 of classic blazer collar to complete pattern.

Wider collar shape The fall of the collar can be increased but the style line of the collar will have to be cut and opened at A, B and C (the amount varies with the depth of the collar).

12 CHANGING THE STYLE LINE

(e.g. double breasted reefer collar)

Using the standard collar and rever draft, the style line of the collar and rever can be changed.

Trace round front section of the block required.

Mark buttonholes and buttonstand for double breasted front (ref. 2, page 120); mark break point.

Construct standard collar and rever, drawing in style lines for reefer collar and rever as shown.

Note For other designs, the neckline can be lowered or raised and the rever angle changed.

10 Standard blazer collar

11 Standard rever collar

12 Changing the style line

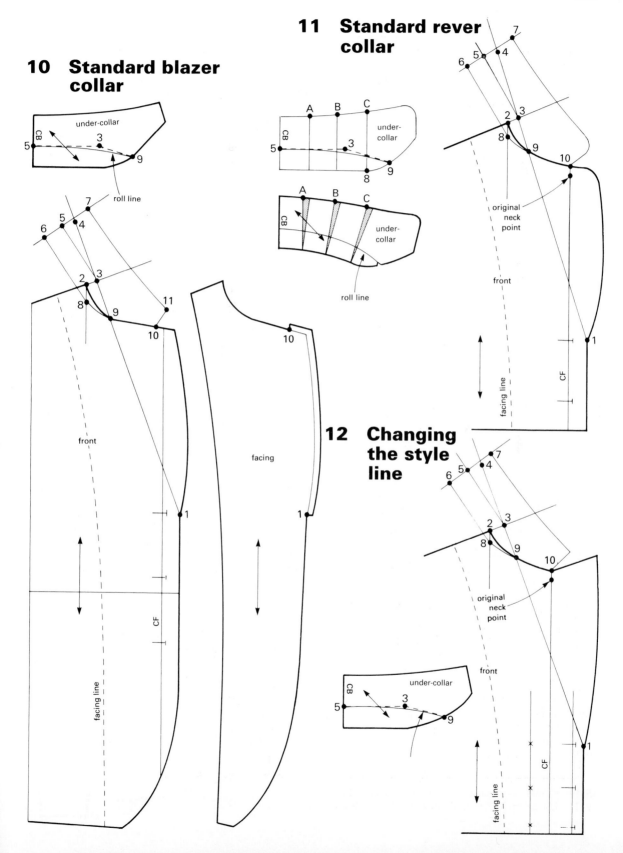

MEASUREMENTS REQUIRED FOR HOODS

Cervical to head crown   This measurement is calculated as height minus cervical height.

$1/2$ neckline measurement

Mark points A, B, C, D at neckline. B–E and C–F = 0.5cm. D–G = 1.5cm. Draw new neckline; measure A–E and F–G.

Both hoods can be attached directly to the garment or can be detachable, secured by zips or buttons.

This wider neckline measurement is required for *both* types of hood. The neckline of the body section of a garment with an attached hood will require the same adaptation.

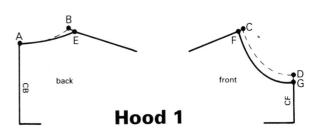

Hood 1

1   HOOD 1

Hood

Square both ways from 0.

0 – 1 $1/2$ neckline measurement minus 1cm; square up.

0 – 2   Cervical to head crown plus 4cm; square across. Mark point 3.

2 – 4 $1/3$ measurement 2–3 plus 2cm.

4 – 5 $1/3$ measurement 2–3 plus 0.5cm; square up.

5 – 6   The measurement 4–5; square across to 7.

0 – 8 $1/2$ measurement 0–1 minus 1cm.

0 – 9   0.75cm: join 9–8 and 9–4 with curves.

1 –10 $1/5$ measurement 0–1; square out.

Join 8–10 with a curve. 10–11 1cm.

3 –12 $1/3$ measurement 1–3; join 11–12 with a curve.

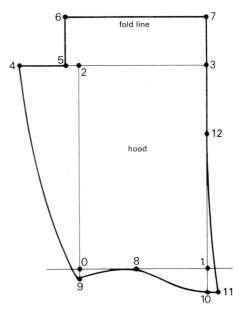

2   HOOD 2

Hood

0 – 1 $1/2$ neckline measurement plus 1.5cm; square up.

0 – 2 $1/5$ measurement 0–1; join 1–2.

2 – 3 $1/2$ measurement 1–2 plus 1cm.

Curve the line 1–3 0.5cm and 2–3 0.5cm.

1 – 4   Cervical to head crown:

    80–116cm height   plus 4cm

    122–152cm height   plus 4.5cm

    158–170cm height   plus 5cm;

    square across to 5.

5 – 6 $1/5$ measurement 4–5; square down to 7.

6 – 8 $1/2$ measurement 6–7.

6 – 9   1.5cm; square out. 9–10 1.5cm.

Square up from the line 1–2 to touch the line 0–1 at 11.

Draw in face curve 10, 8, 11.

Add the same buttonstand as garment from line 2–11.

4 –12 $1/3$ measurement 1–4   plus 2cm.

12–13 $1/5$ measurement 0–1   plus 0.5cm.

4 –14 $1/2$ measurement 4–6: Draw in head curve 1, 13, 14, 10.

Hood gusset

Square down and across from 15.

15–16   Length of outer line of hood from 1–10; square across.

16–17   80–116cm height   5cm

    122–152cm height   6cm

    158–170cm height   7cm; square up to 18.

15–19 $1/4$ measurement 15–16; square across to 20.

19–21   1.5cm; 20–22 1.5cm. Draw curved outer lines.

Hood 2

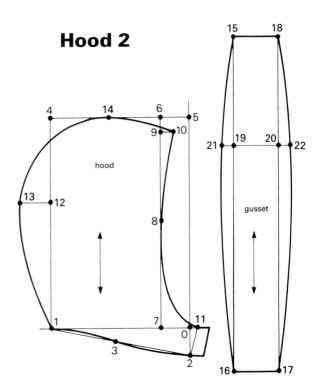

Part Two: Classic 'Form' Pattern Cutting Boys and Girls

12   CLASSIC BODY BLOCK ADAPTATIONS

SPECIAL NOTE

The classic body blocks produce a very basic fit for the garment at the body and at the armhole; they are used for classic garments closely related to the different body shapes of boys and girls. This is important for simple classic garments in woven fabrics where a bad 'body fit' or balance can be very apparent.

If slightly more ease is required in the body and armhole shape, the adaptation for a lowered armhole (page 108) must be completed before proceeding with the styling. For more easy-fitting or casual styles use the 'flat' blocks in the section Simple 'Flat' Pattern Cutting.

1

dress with two-piece sleeve

2

dress with short sleeve

CLASSIC DRESS SHAPES

These dress shapes are semi-fitting or are slightly flared.
A better shape is achieved if the classic blocks are used.
Variations of the sleeves or collars can be used with all the
dresses, which can also be adapted into pinafore dresses.

1 CLASSIC PRINCESS LINE DRESS

Trace off back and front body sections of the classic
bodice block. Mark the waistline.

Back   Draw in panel line on bodice to the waistline.
Mark point A.

A–B   Sizes 80–116cm height   0.5cm
              122–134cm height   1cm
              140–152cm height   2cm.

C is midway between A–B; square down to D on
hemline. D–E 1cm; D–F 1cm. These amounts of flare
can be varied. Join A–E and B–F.

Mark G at centre back waistline, H at the hemline.
G–I 0.5cm; H–J 1cm. Join I–J.

Trace off back and side back sections.

Front   Mark point K at the front waistline.

K–L is the measurement 3–23 on the classic bodice
blocks.

Join to side waist point at M for new front waistline.
Draw in panel line on bodice to the waistline.
Mark point N.

N–O   Sizes 80–116cm height   1cm
              122–134cm height   2cm
              140–152cm height   3cm.

P is midway between N–O; square down to Q from the
new waistline M–L.

Q–R 1cm; Q–S 1cm. These amounts of flare can be
varied.

Join O–R and N–S.

Draw in buttonholes, buttonstand; add extended facing
(ref. 1b, page 120).

Trace off front and side front sections.

Draw grain line on side front section parallel to the line
P–Q.

Collar   Construct a convertible collar (ref. 2, page 122).

Sleeve   Construct a short sleeve (ref. 1, page 108).

2 CLASSIC 'A' LINE DRESS

Back and front sections   Trace off back and front body
sections of the classic dress block.

Draw in lowered armhole and neckline as required.

Drop vertical lines from the centre of the new shoulder
lines and necklines.

Join the underarm point to the hem with a straight line.
Trace off back and front sections. Cut up the vertical
lines and open approx. 2cm on the back and front
sections.

Draw in facing lines.

Facings   Trace off back and front facings.

Note   The amount of flare can be varied; the classic
dress block is usually selected for dresses with slight flare
where the body shape balance needs to be retained.

The adaptation shows a pinafore style. If a dress with
sleeves is required, trace off the sections along the
original sleeve and side seam line. Construct the sleeve
required.

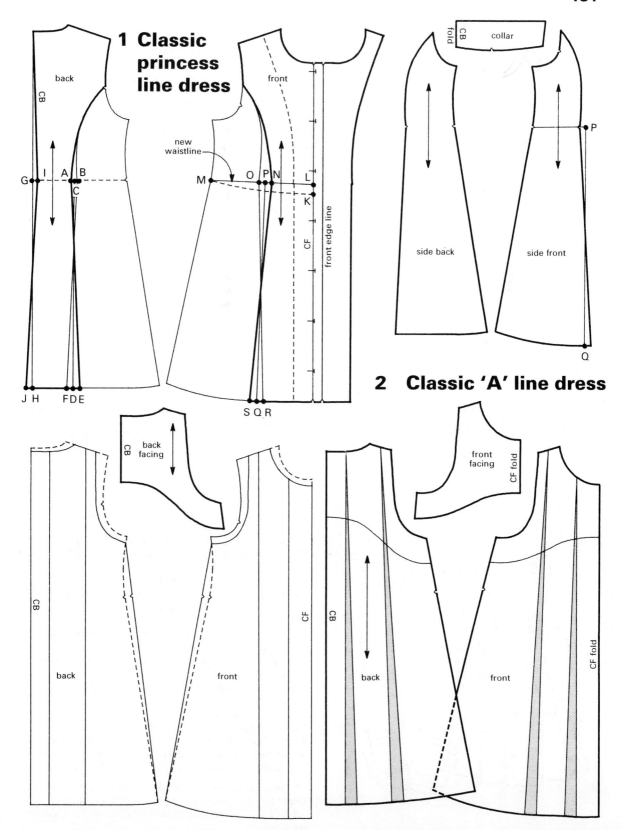

1 Classic princess line dress

back

CB

new waistline

G I A B
C

J H F D E

front

M O P N L
K

CF

front edge line

S Q R

collar

CB fold

side back

side front

P

Q

2 Classic 'A' line dress

back facing

CB

CB

back

CF

front

front facing

CF fold

CB

back

front

CF fold

3 LOW WAISTED DRESSES

Older children can wear simple low waisted dresses cut from the basic bodice blocks, or the 'flat' blocks; however, children up to 98cm height will gain a better fit if the bodice is cut from the classic dress block.

The adaptation shows a dress with a knife pleated skirt, but other types of pleats, gathers or tucks can be used.

Back and front bodice   Trace off bodice block and one-piece sleeve block. Mark points A and B on side seam. B–C $\frac{1}{2}$ waist to hip measurement. Draw new low waistline from C parallel to original waistline.
For waist shaping – draw a curved line from A–C, curve inward 0.5cm at a point mid-way between A and B. Mark D at centre front and centre back of new waistline.
Draw in facing line. Trace off facing.

Back and front skirts   Square both ways from E.
E–F is three times the measurement D–C on back bodice block; square down.
E–G   Skirt length minus the measurement B–C on bodice block; square across.
Construct front skirt as back skirt.

Collar   Construct a flat collar (ref. 4, page 124).

Sleeve   Construct semi-shaped sleeve (ref. 3b, page 108).

Neck tie   Construct rectangle, length approx. 50cm, width approx. 8cm. Draw fold line down centre.

Note   On pleated skirt the two rectangles are seamed and divided by number of pleats required (e.g. 20). The pleat fold is the same width as pleat.

4 PANELLED DRESS

Trace off dress block and one-piece sleeve block.

Back and front   Mark points A and B at shoulder line, C and D at waistline.
A–E $\frac{1}{2}$ measurement A–B; C–F $\frac{1}{3}$ measurement C–D;   square down to G.
Draw in panel lines E, F, G.
Extend shoulder lines for dropped shoulder (ref. 12, page 114).
Cut up panel lines, add 2.5cm flare at G at hem of side panels; add 1.5cm flare at G at hem of back and front.
On back section mark buttonholes, buttonstand; add extended facing.
Add 1cm flare to hem line at H on side seam of side back and side front. Join H to underarm point.

Collar   Construct a two-piece flat collar (ref. 4, page 124).

Sleeve   Complete instructions for a dropped shoulder. Remove cuff depth from bottom of sleeve.
Mark points J and K at hemline.
J–L $\frac{1}{4}$ measurement J–K; square up approx. 6cm.

Cuff   Construct shirt cuff (ref. 1, page 118).

Waist tie   Construct rectangle, length approx. 50cm, width approx. 5cm. Draw fold line down centre.

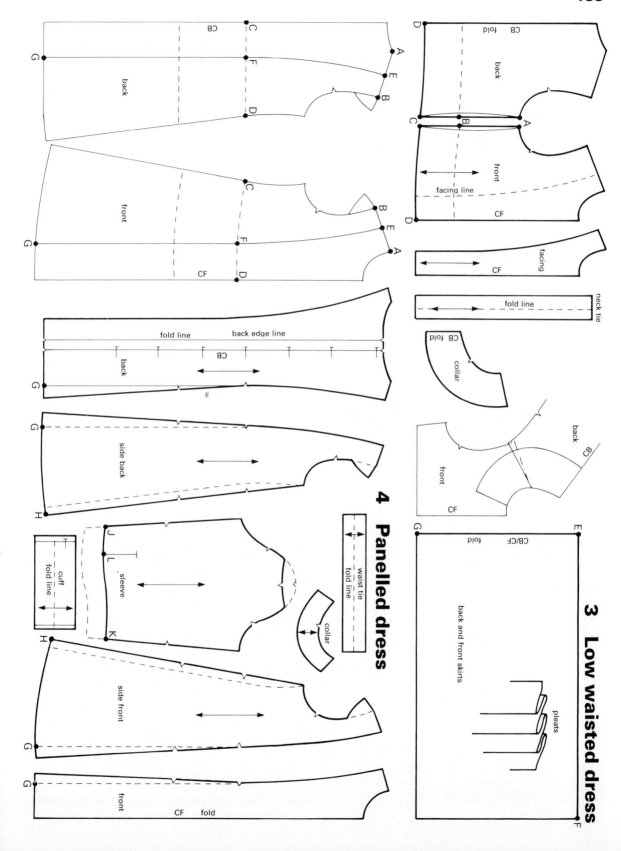

dress with high waistline

5a

CLASSIC WAISTED DRESSES

Young children usually have rounded stomachs and, therefore, many dresses for younger age groups are cut with a high waistline. Approx. 3–5cm is taken off the bodice and added to the skirt.

Note Many styles for younger children accommodate the rounded stomach by cutting dresses with yokes or smocked bodices (see page 54 in Part One 'flat' cutting).

5a CLASSIC WAISTED DRESS 1

Back and front Trace off back and front body sections of the classic bodice block and one-piece sleeve block.
Back bodice Mark A and B at the waistline.
Front bodice Mark C and D on shoulder line, mark E and F on waistline. C–G is $\frac{1}{3}$ measurement C–D. E–H $\frac{1}{2}$ measurement E–F plus 1cm. Draw in panel line. Mark buttonholes, add buttonstand and extended facing (ref. 1b, page 120). Trace of front and side front.
Back and front skirts Square both ways from I.
I–J is the measurement A–B and E–F; square down.
J–K = 1cm; draw in waistline curve.
I–L is skirt length required; square across to M.
M–N = 4cm; join K–M.
Collar Construct an Eton collar (ref. 5, page 124).
Sleeve Design shows a short sleeve (ref. 1, page 108).
Waist tie Construct tie length approx. 50cm, width 5cm.
Mark fold line down the centre.

5b CLASSIC WAISTED DRESS 2

This adaptation is constructed for a dress with an underskirt and a lined bodice.
Back and front (fabric and lining) Trace off back and front body sections of the classic bodice block and one-piece sleeve block. Construct waist shaping (ref. page 106).
Sizes from 122cm height will have a waist dart.
Cut 2cm off the bodice to create a slightly higher waistline.
Mark point A, B, C, D on bodice waistline.
On the back bodice mark buttonholes, add buttonstand and extended facing (ref. 1b, page 120).
Skirt Construct a very gathered skirt to the length required plus the amount taken off the waistline. The width E–F is at least 3 × A–B + C–D on the bodice waistline.
Underskirt Cut a rectangle, the length approx. 9cm less than the fabric skirt, the width is 2 × A–B + C–D on the bodice waistline.
Underskirt yoke Cut a rectangle, length approx. 7cm, the width is A–B + C–D on bodice waistline plus 2cm.
Collar Construct a two-piece flat collar with petal edge (ref. 4, page 124).
Sleeve Construct gathered puff sleeve (ref. 7, page 112).
Cummerbund Height = 2 × the side seam height; length = A–B + C–D minus 2cm; place to fold at CF. Construct a placket 4cm × 4cm.
Bow Construct a bow twice length and width required. Construct tie and knot to length required.

5b

5a Classic waisted dress 1

5b Classic waisted dress 2

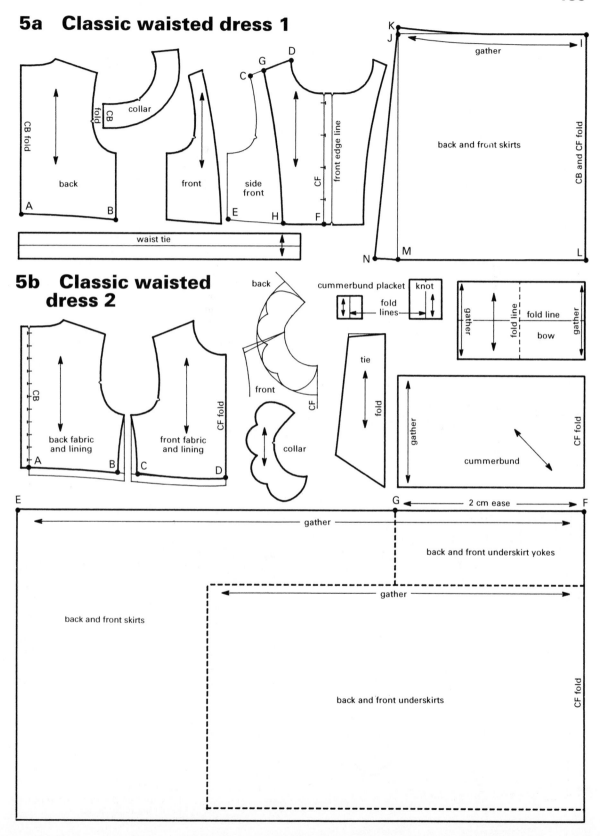

1 CLASSIC BLAZER
Trace off blazer block.
Back Trace off back section.
Front, collar and facing Trace off front section. Construct collar and facing (ref. 10, page 126).
Sleeves Construct a two-piece sleeve for blazer block (page 100).
Pockets Trace off pockets. Add 3cm facing to top of each pocket.

2 CLASSIC FORMAL COAT
Trace off formal coat block.
Back Mark point A at neckline, B at waistline, C at sleeve pitch point, D at underarm point.
B–E 1cm; square down. A–F $\frac{1}{3}$ measurement A–B. Join E–F.
Square down from C to G on waistline, H on hemline. Join D to hemline with straight line. Mark point J.
G–K 2cm. H–L 2cm. Draw in back seam line C, K, L. Curve line from C–K.
Trace off back section.
Front Mark M and N at shoulder points, P at front waistline. Q at front pitch point. R at underarm point. Join R to hemline with a straight line. Mark point S.
Q–T $\frac{1}{2}$ measurement Q–R. S–U the measurement H–J minus 2cm. U–V 2cm.
Join T–V. Mark W on waistline. Curve line from T–W 0.5cm.
W–X $\frac{1}{2}$ measurement W–P plus 1cm. Square down 2cm to Y.
W–Z 5cm. Draw in panel line from shoulder through Y and across to Z.
Draw in welt pocket, depth 2cm.
Mark buttonholes, buttonstand, facing line.
Trace off front section.
Trace off side front; add 3cm pocket facing from Y–Z.
Side section Draw a vertical line. Trace off back and front panels, place to line, square down from C and T to waistline. Join new waist points to hemline.
Facing Trace off facing.
Collar Construct Eton collar (ref. 5, page 124).
Sleeve Construct two-piece sleeve for the formal coat block (page 100).
Pocket Trace off pocket welt and pocket bag.
Belt Construct rectangle, length measurement E–K on back, width 7cm. Draw fold line down centre.

1 Classic blazer

2 Classic formal coat

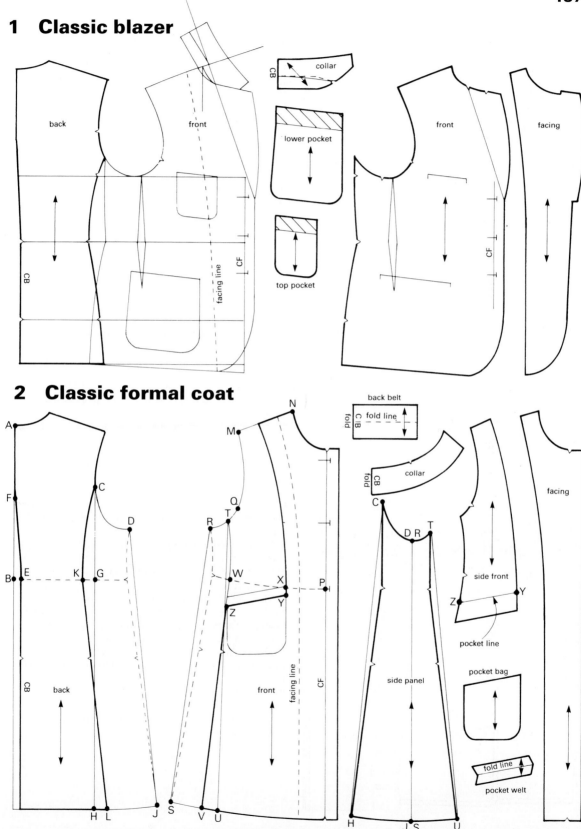

3   CLASSIC RAINCOAT

Trace off overgarment block and one-piece sleeve block.

Draw in finished length with curved front hemline.

Complete adaptation for raglan sleeve (ref. 14, page 116).

For an easier fit – ref. 16, page 116.

Body sections   Complete adaptation for double breasted reefer collar (ref. 12, page 126).

Draw in back yoke line. Draw in welt pocket, pocket bag.

Trace off yoke section. Trace off back section.

Mark A and B on side seam.

B–C   2cm; join A–C.

Add a 4cm–6cm vent pleat at centre back from hipline.

Trace off front section. Mark D and E on side seam.

E–F   3.5cm; join D–F.

Collar and facing   Trace off collar, widen the style line (ref. 11, page 126). Trace off facing, add approx. 0.5cm to rever from break point to collar point.

Pocket and pocket bag   Trace off welt, double its depth, mark fold line at centre. Trace off pocket bag.

Sleeves   Trace off adapted sleeves, mark in strap line. Trace off strap, double its depth, mark fold line.

Belt   Construct belt; G–H $\frac{1}{2}$ waist measurement plus 20cm. G–J twice belt depth required: mark fold line.

4   CLASSIC OVERJACKET OR OVERCOAT

Draw in finished length with curved front hemline.

Body sections

Mark point A at the underarm point.

A–B $\frac{1}{4}$ back width measurement; square down to C on waistline.

C–D and C–E approx. 1cm. Join B–D and B–E with a curve.

Square down to F and G on hemline.

Draw in back yoke line.

Draw in buttonholes, add buttonstand; draw in facing line.

Complete adaptation for a standard rever collar (ref. 11, page 126).

Draw in pocket flap and pocket bag.

Back   Trace off back section.

Back yoke   Trace off back yoke section.

Front   Trace off front section.

Facing   Trace off facing, add approx. 0.5cm to rever from front break point to collar point.

Under-collar   Trace off under-collar.

Top collar   Trace off top collar, add ease (ref. page 122).

Pocket flap   Trace off pocket flap.

Pocket bag   Trace off pocket bag.

Sleeve   Construct a two-piece sleeve for the overgarment block (ref. page 100).

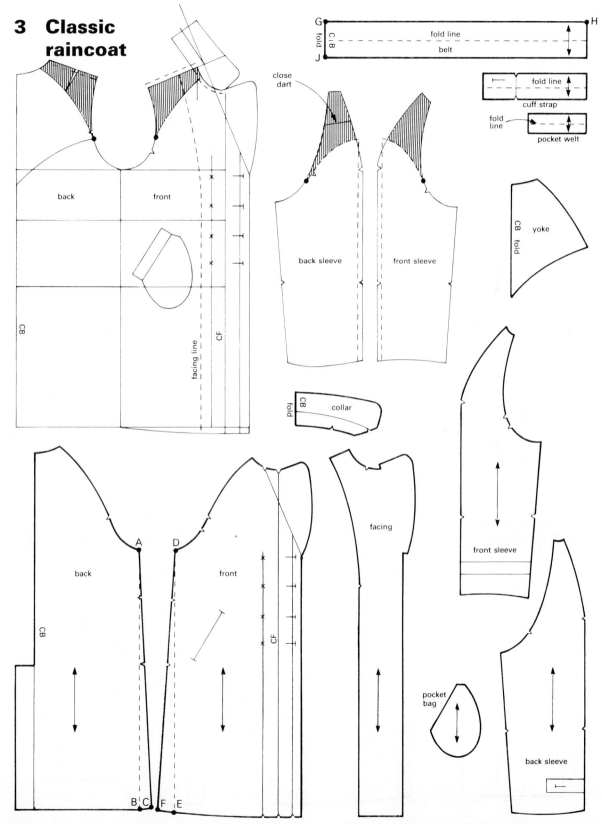

3 Classic raincoat

close dart

fold line
belt

fold line
cuff strap

fold line
pocket welt

back

front

CB

facing line

CF

back sleeve

front sleeve

CB fold yoke

CB fold collar

back

A D

back

CB

front

CF

B C F E

facing

front sleeve

pocket bag

back sleeve

4 Classic overjacket

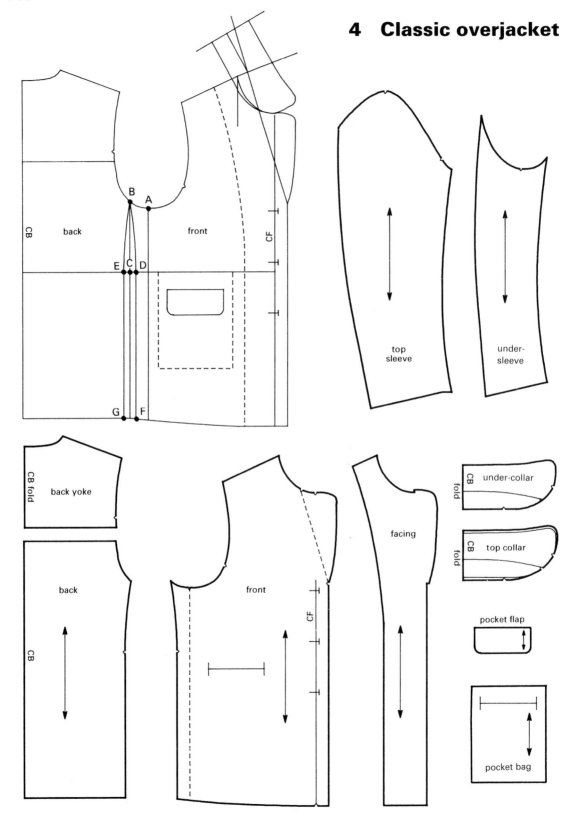

Part Two: Classic 'Form' Pattern Cutting Boys and Girls

13   SKIRTS AND TROUSERS

SPECIAL NOTE
Easy-fitting trousers and dungarees should be cut from the 'flat' trouser blocks in the section Simple 'Flat' Pattern Cutting. The jeans block is also found in that section (page 46).

The Skirt Block

For girls, sizes 80–140cm height
For girls above 140cm height the skirt block which
has more waist shaping should be used (see page 170)

SKIRTS WITHOUT DARTS (80–98cm height)
Girls up to 98cm height have little waist shaping, therefore a basic skirt is not a suitable garment for this group. The skirt block without darting has an easy-fitting waistline (5cm ease). It is usually developed into designs with straps, bib fronts or camisole tops.

MEASUREMENTS REQUIRED TO DRAFT THE BLOCK
(e.g. size 98cm height)
Refer to the size chart (pages 16 and 19) for standard measurements.

Waist	53cm
Hip/seat	56cm
Waist to hip	12cm
Waist to knee	34cm

Back
Square both ways from 0.
0 – 1 Skirt length plus 1cm; square across.
0 – 2 Waist to hip plus 1cm; square across.
2 – 3 $^1/_4$ hip plus 1.5cm; square up to 4 and down to 5.
0 – 6 $^1/_4$ waist plus 1cm.
0 – 7 1cm; join 6–7 with a curve.
5 – 8 2.5cm; draw in side seam 6, 3, 8; curve hipline outwards 0.25cm, curve hemline up 0.25cm at 8.

Front
Square both ways from 9.
9 –10 Skirt length plus 1cm; square across.
9 –11 Waist to hip plus 1cm; square across.
11–12 $^1/_4$ hip plus 2cm; square up to 13, down to 14.
9 –15 $^1/_4$ waist plus 1.5cm.
9 –16 0.5cm; join 15–16 with a curve.
14–17 2.5cm; draw in side seam 15, 12, 17; curve hipline outwards 0.25cm, curve hemline 0.25cm at 17.

Note ELASTICATED WAISTS
Many skirts of all sizes have elasticated waistbands. This adaptation, which allows for the growth of the child, is shown in ref. 3 on page 144.

SKIRTS WITH DARTS (104–140cm height)
Skirts with darts have 1cm ease in the waistline of the skirt. The waistline of the skirt should be eased onto the skirt waistband.

MEASUREMENTS REQUIRED TO DRAFT THE BLOCK
(e.g. size 110cm height)
Refer to the size charts (pages 17 and 19) for standard measurements.

Waist	56cm
Hip	62cm
Waist to hip	13.2cm
Waist to knee	38cm

Back
Square both ways from 0.
0 – 1 Skirt length plus 1cm; square across.
0 – 2 Waist to hip plus 1cm; square across.
2 – 3 $^1/_4$ hip plus 1.5cm; square up to 4 and down to 5.
0 – 6 $^1/_4$ waist:
sizes 104–116cm height   plus 1.2cm
      122–140cm height   plus 1.7cm.
0 – 7 1cm; join 6–7 with a curve.
5 – 8 2.5cm; draw in side seam 6, 3, 8; curve hipline outwards 0.25cm, curve hemline 0.25cm at 8.
9 Mid-way between 6 and 7; square down from the line 6–7.
Construct a dart on this line:
sizes 104–116cm height   length 8cm, width 1cm
      122–140cm height   length 9cm, width 1.5cm.

Front
Square both ways from 10.
10–11 Skirt length plus 1cm; square across.
10–12 Waist to hip plus 1cm; square across.
12–13 $^1/_4$ hip plus 1.5cm; square up to 14, down to 15.
10–16 $^1/_4$ waist:
sizes 104–116cm height   plus 1.3cm
      122–140cm height   plus 1.8cm.
10–17 0.5cm; join 16–17 with a curve.
15–18 2.5cm; draw in side seam 16, 13, 18; curve hipline outwards 0.25cm, curve hemline 0.25cm at 18.
19 Mid-way between 16 and 17; square down from the line 16–17.
Construct a dart on this line:
sizes 104–116cm height   length 6.5cm, width 1cm
      122–140cm height   length 7.5cm, width 1.5cm.

Skirt block without darts 80–98cm height

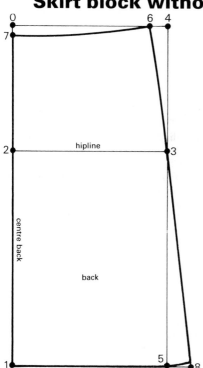
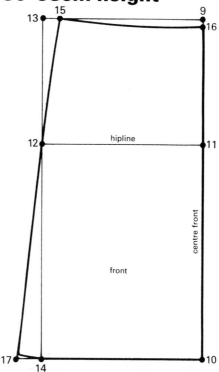

Skirt block with darts 104–140cm height

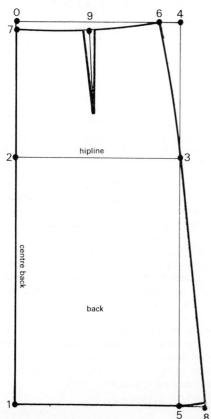
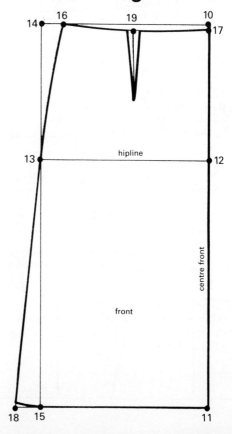

1 CAMISOLE TOP

This type of skirt is suitable for young children (up to approx. 104cm height) who have little waist shaping.
Bodice Trace round sleeveless dress block to waistline. Erase side seam, square down from underarm

points, shape in side seam 0.5cm if required.
Mark A, B, C and D at neckline. E and F at shoulders.
A–G 1cm. B–H, C–J, D–K 2.5cm. E–L, F–M 1cm.
Draw in new neck and armhole curves.
Skirt Trace round skirt block, erase any darts.
Make back and front waistline measurements equal those of front and back bodice. Mark points N and P.
Join N and P to hemline.
The skirt can then be adapted to different styles.

Note The bodice requires an opening at centre back.

WAISTBANDS

Children up to 116cm height often require straps on skirts to hold them in position. Many skirts in all sizes have an elasticated waistband. They hold the skirt in position and they allow for the child's growth.

2 STANDARD WAISTBAND

Skirt without darts A–B $\frac{1}{2}$ waist measurement plus 2.5cm (easy-fitting waistband). B–C 3cm–4cm button extension. Square down from A, B and C.
A–D Twice waistband depth; mark fold line down centre.
Skirt with darts A–B $\frac{1}{2}$ waist measurement. B–C 3cm–4cm button extension. Square down from A, B and C.
A–D Twice waistband depth; mark fold line down centre.

Note For a 'straight' finish at the seam opening the extension is added to only one end of the waistband.

3 ELASTICATED WAISTBAND

Skirts Mark A and B at centre front and back waist. Square up from the hipline to points C and D. Extend waistline curve to C and D. Join C and D to hemline.
Waistband E–F the measurement of A–C and B–D; square down from E and F. E–G twice waistband depth, square across to H. Mark fold line down centre.
On front waistline of skirt B–J $\frac{2}{3}$ measurement B–D.
On waistband E–K the measurement A–C and D–J; square down. E–K is the length of waistband to be elasticated.

Note Skirts with elasticated waistbands do not require an opening. Openings are added only as style features. They are usually placed between B and J on front. Skirts with openings require a button extension on waistband.

4 BIB FRONT

Bib fronts can be added to most skirt styles.
Trace off bodice block. Draw in bib shape required.
Measure the length of strap (A–B plus C–D) required and construct straps the required width.

5 SHAPED WAISTBAND

On skirt block draw lines parallel to waistline; depth 4cm. Cut off back and front sections. Close darts. Place front section to back section. Trace round pattern, add 4cm button extension at centre front.

1 Camisole top

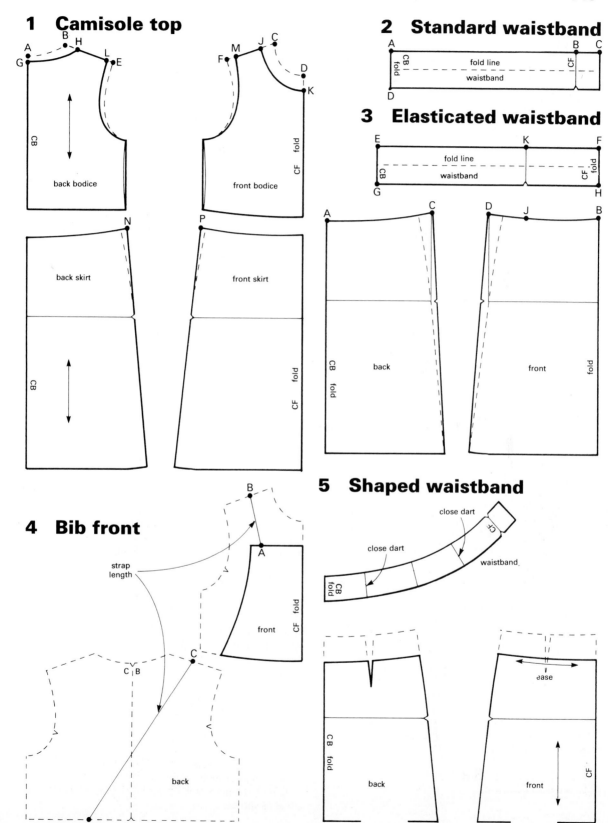

back bodice

front bodice

back skirt

front skirt

2 Standard waistband

fold line
waistband

3 Elasticated waistband

fold line
waistband

back

front

4 Bib front

strap length

front

back

5 Shaped waistband

close dart

close dart

waistband

ease

back

front

6   KILT – WORK DIRECTLY ON CLOTH

Square both ways from A.

A–B   Skirt length plus hem.

A–C   80–92cm height   10cm
      104–116cm height   12cm
      122–152cm height   16cm
      158–164cm height   20cm.

A–D $\frac{1}{2}$ measurement A–C; square down, mark centre front.

C–E   3 times (hip measurement minus A–C).

E–F   80–92cm height   10cm
      104–116cm height   12cm
      122–152cm height   16cm
      158–164cm height   20cm; square down to G.

E–H $\frac{1}{2}$ measurement E–F; square down, mark centre front.

Add 2cm to A–B and F–G for facings.

Pleat section C–E. Decide number of pleats (e.g. 20). Divide C–E into 20 sections. Divide each section into three and mark with pin lines as shown.

Waist shaping   Fold pleats and tack to hipline. To shape waist take the edge of each pleat and lap it over amount required to make a correct waist measurement.

Method   Hip meas. minus waist meas. divided by pleat number, e.g. size 110cm: hips 62cm minus waist 56cm divided by number of pleats $(62 - 56) \div 20 = 0.3$cm lap.

7a   SLIGHTLY GATHERED SKIRT

Trace skirt block, erase any darts. Divide waistline into three sections, mark points A and B; square down. Cut up lines and open sections required amount. Trace round pattern.

7b   VERY GATHERED SKIRT

Back   Square both ways from A.

A–B   Three times half hip measurement; square down.

A–C   Skirt length; square across.

A–D   Mid-way A–B; square down. Mark the line centre back.

Front   Construct pattern as for back.

8a   CIRCULAR SKIRT

The construction of a circular skirt is based on a circle. Make the waist measurement the circumference. Calculate radius from the circumference, see page 10.

A–B is the radius. A–C is the radius.

Draw a quarter circle from B–C.

C–D is skirt length. With a metre stick mark out edge of circle as shown.

8b   HALF CIRCULAR SKIRT

The construction of a half circular skirt is based on a circle. Make the waist measurement the circumference. Calculate the radius from the circumference, see page 10.

A–B is twice the radius. A–C is twice the radius.

Draw a quarter circle from B–C.

C–D is skirt length. With a metre stick mark out edge of circle as shown.

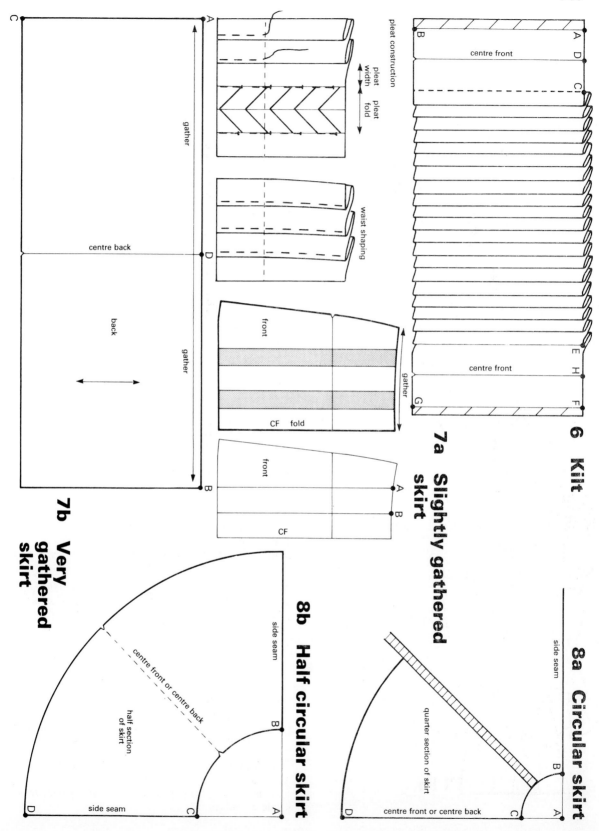

6 Kilt

centre front

B A
D
C

E H
F
G

centre front

7a Slightly gathered skirt

pleat construction

pleat width

pleat fold

waist shaping

front

CF fold

gather

front

A
B

CF

7b Very gathered skirt

C A

gather

centre back

D

back

gather

B

8b Half circular skirt

side seam

centre front or centre back

half section of skirt

B

side seam

D

C

A

8a Circular skirt

side seam

quarter section of skirt

B

centre front or centre back

D

C

A

10

9

11a

11b

Note If an elasticated waistband is required, make the adaptation (ref. 3, page 144) before commencing the design.

9 FLARED SKIRTS

Skirts without darts Trace round back and front sections of the skirt block. Divide waistline into four sections.
Mark points A, B and C; square down. Cut up lines and open at hemline required amount. Trace round pattern.
Skirts with darts Trace round back and front sections of the skirt block. Measure the darts then erase them. Divide waistlines into four sections. Mark points A, B and C; square down.
Construct three darts at A, B and C; the measurement of each dart is one third the dart allowance for that pattern piece.
Cut up lines, close darts, open at hem line the required amount. Trace round pattern.

10 FOUR GORED SKIRT

A four gored skirt is constructed from a flared skirt. It has a centre back and front seams. This skirt hangs well on the figure because it can be cut with the grain line down the centre of each panel.
Back and front Mark in hipline, mark points A and B at hipline, C and D at hemline. D–E 2.5cm, join B–E. F is mid-way A–B, G is mid-way C–E; join F–G.
This becomes the grain line.

11 SECTIONED SKIRTS

Extra flare can be added to sections of skirts.
Trace off skirt block or flared skirt pattern (e.g. flared skirt).
Mark A at centre of waistline, B at centre of hemline. Join A–B. Draw curved style lines at required depth. Divide each curved lower section into four equal parts.
Flared section Cut up lines, open at hemline the required amount. Trace round pattern.
Flared and gathered section Cut up lines, open sections 3cm at top 6cm at hemline (extra or less can be inserted). Trace round pattern as shown.

Note It is necessary to ensure that when curved pattern pieces are opened at the top, each section is laid on a line squared out from the line of previous section (e.g. line C–D).

9 Flared skirt without darts

(diagram labels: A B C; CB; back; C B fold; back; front; CF fold; front; C B A; CF)

10 Four gored skirt

(diagram labels: A F B; C B; back; C G E D)

9 Flared skirt with darts

(diagram labels: close darts; front; CF fold; C B A; front; CF)

11 Sectioned skirts

(diagram labels: A; C B fold; back; B)

11a Flared section

11b Flared and gathered section

(diagram labels: lower back; gather; lower back; gather; C; D)

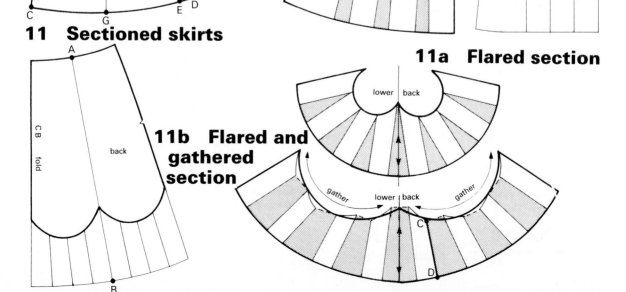

Note If the elasticated waistband is required, make the adaptation (ref. 3, page 144) before commencing the design.

12 SKIRT WITH VENT PLEAT – BOX PLEAT
Trace off skirt block.
Back Mark centre back the pleat stitch line.
Add a pleat to this line width approx.:
 80–98cm height   3cm
104–116cm height   4cm
122–152cm height   5cm
158–164cm height   6cm.
Fold pleat into finished position; cut out pattern.
Front Mark A at pleat position on waistline; square down, cut up line and open twice back pleat width.
Mark fold line down centre. Fold pleat into finished position. Cut out pattern.

13 SKIRT WITH INVERTED PLEATS
Trace off skirt block.
Back Mark A at centre back waistline, square out.
A–B twice pleat width approx.:
 80–98cm height   6cm
104–116cm height   8cm
122–152cm height   10cm
158–164cm height   12cm; square down.
Mark fold line down centre. Fold pleat into finished position. Cut out pattern.
Front Mark C at pleat position on waistline; square down.
Cut up line. C–D four times pleat width approx.:
 80–98cm height   12cm
104–116cm height   16cm
122–152cm height   20cm
158–164cm height   24cm.
Divide C–D into four sections; square down from E, F, G.
Mark lines from E and G fold lines.
Fold pleat into finished position. Cut out pattern.

14 SKIRT WITH BACK AND FRONT PLEATS
Trace off skirt block.
Back Mark A and B at pleat positions on waistline; square down.
Cut up lines. A–C and B–D twice the measurement A–B.
Mark fold line down centre of each opening.
Fold pleats into finished position. Cut out pattern.
Front Construct front as for back.

SKIRTS WITH DARTS
Trace off skirt block.
Measure dart allowance, erase darts. Construct pleats.
Skirts with one pleat Draw in dart on pleat line; complete pattern.
Skirts with two pleats Draw a dart (half dart allowance) on each pleat line; complete pattern.

12 Skirt with vent pleat — box pleat

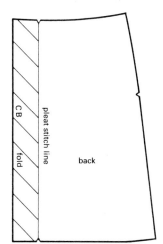

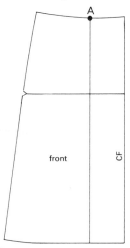

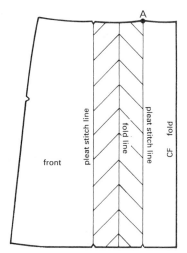

13 Skirt with inverted pleats

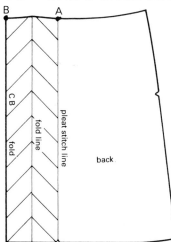

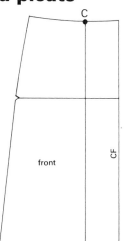

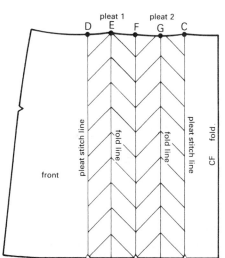

14 Skirt with back and front pleats

Skirt with darts

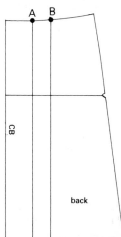

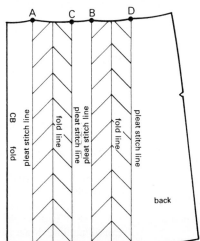

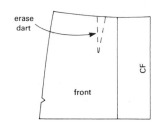

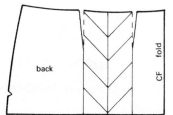

The Classic Trouser Block

For children 92–116cm height, and boys 122–170cm height. For girls, 122–140cm height

The trouser block draft starts at size 92cm height. Below this size use the trouser block in the Babywear Blocks section (ref. page 23) which has a special ease allowance to accommodate nappies.

The earliest figure difference that occurs between boys and girls is that of waist/hip relationship. For girls above 140cm height use the girls' trouser block on page 181 as this block has more waist shaping. Sizes up to 116cm height require more ease in the front of the trousers; this front–back proportion is systematically reduced as the size is increased.

Note 1 There is 1cm ease in the waistline of the trousers. The waistline of trousers should always be eased onto the waistband.

Note 2 The top of the waistband of the basic trouser block for children up to 116cm height and boys, sits on the waistline. For girls above 116cm height the bottom of the waistband sits on the waistline.

MEASUREMENTS REQUIRED TO DRAFT THE BLOCK
(e.g. boys and girls size 134cm height)
Refer to the size charts (pages 16–18) for standard measurements.

	Girls	Boys
Hip/seat	74cm	73cm
Waist	61cm	64cm
Body rise	22.4cm	22cm
Inside leg	62cm	61cm
Trouser bottom width	19cm	19cm
Waist to hip	15.6cm	15.6cm
Waist band depth	3cm	3cm

Front
Square down and across from 0.

Children, 92–116cm height; boys, 122–170cm height
0 – 1 Body rise plus 1cm, minus waistband depth; square across.
0 – 2 Waist to hip plus 1cm, minus waistband depth; square across.
Girls, 122–140cm height
0 – 1 Body rise; square across.
0 – 2 Waist to hip; square across.

1 – 3 Inside leg; square across.
1 – 4 $^1/_2$ measurement 1–3:
  sizes 92–116cm height minus 3cm
  122–152cm height minus 3.5cm
  158–170cm height minus 4cm;
square across.
1 – 5 $^1/_{12}$ hip/seat plus 1.5cm; square up to 6 and 7.

6 – 8 $^1/_4$ hip/seat:
  sizes 92–116cm height plus 1.5cm
  122–152cm height plus 1cm
  158–170cm height plus 0.5cm.
5 – 9 $^1/_{16}$ hip/seat plus 0.5cm. 7–10 1cm.
Join 10–6; join 6–9 with a curve touching a point:
  sizes 92–116cm height 2.25cm from 5
  122–152cm height 2.5cm from 5
  158–170cm height 2.75cm from 5.

Children, 92–116cm height; boys 122–170cm height
10–11 $^1/_4$ waist:
  sizes 92–116cm height plus 0.75cm
  122–170cm height plus 0.25cm.
Girls, 122–140cm height
10–11 $^1/_4$ waist plus 1.25cm.
Construct a dart on line from 0; length 8cm, width 1cm.

3 –12 $^1/_2$ trouser bottom width minus 0.5cm.
4 –13 The measurement 3–12 plus 1cm.
3 –14 $^1/_2$ trouser bottom width minus 0.5cm.
4 –15 The measurement 3–14 plus 1cm.
Draw in side seam through points 11, 8, 13, 12; curve hipline outwards 0.25cm.
Draw inside leg seam 9, 15, 14; curve 9–15 in 0.75cm.

Back
5 –16 $^1/_4$ measurement 1–5; square up to 17 on hip/seat line, 18 on waistline.
16–19 $^1/_2$ measurement 16–18.
18–20 1.5cm. 20–21 1.5cm.
21–22 $^1/_4$ waist:
  sizes 92–116cm height plus 1.25cm
  122–152cm height plus 2.25cm
  158–170cm height plus 2.75cm.
Join 21–22 to touch the horizontal line from 0.
9 –23 $^1/_2$ measurement 5–9, 23–24 0.25cm.
Join 21–19, join 19–24 with a curve touching a point:
  sizes 92–116cm height 3.5cm from 16
  122–152cm height 3.75cm from 16
  158–170cm height 4cm from 16.
17–25 $^1/_4$ hip/seat:
  sizes 92–116cm height plus 1cm
  122–170cm height plus 1.25cm.
12–26 1cm. 13–27 1cm. 14–28 1cm 15–29 1cm.
Draw in side seam through points 22, 25, 27, 26; curve hipline outwards 0.25cm, 25–27 inwards 0.25cm.
Draw inside leg seam 24, 29, 28; curve 24–29 1.25cm.
21–30 $^1/_2$ measurement 21–22; square down from the line 21–22.
Construct a dart on this line:
Sizes 92–116cm height length 7.5cm, width 1.5cm
  122–152cm height length 9cm, width 2cm
  158–170cm height length 11cm, width 2.5cm.
Curve hemline down 1cm at 3.

Classic trouser block

Children 92–116cm height
Boys 122–170cm height

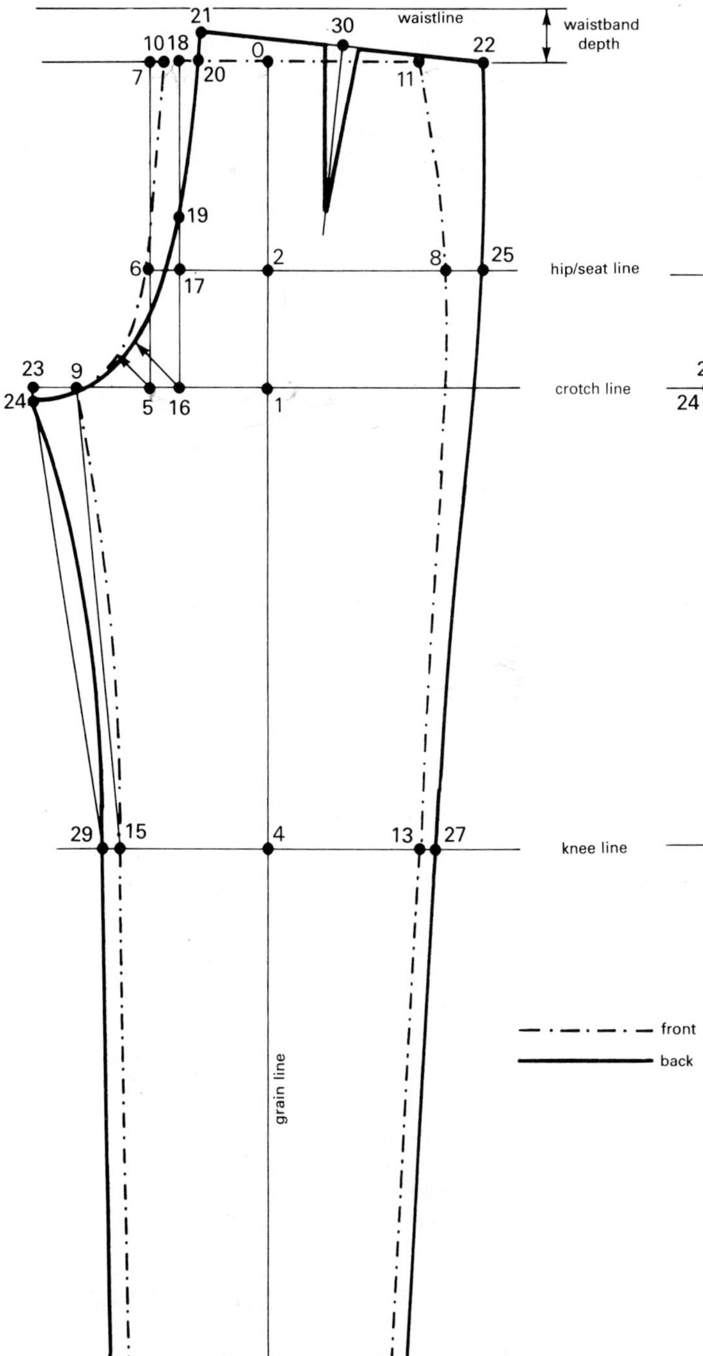

Girls 122–140cm height

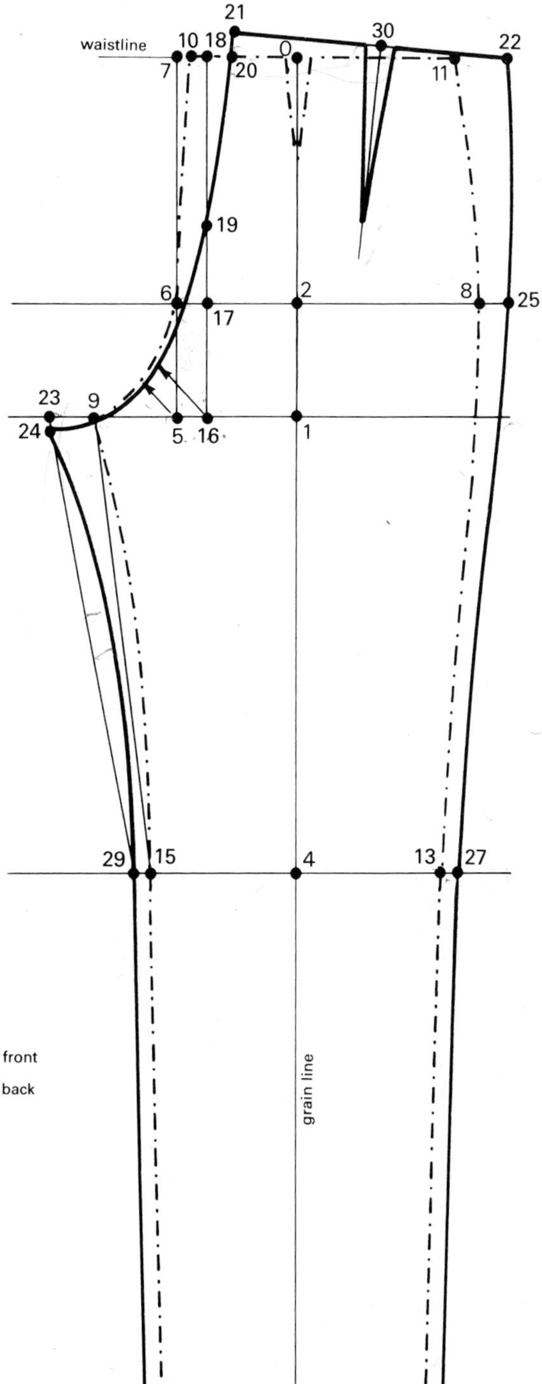

waistline

waistband depth

hip/seat line

crotch line

knee line

grain line

front
back

1 BOYS' BASIC TROUSERS (adjustable waistband)
Boys' basic trousers are worn mainly for school wear.
The waistband has 5cm ease and it is adjustable to allow
for growth.
Adaptation 1 Simple elasticated double cloth
waistband.
Adaptation 2 Single cloth waistband, tailored finish
with elasticated straps.

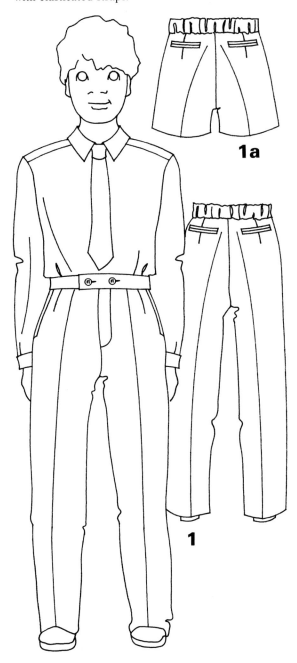

1a

1

Front Trace off front section of trousers.
Mark points 0, 4, 9, 10, 11.
Cut along knee line and along grain line from 0–4.
Open at waistline: 92–116cm height 2cm
                    122–152cm height 3cm
                    158–170cm height 4cm.
11–A 2cm. Draw in new side seam line from A.
Erase old line from 11.
Trace round pattern.
A–B $^1/_6$ measurement 10–A minus 0.5cm.
A–C $^1/_5$ waist measurement plus 1cm.
Join B–C for pocket line. C–D 2cm.
B–E and D–F: 92–116cm height 3cm
              122–152cm height 3.5cm
              158–170cm height 4cm.
Join E–F and F–D for pocket facing.
10–G $^2/_3$ measurement 9–10.
10–H 92–116cm height 3cm
      122–152cm height 3.5cm
      158–170cm height 4cm.
Draw in fly piece as shown. Draw in pocket bag.
B–J $^1/_2$ measurement B–0. Mark tuck at 0, 1cm less
than amount trousers have been opened. Mark 2cm
tuck at J. Trace off frontside piece.

Back Trace off back section of trousers.
Mark in points 17, 21, 22, 24, 25, 30.
Cut along seat line and open a wedge at 17.
17–K 92–116cm height 1.5cm
      122–152cm height 2cm
      158–170cm height 2.5cm.
17–L 0.5cm; draw in new crotch line from 21–24.
22–M 1.5cm; draw new side seam from M to crotch
      line.
30–N $^1/_4$ measurement 21–M minus 1cm. Draw in
      pocket mouth and pocket bag as shown.

Fly piece, pocket facing and pocket bags Trace off
these pattern pieces from front and back sections.

Waistband, double cloth
P–Q $^1/_2$ waist measurement plus 2.5cm; square down.
Q–R Width of fly piece; square down.
P–S Twice waistband depth; square across. Mark
fold line down centre.
P–T $^2/_3$ measurement P–Q; square down. P–T is the
length of waistband to be elasticated.
Waistband, single cloth
P–Q $^1/_2$ waist measurement plus 2.5cm; square down.
Q–R Width of fly piece; square down.
P–S Waistband depth; square across.
P–T $^1/_3$ measurement P–Q plus 3cm; square down to
     U.
Cut up line T–U. Add 2.5cm facing pieces to each
section. Construct small strap.
Cut cloth facing for front waistband, length 5cm.

1a SHORT TROUSERS
For short trousers cut across trouser draft at length
required. Curve hemline down 1cm at centre back.

1 Boys' basic trousers

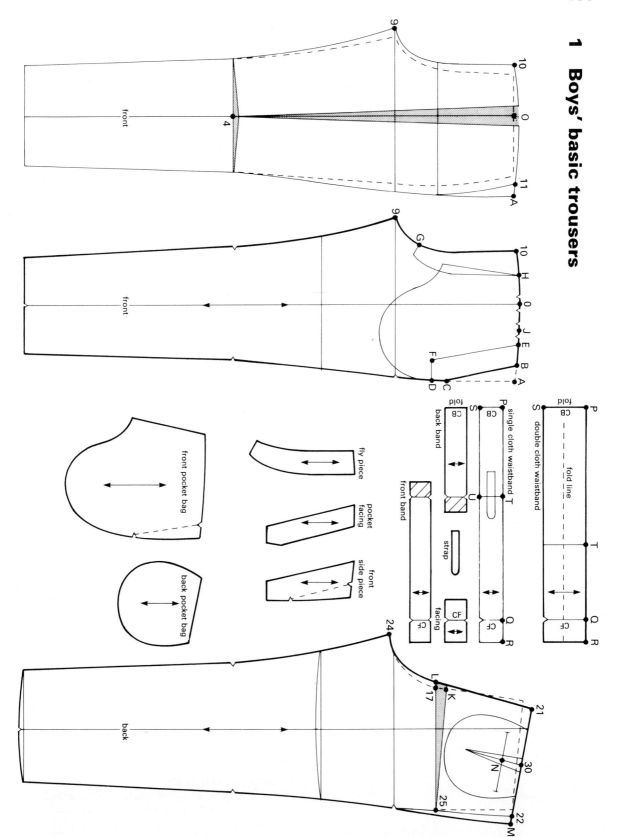

FASHION TROUSERS FOR BOYS AND GIRLS

Simple adaptations can be made to the trouser block. Trouser legs can be narrowed or widened (ref. 2 and 3, this page). Extra ease can be added for elasticated waists (ref. 3, this page). Tucks can be added (ref. 1, page 154). The designs illustrated are based on the girls' trouser block, but the adaptations can also be used with the boys' block.

2 TROUSERS – SLIMLINE

Trace off basic trouser block, reverse front section.

Front   Mark points 0, 8, 9, 10, 11, 12, 13, 14, 15.

0–A $\frac{1}{2}$ measurement 0–11.

11–B $\frac{1}{2}$ measurement 8–11; join A–B with a curve.

Draw in pocket bag as shown.

10–C $\frac{1}{2}$ measurement 9–10 plus 1cm; square out.

Square out from 10. 10–D 3cm; square down.

12–E   1cm; 14–F 1cm; join 13–E and 15–F.

Trace off side piece, add 3cm from A–B.

Trace off pocket bags as shown.

Back   Mark points 17, 24, 25, 26, 27, 28, 29.

Cut across seat line; open a wedge at 17 1cm–1.5cm.

17–G   0.5cm; draw in new crotch line from 21–24.

26–H   1cm; 28–J 1cm; join 27–H and 29–J.

Waistband   Square both ways from K.

K–L   Waist measurement; L–M 3cm; K–N $\frac{1}{2}$ measurement K–L.

Square down from K, L, M, N.

K–P   Twice waistband depth; square across.

Mark fold line through centre.

3 FASHION TROUSERS

Trace off basic trouser block, reverse front section.

Front   Mark points 0, 8, 9, 10, 11, erase any darts.

11-A   4cm; join A to crotch line.

0–B $\frac{1}{5}$ measurement 0–A.

9–C $\frac{1}{4}$ measurement 9–10; join B–C.

B–D $\frac{1}{4}$ measurement B–C.

A–E $\frac{1}{2}$ measurement A–8; join D–E. Draw in pocket bag.

10–F $\frac{1}{2}$ measurement 9–10 plus 1cm.

Square out from 10; 10–G 3cm; square down.

Trace off front, yoke, side piece and pocket bag.

Re-shape trouser leg seams as required. Example shows trousers shaped in at 13 and 15 and out at the hem.

Back   Mark points 17, 21, 22, 24, 25, 27, 29.

Cut across the seat line: open a wedge at 17 1.5cm–2cm.

17–H   0.5cm: draw in new crotch line from 21–24.

22–J   2cm: join J–27 with a curve. Mark K on hipline.

J–L $\frac{1}{2}$ measurement J–21: join K–L.

Trace off back and back side piece.

Re-shape trouser leg seams as required. Example shows trousers shaped in at 27 and 29 and out at the hem.

Waistband   M–N The measurement 21–J on back.

M–P   The measurement A–10 on front, P–Q 3cm.

Square down from M, N, P, Q.

M–R   Twice waistband depth; square across.

Mark fold line down centre.

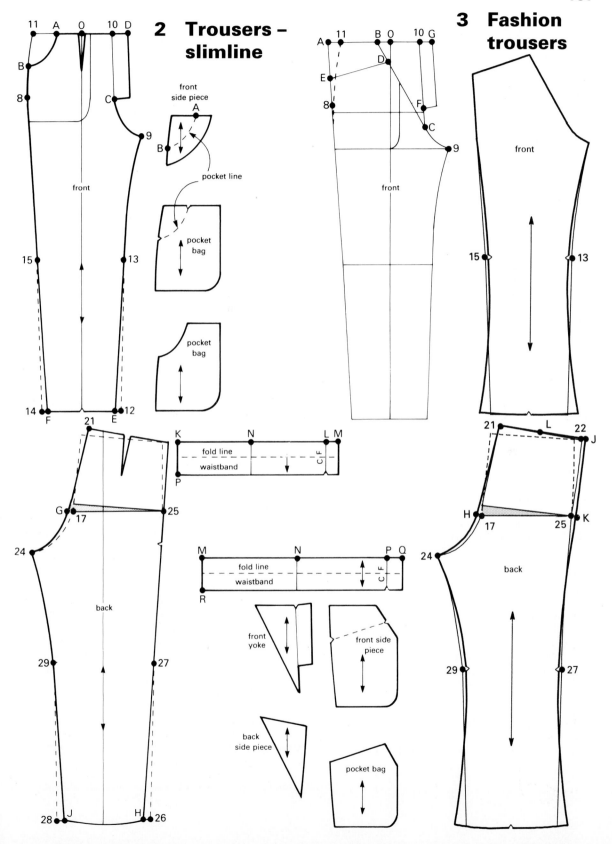

2 Trousers – slimline

front side piece

pocket line

pocket bag

pocket bag

front

fold line

waistband

C.F

back

3 Fashion trousers

front

front

back

fold line

waistband

C.F

front yoke

front side piece

back side piece

pocket bag

back

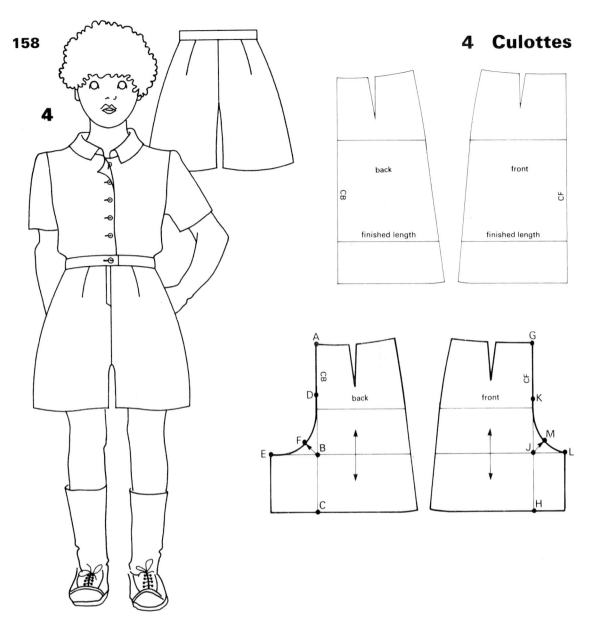

4   CULOTTES

Trace off skirt block to required culotte length.

Back   Mark A at centre back waistline.

A–B body rise: 92–134cm height   plus 1cm
                        140–164cm height   plus 1.5cm;
square across.

A–C   Finished length; square across.

A–D $^1/_2$ measurement A–B minus 1cm.

B–E $^1/_8$ hip: 92–134cm height   plus 1cm
                        140–164cm height   plus 1.5cm;
square down to hemline.

B–F   92–134cm height   2.5cm
          140–164cm height   3cm.

Join D–E with a curved line touching point F.

Front   Mark G at centre front waistline.

G–H   Finished length; square across.

G–J body rise: 92–134cm height   plus 1cm
                        140–164cm height   plus 1.5cm;
square across.

G–K $^1/_2$ measurement G–J.

J–L $^1/_8$ hip: 92–134cm height   minus 2.25cm
                        140–164cm height   minus 2cm;
square down to hemline.

J–M   92–134cm height   3.5cm
          140–164cm height   4cm.

Join K–L with a curved line touching point M.

Waistband   Construct waistband required (page 144).

Part Two: Classic 'Form' Pattern Cutting Girls – Developing Figures

14 THE BASIC BLOCKS AND SIZE CHARTS

Approximate age: 11–14 years

Body measurements
Girls (developing figures) 146–164cm height
Approximate age 11–14 years

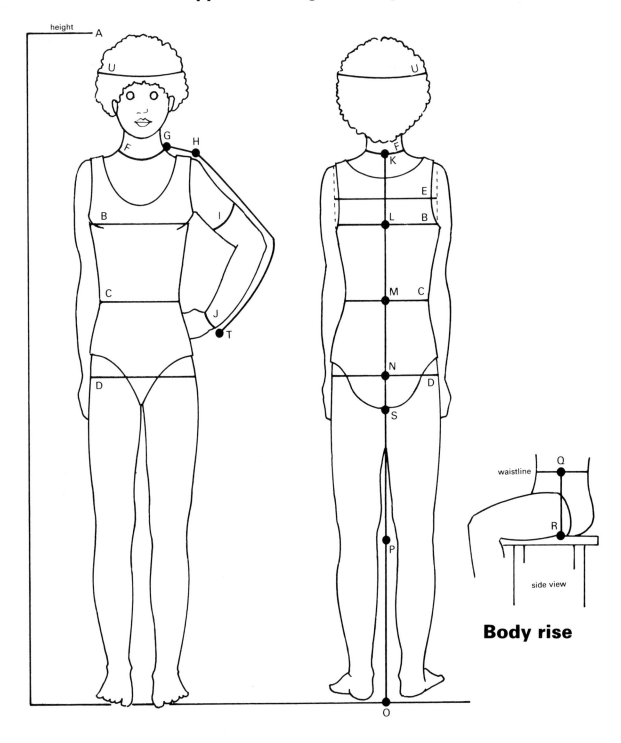

height

Body rise

waistline

side view

Standard Body Measurements

Girls (developing figures), 146–164cm height: approx. age 11–14 years

The size charts and blocks in this section are constructed for girls who are in the process of figure development. They are usually growing fast and experiencing quite rapid changes in their measurements. The blocks are particularly concerned with the size of the bust; they are constructed for bust shapes A and B (girls who have reached mature size C require blocks constructed for women).

At this period of development the increasing variance in the bust sizes of girls in a height group means that the customer needs to refer to bust and hip sizes as well as height. Most manufacturers include this additional information on the labels from 146cm height.

INDIVIDUAL BLOCKS
Read the section on methods of measuring body dimensions and drafting the blocks for individual figures, page 12.

The dart size should relate to the shape of the bust:
Stage A – use a dart size of 2–3cm;
Stage B – use a dart size of 4–5cm;
Stage C – the blocks in this book are unsuitable for mature figures (use blocks constructed for women).

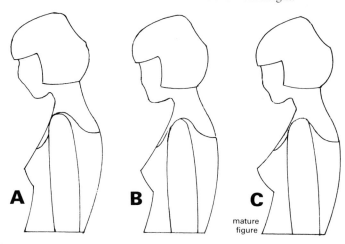

A   B   C

mature figure

A	HEIGHT	146	152	158	164
	APPROXIMATE AGE	11 – – – – – – – – – 14			
B	BUST	78	81	84	87
C	WAIST	65	66	67	68
D	HIP	83	86	89	92
E	ACROSS BACK	31	32.2	33.4	34.6
F	NECK SIZE	33	34	35	36
G–H	SHOULDER	11	11.4	11.8	12.2
	DART	2	3	4	5
I	UPPER ARM	23.2	24	24.8	25.6
J	WRIST	15.2	15.6	16	16.4
K–L	SCYE DEPTH	18.4	19	19.6	20.2
K–M	NECK TO WAIST	34.8	36.2	37.6	39
M–N	WAIST TO HIP	17.6	18.4	19.2	20
K–O	CERVICAL HEIGHT	123.6	129	134.4	139.8
M–P	WAIST TO KNEE	50	52	54	56
Q–R	BODY RISE	24	25	26	27
S–O	INSIDE LEG	68	71	74	76
H–T	SLEEVE LENGTH	54	56	58	59
U	HEAD CIRCUMFERENCE	55.2	55.6	56	56.4
Extra measurements (garments)					
CUFF SIZE, TWO-PIECE SLEEVE		13	13.3	13.6	13.9
CUFF SIZE, SHIRTS		19	20	20.5	21
TROUSER BOTTOM WIDTH		20	20.5	21	21.5
JEANS BOTTOM WIDTH		18	18.5	19	19.5

The Classic Bodice Block

For girls, sizes 146–164cm height

The relationship between height and bust development can vary considerably during puberty, therefore the dart size is only a general guide to the average figure. When drafting for individual figures the dart size which relates to the correct stage of development should be chosen. If a girl has a fully developed figure an adult block will be required.

MEASUREMENTS REQUIRED TO DRAFT THE BLOCK
(e.g. size 158cm height)
Refer to the size chart (page 161) for standard measurements.

Bust	84cm
Across back	33.4cm
Neck size	35cm
Shoulder	11.8
Neck to waist	37.6
Scye depth	19.6cm
Dart	4cm
Waist to hip	19.2cm

Body sections
Square both ways from 0.

0 – 1 Neck to waist plus 1.5cm; square across.

1 – 2 Waist to hip; square across.

0 – 3 $\frac{1}{2}$ bust plus 5cm; square down to 4 and 5 (e.g. 158cm (84 ÷ 2) + 5 = 47).

0 – 6 1.5cm.

6 – 7 Scye depth plus 1cm; square across to 8.

6 – 9 $\frac{1}{2}$ measurement 6–7; square out.

6 –10 $\frac{1}{4}$ scye depth minus 2cm; square out.

0 –11 $\frac{1}{5}$ neck size minus 0.2cm; draw in neck curve.

7 –12 $\frac{1}{2}$ across back plus 0.5cm; square up, mark point 13.

11–14 Shoulder measurement plus 0.8cm ease.

3 –15 $\frac{1}{5}$ neck size minus 0.7cm.

3 –16 $\frac{1}{5}$ neck size minus 0.2cm; draw in neck curve.

16–17 $\frac{1}{2}$ measurement 8–16;
sizes 146–152cm height   plus 1.5cm
          158–164cm height   plus 1.75cm;
square across.

8 –18 The measurement 7–12 plus 0.5cm, plus $\frac{1}{4}$ dart measurement; square up to 19.

14–20 Sizes 146–152cm height   1cm
            158–164cm height   1.25cm;
square across.

15–21 The measurement of the dart.

21–22 Shoulder measurement; draw front shoulder line to touch the line from 20.

8 –23 $\frac{1}{2}$ measurement 8–18.

23–24 1.5cm; join 15–24 and 21–24 to form dart.

18–25 $\frac{1}{2}$ measurement 12–18; square down to 26 and 27.

Draw in armscye shape as shown; measurement of curve: from 12 2.5cm; from 18 2cm.
There is 0.8cm ease on back shoulder, this can be eased into front shoulder during making-up or a dart can be constructed.

11–28 $\frac{1}{2}$ measurement 11–14; square down 5cm from the line 11–14. Construct a dart 0.8cm wide on this line.

Waisted dresses
4 –29 1cm; join 1–29 with a curve.

Sleeve
Draft a one-piece sleeve (page 98) or a two-piece sleeve (page 100) to fit armscye measurement.

THE DART
The bodice block for developing figures can be used for most children's wear styles. The dart position has to be changed depending on the style. For most designs the dart can be swung to the underarm position.

Method   Draw a line from the centre of the side seam to the bust point. Cut up the line. Close the original dart and secure with tape. Shorten the dart by 2cm. For more advanced methods of changing the dart position read the section on dart manipulation in *Metric Pattern Cutting* or other books concerned with women's wear. Because the blocks for girls with developing figures have bust darts they can be adapted easily into the more mature designs shown in these books.

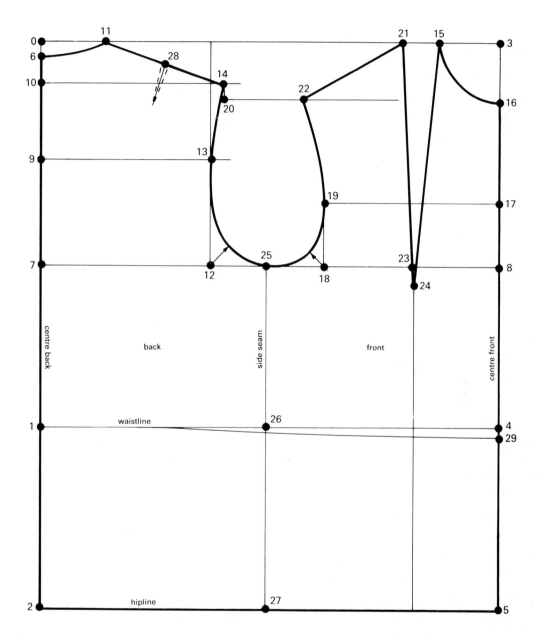

Shaping the Bodice Block

Note Standard ease allowed on a shaped waisted dress is 6cm.

SHAPED BODICE BLOCK TO WAISTLINE
Trace off bodice block to waistline.
Mark points 1, 7, 8, 12, 18, 24, 25, 29 on the bodice block.
7–A $\frac{1}{2}$ measurement 7–12; square down to B.
Square down from 24–C. A–D and 24–E 2cm.
1–F $\frac{1}{4}$ waist:
   sizes 146–152cm height   plus 4cm
        158–164cm height   plus 4.5cm.
29–G $\frac{1}{4}$ waist:
   sizes 146–152cm height   plus 4.5cm
        158–164cm height   plus 5cm.
Draw in curved side seams from 25–F and 25–G.
Construct back dart on the line D–B:
   sizes 146–152cm height   2.5cm dart
        158–164cm height   3cm dart.
Construct front dart on the line E–C:
   sizes 146–152cm height   3cm dart
        158–164cm height   3.5cm dart.

SHAPED BODICE BLOCK TO HIPLINE
Trace off bodice block to hipline, omit point 29 and the line 26–27.
Complete instructions above for shaped bodice block.
Extend the line A–B to H. H–J 5cm.
Extend the line 24–C to K. K–L 7cm.
Complete darts as shown.
M is mid-way between 2–5.
Complete back side seam 25, F, M and front side seam 25, G, M with slightly curved hiplines.

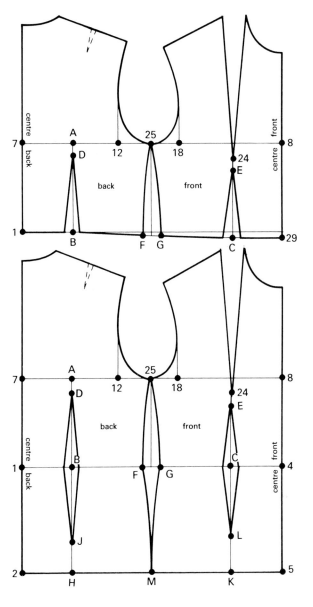

The Dress Block

Trace round standard bodice block to hipline.
Mark side seam to waistline only. Mark points 2, 5, 7, 8, 12, 18, 25, 26.
5–A $\frac{1}{2}$ measurement 2–5; square down to B.
26–C 1.5cm; B–D 3cm. Draw in back side seam 25, C, A, D.
Curve 25–C inwards 0.25cm, curve C–A outwards slightly.
26–E 2cm; B–F 3cm. Draw in front side seam 25, E, A, F.
Curve 25–E inwards 0.25cm. Curve E–A outwards slightly.
Shape up hemline 0.25cm at D and F.

Extra waist shaping
Construct back and front darts as shown on this page – 'Shaped bodice block to hipline'.

Extra flare
Drop perpendicular lines from the base of back and front darts on shoulder. Cut up lines.
Open block at hemline the required amount.
It is usual to include more flare in the front section of the block.

The dress block

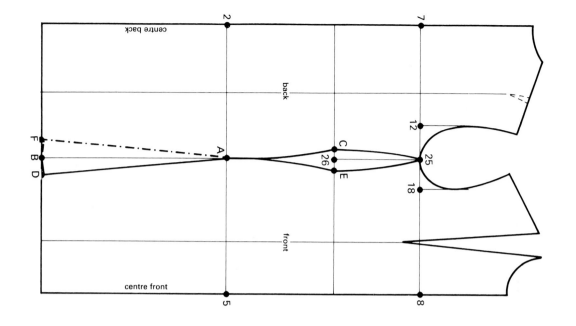

The dress block with extra flare

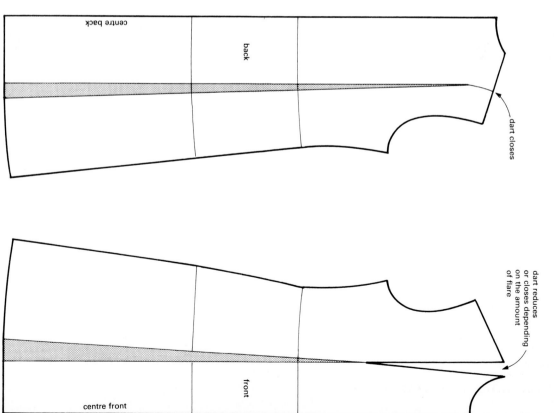

The Classic Overgarment Block

For girls, sizes 146–164cm height

The overgarment block is a base for casual wear designs; i.e. anoraks and duffle coats. These garments require more ease in the body so that they can be worn over trousers, skirts and sweaters.

MEASUREMENTS REQUIRED TO DRAFT THE BLOCK
(e.g. size 158cm height)
Refer to the size chart (page 161) for standard measurements.

Bust	84cm
Across back	33.4cm
Neck size	35cm
Shoulder	11.8cm
Neck to waist	37.6cm
Scye depth	19.6cm
Dart	4cm
Waist to hip	19.2cm

Body sections
Square both ways from 0.

0 – 1 Nape to waist plus 2cm; square across.
0 – 2 $\frac{1}{2}$ bust plus 10cm; square down, mark point 3 on waistline.
0 – 4 2cm.
4 – 5 Scye depth plus 3.5cm; square across to 6.
4 – 7 $\frac{1}{2}$ measurement 4–5; square out.
4 – 8 $\frac{1}{4}$ scye depth; square out.
5 – 9 $\frac{1}{2}$ across back plus 1.5cm; square up to 10 and 11.

11–12 2cm; square out.
0 –13 $\frac{1}{5}$ neck size plus 0.3cm; draw in neck curve.
13–14 Shoulder measurement plus 1.75cm.
2 –15 $\frac{1}{5}$ neck size minus 0.2cm.
2 –16 $\frac{1}{5}$ neck size plus 0.3cm; draw in neck curve.
16–17 $\frac{1}{2}$ measurement 6–16 plus 2cm; square across.
6 –18 The measurement 5–9 plus 0.5cm plus $\frac{1}{4}$ dart measurement.
15–20 Dart measurement.
Join 20 to 11 with a straight line.
20–21 The measurement 13–14 minus 0.5cm.
21–22 1.5cm; join 20–22 with slight curve.
6 –23 $\frac{1}{2}$ measurement 6–18; square up 1cm to 24.
Join 15 to 24 and 20 to 24.
18–25 $\frac{1}{2}$ measurement 9–18 plus 0.5cm; square down.
Mark point 26 on waistline.
Draw in armscye shape as shown, to touch points: 3cm from 9 and 2.5cm from 18.
4 –27 Finished length; square across to 28 and 29.
29–30 1cm; join 28–30 with a curved line.
1 –31 waist to hip; square across.

Note There is 0.5cm ease on the back shoulder.

Sleeve
Draft a one-piece sleeve (page 98) or two-piece sleeve (page 100) to fit armscye measurement.

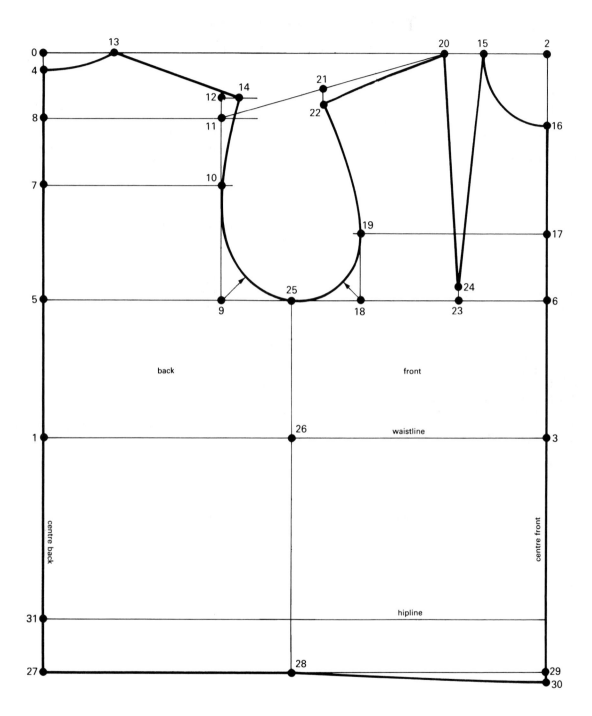

The Classic Trouser Block

For girls, sizes 146–164cm height

Note 1   The bottom of the waistband of the girls' trouser block sits on the waistline.
Note 2   There is 1cm ease in the waistline of the trousers. The waistline of trousers should always be eased onto the waistband.

MEASUREMENTS REQUIRED TO DRAFT THE BLOCK
(e.g. size 158cm height)
Refer to the size charts (pages 17 and 161) for standard measurements.

Hip	89cm
Waist	67cm
Body rise	26cm
Inside leg	74cm
Trouser bottom width	21cm
Waist to hip	19.2cm

Front
Square down and across from 0.
0 – 1   Body rise; square up.
0 – 2   Waist to hip; square across.
1 – 3   Inside leg; square across.
1 – 4 $\frac{1}{2}$ measurement 1–3 minus 4cm; square across.
1 – 5 $\frac{1}{12}$ hip plus 1.5cm; square up to 6 and 7.
6 – 8 $\frac{1}{4}$ hip plus 0.5cm; square up.
5 – 9 $\frac{1}{16}$ hip plus 0.5cm.
7 –10   1cm; join 10–6 and 6–9 with a curve touching a point 2.75cm from 5.
10–11 $\frac{1}{4}$ waist:
    sizes 146–152cm height   plus 1.6cm
        158–164cm height   plus 2cm.
3 –12 $\frac{1}{2}$ trouser bottom width minus 0.5cm.
4 –13   The measurement 3–12 plus 1cm.
3 –14 $\frac{1}{2}$ trouser bottom width minus 0.5cm.
4 –15   The measurement 3–14 plus 1cm.
Draw side seam through points 11, 8, 13, 12; curve hipline outwards 0.25cm.

Draw inside leg seam 9, 15, 14. Curve 9–15 inwards 0.75cm.
Construct a dart on the line from 0:
    sizes 146–152cm height 7.5cm long, 1.4cm wide
        158–164cm height 8.5cm long, 1.8cm wide.

Back
5 –16 $\frac{1}{4}$ measurement 1–5; square up to 17 on hipline, 18 on waistline.
16–19 $\frac{1}{2}$ measurement 16–18.
18–20   1.5cm.
20–21   1.5cm.
21–22 $\frac{1}{4}$ waist:
    sizes 146–152cm height   plus 2.7cm
        158–164cm height   plus 3.5cm.
Join 21–22 to touch horizontal line from 0.
9 –23 $\frac{1}{2}$ measurement 5–9.
23–24   0.25cm.
Join 21–19 and 19–24 with a curve touching a point 4cm from 16.
17–25 $\frac{1}{4}$ hip   plus 1.25cm.
12–26   1cm.
13–27   1cm.
14–28   1cm.
15–29   1cm.
Draw in side seam through points 22, 25, 27, 26.
Curve hipline outwards 0.25cm; 25–27 inwards 0.25cm.
Draw inside leg seam 24, 29, 28. Curve 24–29 inwards 1.25cm.
Divide the line 21–22 into three parts. Mark points 30 and 31. Using the line 21–22 square down from 30 and 31.
Sizes 146–152cm height   30–32 10cm; 31–33 8cm
    158–164cm height   30–32 12 cm; 31–33 10cm.
Construct darts on these lines:
sizes 146–152cm height   1.2cm wide
    158–164cm height   1.6cm wide.
Curve hemline down 1cm at 3.

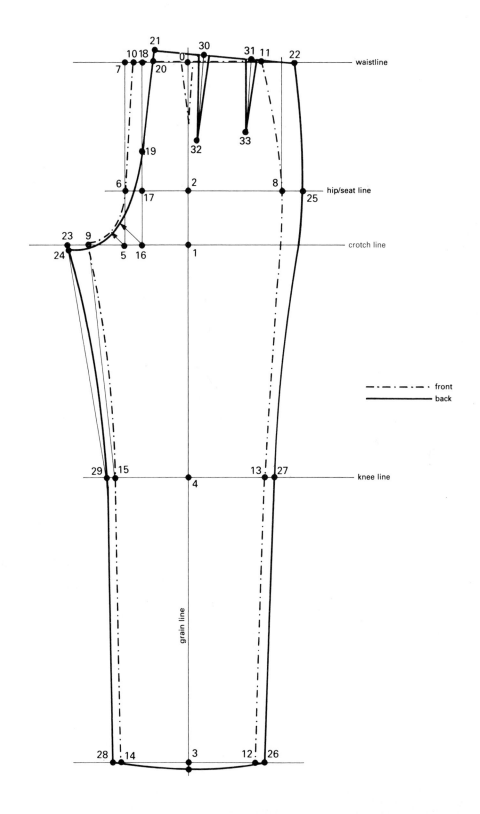

waistline

hip/seat line

crotch line

— · — · — front
———— back

knee line

grain line

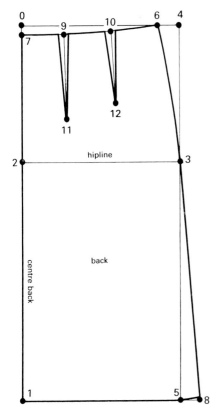

The Skirt Block

For girls, sizes 146–164cm height

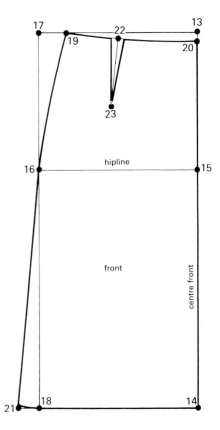

Note 1   There is 1cm ease in the waistline of the skirt. The waistline of the skirt should always be eased onto the waistband.

Note 2   The adaptation for the elasticated back waistband is shown on page 144, ref. 3.

MEASUREMENTS REQUIRED TO DRAFT THE BLOCK
(e.g. size 158cm height)
Refer to the size chart (pages 17 and 161) for standard measurements.

Waist	67cm
Hip	89cm
Waist to hip	19.2cm
Skirt length	54cm

Back

Square both ways from 0.

0–1   Skirt length required plus 1cm; square across.

0–2   Waist to hip plus 1cm; square across.

2–3 $^1/_4$ hip plus 1.5cm; square up to 4 and down to 5.

0–6 $^1/_4$ waist:
sizes 146–152cm height   plus 2.6cm
          158–164cm height   plus 3.4cm.

0–7   1cm; join 6–7 with a curve.

5–8   3cm. Draw in side seam 6, 3, 8; curve hipline outwards 0.4cm; curve hemline 0.25cm at 8.

Divide the line 6–7 into three parts. Mark points 9 and 10. Square down from the line 6–7.
Sizes 146–152cm height 9–11 10cm; 10–12 8cm
          158–164cm height 9–11 12cm; 10–12 10cm.
Construct darts on these lines:
sizes 146–152cm height   1.2cm wide
          158–164cm height   1.6cm wide.

Front

Square up both ways from 13.

13–14   Skirt length required plus 1cm; square across.

13–15   Waist to hip plus 1cm; square across.

15–16 $^1/_4$ hip plus 1cm; square up to 17 and down to 18.

13–19 $^1/_4$ waist:
sizes 146–152cm height   plus 1.8cm
          158–164cm height   plus 2.3cm.

13–20   1cm; join 19–20 with a curve.

18–21   3cm. Draw in side seam 19, 16, 21; curve hipline outwards 0.25cm. Curve hemline 0.25cm at 21.

19–22 $^1/_2$ measurement 19–20 minus 2cm; square down from the line 19–20.

22–23   Sizes 146–152cm height   8cm
          158–164cm height   9cm.
Construct the dart:
sizes 146–152cm height   1.5cm wide
          158–164cm height   2cm wide.

15   GRADING

Pattern Grading

Pattern grading is a technique used to reproduce a
pattern in other sizes. An accurate method is to draft the
smallest size and the largest size (within a size group),
then stop off the sizes between on lines drawn through
the basic points. Although computers are being used
increasingly, to give the correct data to the computer it
is necessary to understand the principles.

GRADING BLOCK PATTERNS ONE SIZE UP
The method of finding a point by measuring
horizontally then vertically is shown. From base point 1
square across. Measure horizontally the required
measurement. Mark point 2, square up. Measure
vertically the required measurement to point 3. Draw a
line through points 1 and 3 for a grading line. Points for
further grading can be made along the line.

Important   The blocks are drafted with variations of
ease in relation to size groupings; therefore in some
cases the grades are applied to the first pattern size in
any group, i.e. 92cm height, 122cm height. The groups
will be stated in the instructions. The blocks are graded
to the size charts (pages 16 and 19). However, in some
cases the grades have been adjusted slightly to give very
simple regular grades.

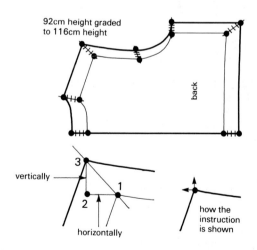

92cm height graded
to 116cm height

back

vertically

horizontally

how the
instruction
is shown

The 'Flat' Blocks for Babies and Infants

Sizes 56–92cm height, 8cm and 6cm height intervals

The first figures in the instruction lines refer to the height group 56cm–72cm, the figures in brackets refer to the height group 80cm–98cm.

BODY AND OVERGARMENT BLOCKS
Back
1   Measure 8mm (6mm) hor.
2   Measure 8mm (6mm) hor. 2.5mm (1.2mm) vert.
3   Measure 6mm (4.5mm) hor. 7mm (5mm) vert.
4   Measure 4mm (3mm) hor. 6mm (4mm) vert.
5   Measure 7.5mm (5mm) vert.
6   Measure 4mm (6mm) hor. 7.5mm (5mm) vert.
7   Measure 4mm (6mm) hor.
Front
7   Measure 6mm (4.5mm) hor.
Sleeve
1   Measure 5.8mm (3.8mm) vert.
2   Measure 4mm (3mm) hor.
3   Measure 21mm (22mm) hor.
4   Measure 21mm (22mm) hor. 4mm (2mm) vert.

TWO-PIECE TROUSER BLOCK
Back
1   Measure 9.8mm hor. 3.8mm (2.5mm) vert.
2   Measure 10mm hor. 3.8mm (2.5mm) vert.
3   Measure 3.8mm (2.5mm) vert.
4, 5   Measure 30mm (35mm) hor. 2.5mm (1.6mm) vert.
6   Measure 6.2mm (4.8mm) vert.
7   Measure 5mm hor. 6.2mm (4.8mm) vert.
Front
8, 9   Measure 10mm hor. 3.8mm (2.5mm) vert.
10   Measure 2.5mm hor. 3.8mm (2.5mm) vert.
11   Measure 5.5mm (3.7mm) vert.
12, 13   Measure 30mm (35mm) hor. 2.5mm (1.6mm) vert.
14   Measure 3.8mm (2.5mm) vert.

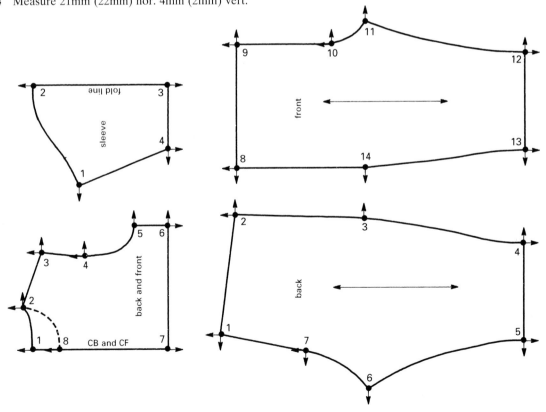

The 'Flat' Body, Shirt and Overgarment Blocks

**Unisex sizes 80–164cm height
12cm height intervals**

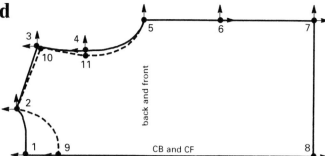

In accurate garment sizing it is important that the grades are made on the two blocks which are constructed in each particular size grouping; Unisex Size Chart, page 19.

The first figures in the instruction lines refer to the height group 80cm–116cm, the figures in brackets refer to the height group 128cm–164cm.

BODY AND SHIRT BLOCKS
Back
1 Measure 12mm (14mm) hor.
2 Measure 12mm (14mm) hor. 2.4mm (4.8mm) vert.
3 Measure 9mm (10.5mm) hor. 10mm (14mm) vert.
4 Measure 6mm (7mm) hor. 8mm (12mm) vert.
5 Measure 10mm (15mm) vert.
6 Measure 12mm (14mm) hor. 10mm (15mm) vert.
7 Measure 24mm (26mm) hor. 10mm (15mm) vert.
8 Measure 24mm (26mm) hor.

Front
9 Measure 9mm (10.5mm) hor.
10 Measure 6mm (7mm) hor. 8mm (12mm) vert.
11 Measure 8mm (10mm) hor.

Basic sleeve
1 Measure 7.5mm (11mm) vert.
2 Measure 6mm (7mm) hor.
3 Measure 44mm (38mm) hor.
4 Measure 44mm (38mm) hor. 5mm (7mm) vert.

Shirt sleeve
1 Measure 9mm (13.5mm) vert.
2 Measure 4mm (4.5mm) hor.
3 Measure 46mm (40.5mm) hor.
4 Measure 46mm (40.5mm) hor. 6mm (9mm) vert.

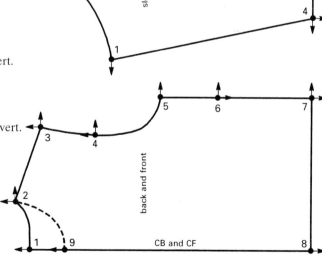

OVERGARMENT BLOCK
Back and front
1 Measure 12mm (14mm) hor.
2 Measure 12mm (14mm) hor. 2.4mm (4.8mm) vert.
3 Measure 9mm (10.5mm) hor. 10mm (14mm) vert.
4 Measure 6mm (7mm) hor. 8mm (12mm) vert.
5 Measure 10mm (15mm) vert.
6 Measure 12mm (14mm) hor. 10mm (15mm) vert.
7 Measure 24mm (26mm) hor. 10mm (15mm) vert.
8 Measure 24mm (26mm) hor.
9 Measure 8mm (10mm) hor.

Basic sleeve
1 Measure 7.5mm (11mm) vert.
2 Measure 6mm (7mm) hor.
3 Measure 44mm (38mm) hor.
4 Measure 44mm (38mm) hor. 5mm (7mm) vert.

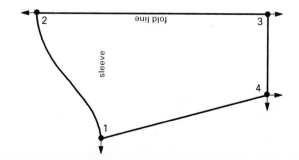

The 'Flat' Trouser Block

**Unisex sizes 80–164cm height
12cm height intervals**

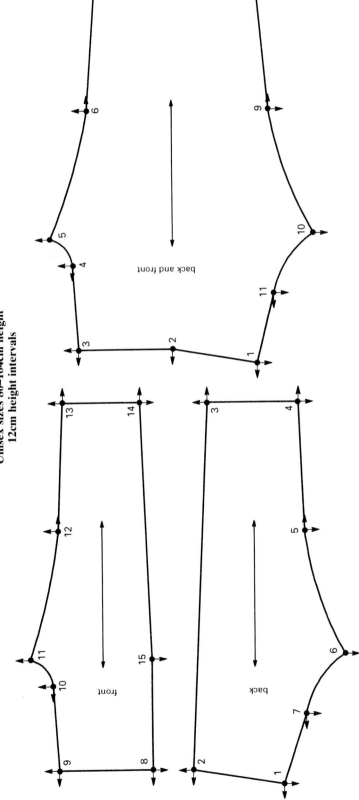

In accurate garment sizing it is important that the grades are made on the two blocks which are constructed in each particular size grouping; Unisex Size Chart, page 19.

TWO-PIECE TROUSER BLOCK

Back

1 Measure 17.5mm hor. 6.2mm (7.5mm) vert.
2 Measure 18mm hor. 6.2mm (7.5mm) vert.
3,4 Measure 70mm hor. 4.7mm (7.5mm) vert.
5 Measure 35mm hor. 4.7mm (7.5mm) vert.
6 Measure 12.4mm (15mm) vert.
7 Measure 9mm hor. 12.5mm (15mm) vert.

Front

8,9 Measure 18mm hor. 6.2mm (7.5mm) vert.
10 Measure 4.5mm hor. 6.2mm (7.55mm) vert.
11 Measure 9.4mm (11.2mm) vert.
12 Measure 35mm hor. 4.7mm (7.5mm) vert.
13,14 Measure 70mm hor. 4.7mm (7.5mm) vert.
15 Measure 6.2mm (7.5mm) vert.

ONE-PIECE TROUSER BLOCK

Back and front

1 Measure 17.5mm hor. 12.5mm (15mm) vert.
2 Measure 18mm hor.
3 Measure 18mm hor. 12.5mm (15mm) vert.
4 Measure 4.5mm hor. 12.5mm (15mm) vert.
5 Measure 15.5mm (18.5mm) vert.
6 Measure 35mm hor. 9.4mm (15mm) vert.
7,8 Measure 70mm hor. 9.4mm (15mm) vert.
9 Measure 35mm hor. 9.4mm (15mm) vert.
10 Measure 19mm (22.5mm) vert.
11 Measure 9mm hor. 12.5mm (15mm) vert.

The Skirt Blocks

For girls, sizes 80–140cm height

SKIRT BLOCK (80–98cm height)

Back
1 Measure 6mm hor.
2 Measure 6mm hor. 5mm vert.
3 Measure 5mm vert.
4 Measure 14mm hor. 6.5mm vert.
5 Measure 14mm hor.

Front
6 Measure 6mm hor.
7 Measure 6mm hor. 5mm vert.
8 Measure 5mm vert.
9 Measure 14mm hor. 6.5mm vert.
10 Measure 14mm hor.

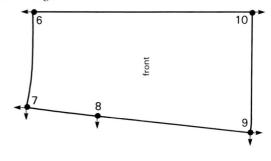

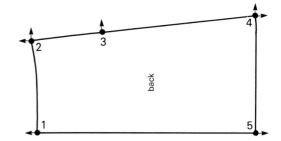

SKIRT BLOCK (104–140cm height)
Note that 104–122cm blocks have 1cm waist darts,
128–140cm blocks have 1.5cm waist darts. The grades
shown below have to be applied after the construction
of the first pattern 104cm, 110cm in each group.

Back
1 Measure 6mm hor.
2, 3, 4 Measure 6mm hor. 2.5mm (1.3mm) vert.
5 Measure 6mm hor. 5mm (2.5mm) vert.
6 Measure 5mm (7.5mm) vert.
7 Measure 14mm hor. 6.5mm (9mm) vert.
8 Measure 14mm hor.

Front
9 Measure 6mm hor.
10, 11, 12 Measure 6mm hor. 2.5mm (1.3mm) vert.
13 Measure 6mm hor. 5mm (2.5mm) vert.
14 Measure 5mm (7.5mm) vert.
15 Measure 14mm hor. 6.5mm (9mm) vert.
16 Measure 14mm hor.

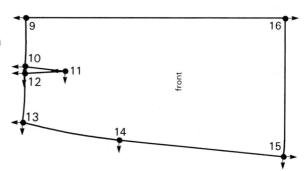

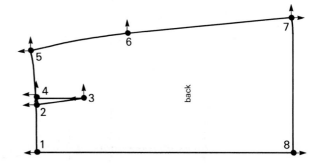

The Classic Bodice and Overgarment Blocks – Infants

For boys and girls, sizes 80–98cm height; approximate age 1–3 years

Back
1 Measure 6mm hor.
2 Measure 6mm hor. 1.2mm vert.
3 Measure 4.5mm hor. 5mm vert.
4 Measure 2.5mm hor. 4mm vert.
5 Measure 2mm hor. 4mm vert.
6 Measure 5mm vert.
7 Measure 6mm hor. 5mm vert.
8 Measure 12mm hor. 5mm vert.
9 Measure 12mm hor.

Front
10 Measure 4mm hor.
11 Measure 6mm hor. 1.2mm vert.
12 Measure 4.5mm hor. 5mm vert.
13 Measure 1mm hor. 4mm vert.
14 Measure 5mm vert.
15 Measure 6mm hor. 5mm vert.
16 Measure 12mm hor. 5mm vert.
17 Measure 12mm hor.

ONE-PIECE SLEEVE
1 Measure 3mm vert.
2 Measure 2mm hor. 2.5mm vert.
3 Measure 3.5mm hor.
4 Measure 1mm hor. 2mm vert.
5 Measure 3mm vert.
6 Measure 22mm hor. 2mm vert.
7 Measure 22mm hor.
8 Measure 22mm hor. 2mm vert.

TWO-PIECE SLEEVE
Top sleeve
1 Measure 22mm hor. 2mm vert.
2 Measure 2.5mm hor. 4.5mm vert.
3 Measure 3.5mm hor. 2mm vert.
4 Measure 22m hor.

Under-sleeve
5 Measure 22mm hor. 2mm vert.
6 Measure 2.5mm hor. 4mm vert.
7 Measure 1mm vert.
8 Measure 22mm hor.

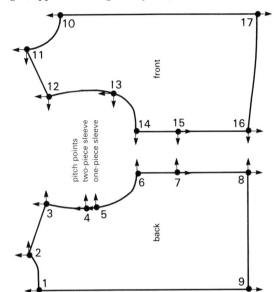

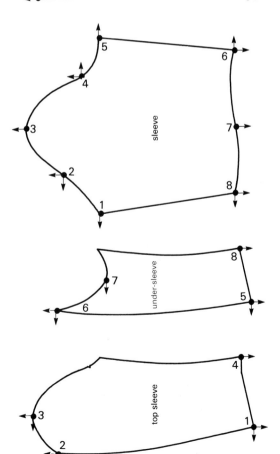

The Classic Bodice and Overgarment Blocks – Girls

For girls (undeveloped figures), sizes 104–152cm height; approximate age 4–12 years

The first figures in the instruction lines refer to the height group 104–116cm, the figures in brackets refer to the height group 122–152cm.

In accurate classic garment sizing it is important that the grades are made on the two blocks which are constructed in each particular size grouping.

Back
1 Measure 6mm hor.
2 Measure 6mm hor. 1.2mm (2.4mm) vert.
3 Measure 4.5 hor. 5mm (7mm) vert.
4 Measure 2.5mm hor. 4mm (6mm) vert.
5 Measure 2mm hor. 4mm (6mm) vert.
6 Measure 5mm (7.5mm) vert.
7 Measure 6mm hor. 5mm (7.5mm) vert.
8 Measure 12mm hor. 5mm (7.5mm) vert.
9 Measure 12mm hor.

Front
10 Measure 4mm hor.
11 Measure 6mm hor. 1.2mm (2.4mm) vert.
12 Measure 4.5mm hor. 5mm (7mm) vert.
13 Measure 1mm hor. 4mm (6mm) vert.
14 Measure 5mm (7.5mm) vert.
15 Measure 6mm hor. 5mm (7.5mm) vert.
16 Measure 12mm hor. 5mm (7.5mm) vert.
17 Measure 12mm hor.

ONE-PIECE SLEEVE
1 Measure 3mm (4.5mm) vert.
2 Measure 2mm hor. 2.5mm (3.5mm) vert.
3 Measure 3.5mm hor.
4 Measure 1mm hor. 2mm (3.5mm) vert.
5 Measure 3mm (4.5mm) vert.
6 Measure 22mm hor. 2mm (3mm) vert.
7 Measure 22mm hor.
8 Measure 22mm hor. 2mm (3mm) vert.

TWO-PIECE SLEEVE
Top sleeve
1 Measure 22mm hor. 2mm (5mm) vert.
2 Measure 2.5mm hor. 4.5mm (5mm) vert.
3 Measure 3.5mm hor. 2mm (2.5mm) vert.
4 Measure 22mm hor.

Under-sleeve
5 Measure 22mm hor. 2mm (5mm) vert.
6 Measure 2.5mm hor. 4mm (4.5mm) vert.
7 Measure 1mm (1.5mm) vert.
8 Measure 22mm hor.

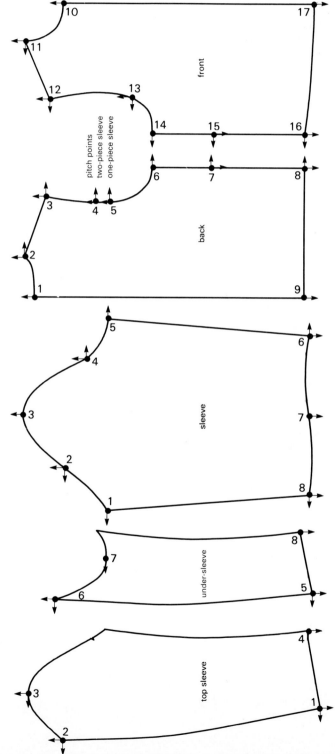

The Classic Overgarment Block – Boys

For boys, sizes 104–170cm height; approximate age 4–14 years

The first figures in the instruction lines refer to the height group 104–116cm; the figures in brackets refer to the height groups 122–152cm, 158–170cm.

These grades are constructed to retain the balance between the front and back block sections, this reflects the increasing back length for the growing boy's form. In accurate classic garment sizing it is important that the grades are made on three blocks which are constructed in each particular size grouping.

Back
1 Measure 6mm (8mm) (10mm) hor.
2 Measure 6mm (8mm) (10mm) hor. 1.2mm (2.4mm) (2.4mm) vert.
3 Measure 4.5mm (6.5mm) (8.5mm) hor. 5mm (7mm) (9mm) vert.
4 Measure 2.4mm (3.5mm) (4.5mm) hor. 4mm (6mm) (8mm) vert.
5 Measure 2mm (3mm) (4mm) hor. 4mm (6mm) (8mm) vert.
6 Measure 5mm (7.5mm) (10mm) vert.
7 Measure 6mm hor. 5mm (7.5mm) (10mm) vert.
8 Measure 12mm (12mm) (14mm) hor. 5mm (7.5mm) (10mm) vert.
9 Measure 12mm (12mm) (14mm) hor.

Front
10 Measure 4mm (6mm) (8mm) hor.
11 Measure 6mm (8mm) (10mm) hor. 1.2mm (2.4mm) (2.4mm) vert.
12 Measure 4.5mm (6.5mm) (8.5mm) hor. 5mm (7mm) (9mm) vert.
13 Measure 1mm (1.2mm) (1.5mm) hor. 4mm (6mm) (8mm) vert.
14 Measure 5mm (7.5mm) (10mm) vert.

15 Measure 6mm hor. 5mm (7.5mm) (10mm) vert.
16 Measure 12mm (12mm) (14mm) hor. 5mm (7.5mm) (10mm) vert.
17 Measure 12mm (12mm) (14mm) hor.

ONE-PIECE SLEEVE
1 Measure 3mm (5mm) (7mm) vert.
2 Measure 2mm (2.2mm) (2.5mm) hor. 2mm (2.5mm) (3mm) vert.
3 Measure 3.5mm (4.5mm) (5.5mm) hor.
4 Measure 1mm (1.2mm) (1.4mm) hor. 2mm (3.5mm) (5mm) vert.
5 Measure 3mm (5mm) (7mm) vert.
6 Measure 22mm (22mm) (16.5mm) hor. 2mm (3.5mm) (3.5mm) vert.
7 Measure 22mm (22mm) (16.5mm) hor.
8 Measure 22mm (22mm) (16.5mm) hor. 2mm (3.5mm) (3.5mm) vert.

TWO-PIECE SLEEVE
Top sleeve
1 Measure 22mm (22mm) (16.5mm) hor. 2mm (5mm) (5mm) vert.
2 Measure 2.5mm (3mm) (3.5mm) hor. 5.5mm (6.5mm) (7.5mm) vert.
3 Measure 3.5mm (4.5mm) (5.5mm) hor. 3mm (3.5mm) (4mm) vert.
4 Measure 22mm hor.

Under-sleeve
5 Measure 22mm (22mm) (16.5mm) hor. 2mm (5mm) (5mm) vert.
6 Measure 2.5mm (3mm) (3.5mm) hor. 4.5mm (4.8mm) (5mm) vert.
7 Measure 1.5mm (2.2mm) (3mm) vert.
8 Measure 22mm (22mm) (16.5mm) hor.

The Classic Overgarment Block – Boys

For boys, sizes 104–170cm height; approximate age 4–14yrs

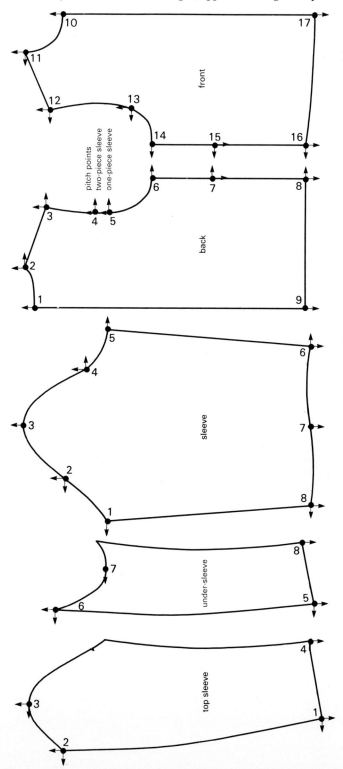

The Classic Trouser Block – Infants

For boys and girls, sizes 80–98cm height

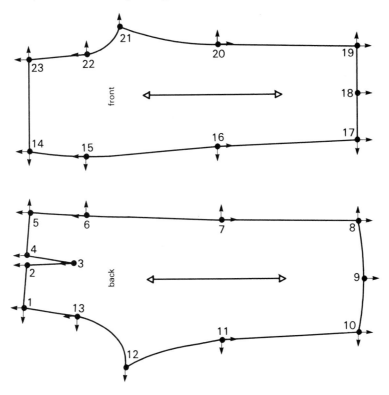

Back

1   Measure 10mm hor. 2mm vert.
2, 3, 4   Measure 10mm hor.
5   Measure 10mm hor. 3mm vert.
6   Measure 4mm hor. 3.5mm vert.
7   Measure 17.5mm hor. 2.5mm vert.
8   Measure 35mm hor. 2.5mm vert.
9   Measure 35mm hor.
10   Measure 35mm hor. 2.5mm vert.
11   Measure 17.5mm hor. 2.5mm vert.
12   Measure 4mm vert.
13   Measure 4mm hor. 2mm vert.

Front

14   Measure 10mm hor. 3.5mm vert.
15   Measure 4mm hor. 3.5mm vert.
16   Measure 17.5mm hor. 2.5mm vert.
17   Measure 35mm hor. 2.5mm vert.
18   Measure 35mm hor.
19   Measure 35mm hor. 2.5mm vert.
20   Measure 17.5mm hor. 2.5mm vert.
21   Measure 3mm vert.
22   Measure 4mm hor. 1.5mm vert.
23   Measure 10mm hor. 1.5mm vert.

The Classic Trouser Block – Girls

For girls, sizes 104–140cm height

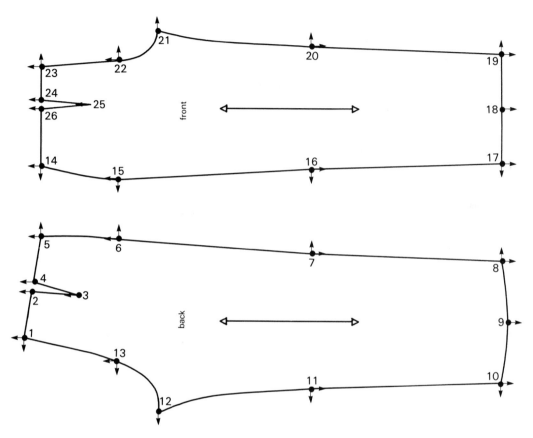

The first figures in the instruction lines refer to the height group 104–116cm, the figures in brackets refer to the height group 122–140cm.

There is a front waist darting on the block on the sizes (122–140cm height); therefore, it is important that the grades are made on the two blocks which are constructed in each particular size grouping.

Back
1 Measure 8mm hor. 2mm (1mm) vert.
2, 3, 4 Measure 8mm hor.
5 Measure 8mm hor. 3mm (1.5mm) vert.
6 Measure 2mm hor. 5mm vert.
7 Measure 17.5mm hor. 2.5mm vert.
8 Measure 35mm hor. 2.5mm vert.
9 Measure 35mm hor.
10 Measure 35mm hor. 2.5mm vert.
11 Measure 17.5mm hor. 2.5mm vert.
12 Measure 5.5mm vert.
13 Measure 2mm hor. 2.5mm vert.

Front
14 Measure 8mm hor. 3mm (0.5mm) vert.
15 Measure 2mm hor. 5mm vert.
16 Measure 17.5mm hor. 2.5mm vert.
17 Measure 35mm hor. 2.5mm vert.
18 Measure 35mm hor.
19 Measure 35mm hor. 2.5mm vert.
20 Measure 17.5mm hor. 2.5mm vert.
21 Measure 5mm vert.
22 Measure 2mm hor. 3mm vert.
23 Measure 8mm hor. 2mm vert.
24, 25, 26 Measure 8mm hor.

The Classic Trouser Block – Boys

For boys, sizes 104–170cm height

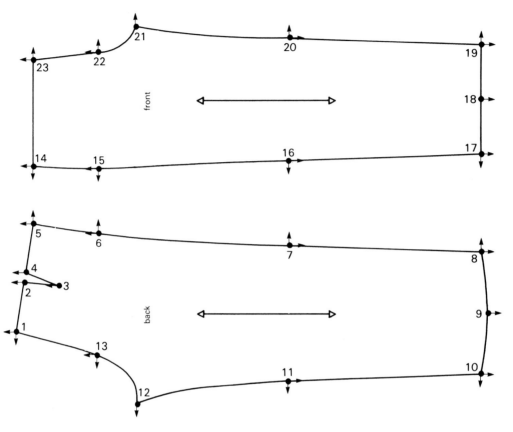

The first figures in the instruction lines refer to the height group 104–152cm, the figures in brackets refer to the height group 158–170cm.

Back
1   Measure 8mm hor. 2mm vert.
2, 3, 4   Measure 8mm hor.
5   Measure 8mm hor. 3mm vert.
6   Measure 2mm hor. 5mm (6.5mm) vert.
7   Measure 17.5mm hor. 2.5mm vert.
8   Measure 35mm hor. 2.5mm vert.
9   Measure 35mm hor.
10   Measure 35mm hor. 2.5mm vert.
11   Measure 17.5mm hor. 2.5mm vert.
12   Measure 5.5mm (7mm) vert.
13   Measure 2mm hor. 2.5mm (3.5mm) vert.

Front
14   Measure 8mm hor. 3mm vert.
15   Measure 2mm hor. 5mm (6mm) vert.
16   Measure 17.5mm hor. 2.5mm vert.
17   Measure 35mm hor. 2.5mm vert.
18   Measure 35mm hor.
19   Measure 35mm hor. 2.5mm vert.
20   Measure 17.5mm hor. 2.5mm vert.
21   Measure 5mm (6mm) vert.
22   Measure 2mm hor. 3mm (4mm) vert.
23   Measure 8mm hor. 2mm vert.

16   BRITISH STANDARD BS 7231

A discussion of the BSI Standard 7231

HISTORY

When the British Standards Institution (BSI) published its standard BS 3728 in 1982 it did not include size charts as it believed that the one used in the previous survey was outdated. BSI did, however, adopt the centilong system which designates children's sizing by height intervals. There was a demand from the manufacturers for new size charts, so the BSI, in conjunction with a consortium of major manufacturers, and with support from the Department of Trade and Industry (DTI) and the National Children's Wear Association (NCWA), decided to begin a series of sizing surveys.

A boys' survey was commissioned by a consortium of retailers, manufacturers and the NCWA. Loughborough University's Human Science Department was asked to undertake the study. In 1986 BSI and the consortium tried to fund a project to measure girls from 5–17. The money was not forthcoming from the DTI, so the consortium proceeded independently. The girls' survey was completed in 1986, but as it was a private survey, the data was not available to the public.

The consortium realised the need to complete the gap in the data (0–5 years). This time the government was prepared to provide half the money, an enlarged consortium provided the remainder of the money on the understanding that they would have access to the earlier data. The data was submitted to the group early in 1988 and released to the BSI for publication.

The transposition of the raw data into commercially usable size charts took place during 1988-1989. This work is now completed and is published as a British Standard (BS 7231). The results are offered in two forms:

Part 1   a statistical report offering the raw data;
Part 2   size charts constructed for manufacturers.

Differences of opinion arose between members of the technical committee; some were not satisfied with the way the measurements were calculated and given in Part 2 of the Standard. For further discussion on the problems see the Bibliography for references of articles in Drapers Record (1990) and Hollings Apparel Industry Review (1990).

Author's comment

The size charts provide a marketing tool, useful for planning size groupings of garments in retail outlets or as a general guide to sizing for clothing manufacturers. However, it is obvious from the text in their Foreword of the Standard, that BSI intended that the size charts should also be used for pattern making; and it is also obvious that they were aware that problems and confusions could arise.

I recommend that manufacturers who wish to use the new British Standard will find it more useful to use the raw data in Part 1 (collected by the University and offered in centile tables) to construct their own size charts. When doing so, the following points quoted directly from the Standard should be noted:

- 'it is also recommended that technicians should take care to identify the children's measurement points that are used in these tables as they are slightly different from those they have used hitherto.'
- 'some of the measurements are slightly different, since it was necessary to use some different points for babies, older girls and older boys.'

These points could cause problems for technicians. Part 1 has photographs of where the measurements were taken and this is helpful when interpreting the measurements. The size groups – infants, boys and girls – were measured at different times, by different people and treated as separate groups. This must be taken into account when constructing charts across the size groupings.

Part 2 is only included in the Appendix as a reference for designers and tutors who may wish to be aware of the anomalies.

SPECIAL NOTE

The author would like it to be recognised that, when the measurement positions of the body are taken into account, a great deal of the raw data (collected by the University of Loughborough and published in Part 1 of BS 7231) correlates closely with the raw data collected in the author's survey. She therefore argues that her size charts offered in the main section of this book are valid and that they are of a sounder construction than those offered in Part 2 of the Standard. They therefore remain as the foundation to her methods of pattern construction. **Supplementary measurements are offered in this book that are taken from Part 1 of the survey.**

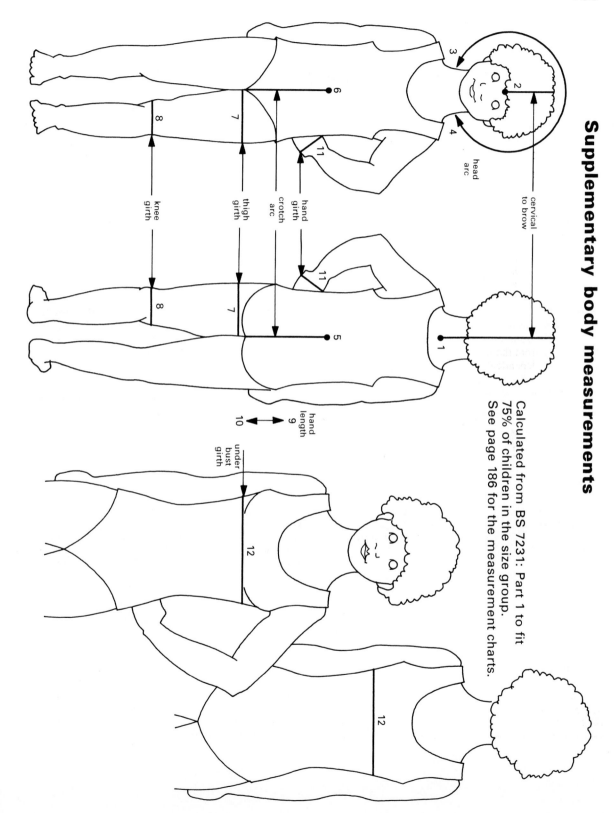

Supplementary body measurements

Calculated from BS 7231: Part 1 to fit
75% of children in the size group.
See page 186 for the measurement charts.

cervical
to brow

head
arc

knee
girth

thigh
girth

crotch
arc

hand
girth

hand
length

under
bust
girth

Supplementary Body Measurements

Calculated from BS 7231 Part 1 to fit 75% of children in the size group

INFANTS

		56	64	72	78	86	92	98
HEIGHT								
APPROXIMATE WEIGHT (kg)		4–5	6–7	8	9–10	11–12	–	–
APPROXIMATE AGE		birth	3m	6m	12m	18m	2	3
1–2	CERVICAL TO BROW	30	32.5	35	36.5	38	39.5	41
3–4	HEAD ARC	–	–	43	45	47	48	49
5–6	CROTCH ARC	–	–	–	–	38	40	43
7	THIGH GIRTH	24	26	28	29	30	31	32.5
9–10	HAND LENGTH	–	–	–	–	10.5	11	11.5
11	HAND GIRTH	–	–	–	–	12.5	13	13.5

GIRLS AND BOYS

		104	110	116	122	128	134	140	146	152	158	164	170
HEIGHT													
APPROXIMATE AGE		4	5	6	7	8	9	10	11	12			14
GIRLS													
5–6	CROTCH ARC	45.5	48	50.5	53	55.5	58	60.5	63	66	69	72	–
7	THIGH GIRTH	35	37	39	41	43	45	47	49	51	53.5	56	–
8	KNEE GIRTH	23	24	25	26	27	28.5	30	31.5	33	34.5	36	–
9–10	HAND LENGTH	12	12.5	13	13.5	14.5	15	15.5	16.5	17	17.5	18	–
11	HAND GIRTH	14.5	15	15.5	16	16.5	17	17.5	18	18.5	19	19	–
12	UND.BUST GIRTH	–	–	–	–	–	70	71	72	73	74	76	–
BOYS													
5–6	CROTCH ARC	43.5	46	48.5	51	53.5	56	59	62	65	68	70.5	73
7	THIGH GIRTH	33.5	35	36.5	38	39.5	41	42.5	44	45.5	47	48.5	50

Appendix

British Standard BS 7231*
Body measurements of boys and girls from birth up to 16.9 years
Part 2. Recommendations of body dimensions for children

FOREWORD

This part of BS 7231 has been prepared under the direction of the Textiles and Clothing Standards Policy Committee. A series of four size survey studies formed the basis for the data which are contained in Part 1 of BS 7231. This Part contains recommended size charts for use by garment manufacturers, derived from the data in Part 1. The measurements in these tables have been carefully selected to be of maximum use to garment manufacturers and pattern technicians. In the range from birth to 4.9 years, the measurements for both sexes are grouped together. In the range from 5 years to 16.9 years, some of the measurements are slightly different, since it was necessary to use some different points for babies, older girls and older boys. The measurements have been rounded to the nearest centimetre of 0.5cm.

The tables are arranged under 6cm size intervals. The six centimetre interval is also expressed in tables as approximate age spans because the average height of children increases by about 12cm from birth to 6 months then 6cm to 12 months, then 6cm every 3 months until 2 years, and thereafter by an average of 6cm per year until fully grown. This height interval is also commonly used in European countries as well as in several other countries in the world.

There are two sets of tables in this Part, each set representing a different combination of centiles, a centile being one of 99 values which divide a variable into 100 groups with equal frequency. The first set of tables uses the 50th centile for height and 50th centile for girth, these being known as the median average measurements of children in the surveys.

The second set of tables uses the 75th centile for height and the 60th centile for girth. Garments made from this set of tables will thus be longer than the average and slightly more roomy. They will tend to favour the children who are in the upper sector of each height interval, rather than those who are in the middle. This combination was chosen following detailed discussions with a wide representation of the children's retailing and manufacturing trades, who take the view that garments can usually be shortened after purchase and that it is advisable to make them slightly roomy to allow for growth.

It is stressed, however, that no matter which combination of percentiles are used, the tables give *body measurements* and not *garment measurements*. In constructing patterns, technicians should use whatever allowances they consider necessary for the style of garment they are manufacturing. It is also recommended that technicians should take care to identify the children's measurement points that are used in these tables, in case they are slightly different from those that they have used hitherto.

In addition to the tables showing body measurements, recommendations regarding labels are included. The girth recommendations are body measurements and not garment measurements. These recommendations represent the minimum required on the labels, and manufacturers are free to provide whatever additional measurements they consider advisable for each style of garment. It is strongly recommended that the information regarding sizing should be given on a sew-in label rather than on a swing ticket.

Compliance with a British Standard does not of itself confer immunity from legal obligations.

Table 2. Baby and infants, 56 cm to 104 cm height, 50th centile height, 50th centile girth, 50th centile height

Dimension	00 Age (approximate)								
	Newborn	0–3 months	3–6 months	6–12 months	12–18 months	18–24 months	2 years	3 years	4 years
01 Weight	3.5	5.5	8.0	9.5	11.0	12.5	–	–	–
10 Height	56	62	68	74	80	86	92	98	104
11 Crown – Crotch	37.0	41.0	43.5	46.5	49.5	52.0	53.5	–	–
12 Cervicale – Foot	–	–	–	–	65.5	69.5	74.0	79.0	84.5
20 Cervicale – Brow	27.5	31.0	33.0	34.5	36.5	38.0	39.5	41.0	41.0
21 Head Arc	33.0	36.5	37.5	43.0	45.0	46.5	47.5	48.5	50.0
22 Head Girth	38.0	42.0	44.0	46.0	48.0	50.0	50.0	50.5	51.0
23 Neck Girth	21.5	23.0	23.5	23.5	24.0	24.5	24.5	25.0	25.0
31 Shoulder Length	5.0	5.5	6.0	6.5	7.0	7.5	8.0	8.5	9.0
33 Arm Scye Depth	4.0	4.5	5.0	5.0	5.5	5.5	6.0	–	–
35 Arm Scye Girth	–	–	–	–	21.5	22.0	23.0	24.0	25.0
40 Axillary Width (back)	15.0	16.0	18.0	19.5	20.5	21.5	22.5	23.5	24.5
41 Axillary Width (front)	14.0	15.0	16.0	16.5	17.5	18.0	19.0	20.0	20.5
46 Chest Girth	38.0	43.0	45.5	47.5	49.5	50.5	51.5	53.0	55.0
51 Front Neck – Waist	–	–	–	–	20.5	21.5	22.5	23.0	24.0
53 Back Neck – Waist	16.0	18.0	19.0	20.5	22.5	23.0	23.0	24.0	24.5
55 Trunk Loop	62.5	69	73.5	77.0	80.0	84.0	87.0	–	–
60 Crotch Arc	–	–	–	–	35.5	38.0	39.0	42.0	44.0
61 Waist – Crotch	7.0	8.5	9.5	10.0	11.0	11.0	11.0	–	–
63 Waist Girth	36.5	39.5	42.0	43.0	44.5	46.0	48.5	50.0	51.0
65 Waist Height	26.0	30.0	34.0	38.0	42.0	45.0	48.5	–	–
66 Waist Hip	–	–	–	–	11.0	12.0	12.5	13.0	14.0
68 Hip Girth	34.0	41.5	44.5	47.0	49.0	50.0	52.0	54.0	56.5
70 Inside Leg	19.0	21.5	24.5	28.0	31.0	34.0	37.5	41.0	44.5
71 Knee Height	–	–	–	–	–	20.5	22.5	24.5	26.5
72 Thigh Girth	19.5	24.0	26.0	27.5	28.5	29.5	30.5	31.5	33.5
74 Ankle Girth	10.0	12.0	13.0	14.0	14.5	14.5	15.0	15.0	15.5
75 Foot Length	8.0	9.0	10.0	11.0	12.0	13.0	14.0	15.5	16.5
80 Elbow Length	–	–	–	–	–	16.5	17.5	18.5	19.5
81 Arm Length	18.5	20.5	22.5	25.0	27.5	29.5	31.5	34.0	36.0
82 Maximum Upper Arm Girth	12.0	14.0	15.0	16.0	16.5	16.5	17.0	17.0	18.0
83 Wrist Girth	9.0	10.5	10.5	11.5	12.0	12.0	12.0	12.0	12.0
90 Hand Girth	–	–	–	–	–	12.0	12.5	13.0	13.5
92 Hand Length	–	–	–	–	–	10.0	10.5	11.5	12.0

NOTE: Weights are in kilograms; all other dimensions are in centimetres.

Table 3. Boys, 110 cm to 164 cm height, 50th centile girth, 50th centile height

Dimension	00 Age (approximate)									
	5 years	6 years	7 years	8 years	9 years	10 years	11 years	12 years	13 years	14 years
10 Height	110	116	122	128	134	140	146	152	158	164
12 Cervicale – Foot	90.5	95.5	101.0	106.5	112.0	117.5	123.0	128.5	134.0	139.5
22 Head Girth	51.5	52.0	52.5	52.5	53.0	53.5	54.0	54.5	55.0	55.5
23 Neck Girth (at larynx)	28.0	28.0	29.0	30.0	30.5	31.5	32.0	33.0	34.0	36.0
35 Arm Scye Girth	26.0	27.0	28.0	29.5	30.5	32.0	33.5	35.0	37.0	38.5
40 Axillary Width (back)	27.0	28.0	29.0	30.0	31.0	32.0	33.0	34.5	35.0	36.5
46 Chest Girth	58.0	59.5	62.0	63.5	66.0	68.5	72.0	76.0	80.0	84.0
53 Back Neck–Waist	26.0	27.0	28.0	29.0	30.0	31.0	32.0	33.0	35.0	37.5
61 Waist to Crotch	17.5	18.0	19.0	20.0	21.0	22.0	23.0	24.0	25.0	26.0
63 Waist Girth	54.0	55.0	56.0	57.0	59.0	61.0	63.5	65.5	67.5	70.0
65 Waist Height	64.5	68.5	72.5	77.5	82.0	86.0	91.0	95.0	99.0	102.5
68 Hip Girth	57.5	60.0	62.5	65.5	68.0	71.0	74.5	78.0	80.0	84.0
70 Inside Leg	47.0	50.5	54.0	58.0	61.0	64.5	68.0	71.0	74.0	77.0
71 Knee Height	28.5	30.0	32.5	34.5	36.5	38.5	40.5	42.5	44.5	46.5
72 Thigh Girth	31.5	33.0	34.5	36.5	38.0	40.0	42.0	43.5	44.5	46.0
80 Elbow Length	22.0	23.0	24.5	25.5	27.0	28.5	30.0	31.0	32.5	34.0
81 Arm Length	35.5	37.5	39.5	42.0	44.5	46.5	49.0	51.5	54.0	56.0
82 Maximum Upper Arm Girth	17.0	17.5	18.0	18.5	19.5	20.5	21.5	22.5	23.5	24.5
83 Wrist Girth	12.0	12.0	12.5	13.0	13.0	13.5	14.0	15.0	15.5	16.0

NOTE. All dimensions are in centimetres.

Table 4. Girls, 110 cm to 164 cm height, 50th centile girth, 50th centile height

Dimensions	00 Age (approximate)									
	5 years	6 years	7 years	8 years	9 years	10 years	11 years	12 years	13 years	14 years
10 Height	110	116	122	128	134	140	146	152	158	164
12 Cervicale – Foot	90.5	95.5	101.0	106.5	112.0	118.0	123.5	129.0	134.0	139.5
22 Head Girth	51.0	51.5	52.0	52.5	53.0	53.5	53.5	54.0	54.5	55.5
23 Neck Girth (at larynx)	25.0	25.5	26.0	27.0	27.5	28.0	29.0	30.0	31.0	32.0
31 Shoulder Length	8.0	8.5	9.0	9.5	10.0	10.5	11.0	11.5	11.5	12.0
35 Arm Scye Girth	26.5	27.5	28.5	30.0	31.5	32.5	34.5	36.0	37.5	39.5
42 Back Width	23.0	24.0	24.5	25.5	26.5	28.0	29.0	30.5	32.0	33.0
43 Chest Width	20.0	21.0	22.0	23.0	24.0	25.0	26.0	27.0	28.0	29.0
46 Chest Girth	55.5	57.5	59.0	61.5	64.0	66.5	71.0	76.0	82.5	86.0
47 Under Bust Girth	–	–	–	–	–	–	67.5	68.5	71.5	73.0
53 Back Neck–Waist	26.0	27.0	28.0	29.0	30.5	32.0	33.5	35.5	37.5	39.0
63 Waist Girth	50.5	52.0	52.5	55.0	56.0	57.5	59.0	61.0	63.0	65.0
64 Side Seam	66.5	70.5	75.0	79.5	84.0	89.0	93.5	97.5	101.5	105.0
66 Waist–Hip	13.0	14.0	14.5	15.5	16.5	17.5	18.5	19.5	20.5	21.5
67 High Hip Girth	–	–	–	–	–	–	75.0	77.0	81.0	83.5
68 Hip Girth	59.0	61.5	64.0	67.0	70.5	74.0	77.0	82.0	88.0	92.0
70 Inside Leg	48.5	51.5	55.0	59.0	62.5	66.0	69.5	72.0	74.0	76.5
71 Knee Height	28.5	30.5	32.5	34.5	36.5	38.5	40.5	41.5	43.0	44.5
72 Thigh Girth	34.5	36.0	38.0	40.0	42.0	44.0	46.0	49.0	52.0	54.0
73 Knee Girth	23.5	24.5	25.5	26.5	28.0	29.0	31.0	32.0	33.0	34.0
74 Ankle Girth	16.0	16.5	17.0	18.0	18.5	19.0	19.5	20.0	21.0	21.5
80 Elbow Length	21.0	22.0	23.0	24.5	25.5	27.0	28.5	29.5	31.0	31.5
81 Arm Length	37.5	39.0	41.5	44.0	46.0	48.5	51.0	53.5	55.5	57.5
82 Maximum Upper Arm Girth	18.0	19.0	19.5	20.5	21.5	22.5	23.5	24.0	25.5	26.5
83 Wrist Girth	12.0	12.5	12.5	13.0	13.5	14.0	14.5	14.5	15.0	15.5
91 Hand Width	6.0	6.0	6.0	6.5	6.5	7.0	7.0	7.0	7.5	7.5
92 Hand Length	12.5	13.0	13.5	14.0	14.5	15.5	16.0	16.5	17.0	17.5

NOTE. All dimensions are in centimetres.

Table 5. Baby and infants, 56 cm to 104 cm height, 60th centile girth, 75th centile height

Dimension	10 Height								
	56	62	68	74	80	86	92	98	104
11 Crown – Crotch	38.0	42.0	45.0	47.0	50.0	53.0	56.0	–	–
12 Cervicale – Foot	–	–	–	–	66.0	70.0	75.0	80.0	85.5
20 Cervicale – Brow	29.0	32.0	34.0	36.0	37.5	39.5	40.5	42.0	42.0
21 Head Arc	37.0	37.5	38.5	43.5	46.0	47.5	49.0	50.0	51.5
22 Head Girth	41.0	44.0	45.0	48.0	49.0	51.0	51.0	51.5	51.5
23 Neck Girth (at larynx)	22.0	24.0	24.0	24.5	24.5	25.0	25.0	25.0	25.0
31 Shoulder Length	5.0	5.5	6.0	6.5	7.0	7.5	8.0	8.5	9.0
33 Arm Scye Depth	4.5	5.0	5.0	5.5	5.5	6.0	6.0	–	–
35 Arm Scye Girth	–	–	–	–	22.0	23.0	24.0	25.0	26.0
40 Axillary Width (back)	15.0	16.5	18.5	20.0	21.0	22.0	23.0	24.0	24.5
41 Axillary Width (front)	14.0	15.5	16.5	17.0	18.0	18.5	19.5	20.5	21.0
46 Chest Girth	38.5	43.5	46.0	48.0	50.0	51.0	52.0	53.5	55.5
51 Front Neck – Waist	–	–	–	–	21.0	22.0	23.0	24.0	25.0
53 Back Neck – Waist	17.0	18.5	19.5	21.5	23.0	23.5	24.0	24.5	25.5
55 Trunk Loop	64.0	71.0	75.0	78.0	82.0	86.0	89.0	–	–
60 Crotch Arc	–	–	–	–	37.0	39.0	41.0	43.0	45.0
61 Waist – Crotch	7.0	8.5	9.5	10.0	11.0	11.0	11.5	–	–
63 Waist Girth	37.0	40.5	42.5	43.5	45.0	46.5	49.0	51.0	52.0
65 Waist Height	27.0	31.0	35.0	39.0	43.0	46.0	50.0	–	–
66 Waist Hip	–	–	–	–	11.5	12.5	13.0	14.0	15.0
68 Hip Girth	36.5	42.5	46.0	48.0	50.0	51.0	53.0	55.0	58.0
70 Inside Leg	20.0	22.5	25.5	29.0	32.0	35.0	38.5	42.5	45.5
71 Knee Height	–	–	–	–	–	21.0	23.0	25.0	27.0
72 Thigh Girth	21.0	25.0	28.0	29.0	30.0	31.0	32.0	33.0	35.0
74 Ankle Girth	11.5	13.0	14.0	14.5	15.0	15.0	15.5	16.0	16.0
75 Foot Length	8.5	9.5	10.5	11.5	12.5	13.5	14.5	16.0	17.0
80 Elbow Length	–	–	–	–	–	17.0	18.0	19.0	20.0
81 Arm Length	19.0	22.0	23.5	26.0	28.0	30.5	32.5	35.0	36.5
82 Maximum Upper Arm Girth	12.5	14.0	15.5	16.0	16.5	17.0	17.5	18.0	18.5
83 Wrist Girth	10.0	10.5	11.0	11.5	12.0	12.0	12.0	12.5	12.5
90 Hand Girth	–	–	–	–	–	12.5	13.0	13.5	14.0
92 Hand Length	–	–	–	–	–	10.5	11.0	11.5	12.0

NOTE. All dimensions are in centimetres.

Table 6. Boys, 110 cm to 164 cm height, 60th centile girth, 75th centile height

Dimension	10 Height									
	110	116	122	128	134	140	146	152	158	164
12 Cervicale – Foot	91.5	97.0	102.5	108.0	113.5	119.0	124.5	130.0	135.5	141.0
22 Head Girth	52.0	53.0	53.5	53.5	54.0	54.0	54.5	55.0	55.5	56.0
23 Neck Girth (at larynx)	29.0	29.5	30.0	30.5	31.5	32.5	33.5	34.5	35.5	37.0
35 Arm Scye Girth	26.5	27.5	28.5	29.5	31.0	32.5	34.0	35.5	37.5	39.5
40 Axillary Width (back)	28.0	29.0	30.0	31.0	32.0	33.0	34.0	35.0	36.0	37.0
46 Chest Girth	58.5	60.0	62.0	64.0	66.5	69.0	73.5	78.5	83.5	86.0
53 Back Neck – Waist	27.0	28.0	29.0	30.0	31.0	32.5	33.5	34.5	36.5	39.0
61 Waist to Crotch	18.5	19.5	20.0	21.0	22.0	23.0	24.5	25.0	26.5	27.0
63 Waist Girth	54.5	55.5	56.5	58.0	60.0	62.0	64.5	67.0	69.5	72.0
65 Waist Height	66.0	70.0	74.0	78.5	83.0	87.5	92.0	96.5	101.0	104.5
68 Hip Girth	58.5	61.0	63.5	66.5	69.5	72.5	76.0	79.5	82.0	85.5
70 Inside Leg	48.5	52.0	55.5	59.0	62.5	66.0	69.5	73.0	76.0	79.0
71 Knee Height	29.0	31.0	33.0	35.0	37.0	39.0	41.0	43.0	45.0	47.0
72 Thigh Girth	32.5	34.0	35.5	37.0	39.0	41.0	43.0	45.0	46.0	47.0
80 Elbow Length	23.0	24.0	25.5	26.5	28.0	29.5	31.0	32.5	34.0	35.5
81 Arm Length	36.5	38.5	41.0	43.0	45.5	48.0	50.5	53.0	55.5	58.0
82 Maximum Upper Arm Girth	17.0	17.5	18.0	18.5	19.5	20.5	21.5	22.5	23.5	24.5
83 Wrist Girth	12.5	12.5	13.0	13.0	13.5	14.0	14.5	15.0	15.5	16.0

NOTE. All dimensions are in centimetres.

Table 7. Girls, 110 cm to 164 cm height, 60th centile girth, 75th centile height

Dimension	10 Height									
	110	116	122	128	134	140	146	152	158	164
12 Cervicale – Foot	92.0	97.0	102.0	107.5	113.0	119.0	125.0	130.0	135.0	140.0
22 Head Girth	52.0	52.5	53.0	53.5	54.0	54.5	55.0	55.0	56.0	56.5
23 Neck Girth (at larynx)	25.0	26.0	26.5	27.5	28.5	29.0	30.0	31.0	32.0	33.0
31 Shoulder Length	8.0	8.5	9.0	9.5	10.0	10.5	11.0	11.5	12.0	12.5
35 Arm Scye Girth	27.0	28.0	29.0	30.5	32.0	33.5	35.0	36.5	38.5	40.0
42 Back Width	23.0	24.0	25.0	26.0	27.0	28.0	29.5	31.0	32.5	34.0
43 Chest Width	20.5	21.5	22.5	23.5	24.5	25.5	26.5	27.5	28.5	29.5
46 Chest Girth	56.0	58.0	60.0	62.0	65.0	68.0	73.0	78.0	83.0	88.0
47 Under Bust Girth	–	–	–	–	–	–	69.0	70.0	72.0	74.0
53 Back Neck–Waist	27.0	28.0	29.0	30.0	31.5	33.0	34.5	36.5	38.5	40.5
60 Crotch Arc	48.0	50.0	52.0	54.0	56.5	59.0	61.5	64.0	67.0	70.0
63 Waist Girth	52.0	53.0	54.0	55.0	57.0	59.0	61.0	63.0	65.0	67.0
64 Side Seam	68.0	72.0	76.0	81.0	86.0	91.0	95.0	99.0	103.0	107.0
66 Waist Hip	14.0	15.0	16.0	17.0	18.0	19.0	20.0	21.0	22.0	23.0
67 High Hip Girth	–	–	–	–	–	–	77.0	79.0	82.0	85.0
68 Hip Girth	60.0	63.0	66.0	69.0	72.0	75.0	79.0	84.0	89.0	94.0
70 Inside Leg	50.0	53.0	56.5	60.0	63.5	67.0	70.5	73.0	75.5	78.0
71 Knee Height	29.0	31.0	33.0	35.0	37.0	39.0	41.0	42.5	44.0	45.5
72 Thigh Girth	35.0	37.0	39.0	41.0	43.5	45.5	47.5	50.5	53.5	56.0
73 Knee Girth	24.0	25.0	26.0	27.5	29.0	30.5	31.5	32.5	33.5	35.0
74 Ankle Girth	17.0	17.0	17.5	18.0	19.0	19.0	20.0	20.0	21.0	22.0
80 Elbow Length	21.0	22.5	24.0	25.5	27.0	28.0	29.0	30.0	31.5	33.0
81 Arm Length	38.5	40.5	42.5	45.0	47.5	50.0	52.5	55.0	57.0	59.0
82 Maximum Upper Arm Girth	18.5	19.0	20.0	21.0	22.0	23.0	24.0	25.0	26.0	27.0
83 Wrist Girth	12.5	12.5	13.0	13.5	14.0	14.0	14.5	15.0	15.5	15.5
91 Hand Width	6.0	6.0	6.0	7.0	7.0	7.0	7.5	7.5	8.0	8.0
92 Hand Length	12.5	13.0	13.5	14.5	15.0	16.0	16.5	17.0	17.5	18.0

NOTE. All dimensions are in centimetres.

Bibliography

Beazley, A. (1990) New Sizing for British Children's wear. Developing patterns from the BSI recent survey of children's measurements. *Hollings Apparel Industrial Review*, Summer, pp. 41–60.

British Standards Institution (1990) *Body measurements of boys and girls from birth up to 16.9 years*, BS 7231. BSI, London.

British Standards Institution (1997) *The design and manufacture of children's clothing to promote mechanical safety*, BS 7907. BSI, London.

Cameron, N. (1978) Methods of auxological anthropometry. In: *Human Growth, Post-natal Growth*, Vol. 2 (eds F. Faulkner and J.M. Tanner). Baillière and Tindall, London.

Carter, N.D. (1980) *Development of Growth and Ageing.* Croom Helm, London.

Kunick, P. (1967) *Sizing, Pattern Construction and Grading for Women's and Children's Garments.* Philip Kunick Ltd, London.

Marshall, W.A. (1970) Physical growth and development. *Brennamann's Practice of Pediatrics*, Vol. 1, Chapter 3. Harper and Row Publishers Inc., Maryland.

Marshall, W.A. (1977) *Human Growth and its Disorders.* Academic Press, London.

Marshall, W.A. (1978) Puberty. In: *Human Growth, Post-natal Growth*, Vol. 2 (eds F. Faulkner and J.M. Tanner). Baillière and Tindall, London.

Rodwell, W. (1970) Towards metric sizing. *Clothing Institute Journal*, **XVI**, Nos 2 and 3, 1968. Supplementary notes.

Tanner, J.M. (1955) *Growth at Adolescence.* Blackwell Science, Oxford.

Tanner, J.M. (1960) *Human Growth*, Vol. III. Pergamon Press, London.

Tanner, J.M., Whitehouse, R.H. & Takaishi, M. (1966) Standards from birth to maturity for height, weight, height velocity and weight velocity: British children, 1965. *Arch. Dis Child*, **41**, 454 and 613.

Further Reading

Cooklin, G. (1991) *Pattern Grading for Children's Clothes.* Blackwell Science, Oxford.